First Edition
Robert A Curedale
Copyright © 2016 by Robert A. Curedale
All rights reserved
First edition March 2016
Published by Design Community College Inc,

The publisher and author accept no liability, regardless of legal basis. Designations used in this book may be trademarks whose use by third parties for their own purposes could violate the rights of the owners. The author and publisher have taken great care with all texts and illustrations in this book. The information contained within this book is strictly for educational purposes. If you wish to apply ideas contained in this book you are taking full responsibility for your actions. There are no representations or warranties, express or implied, about the completeness, accuracy, reliability, suitability or availability with respect to the information, products, services, or related graphics contained in this book for any purpose. Any use of this information is at your own risk. The author has made every effort to ensure the accuracy of the information within this book was correct at time of publication. The publisher and author do not assume and hereby disclaims any liability to any party for any loss, damage, or disruption caused by errors or omissions, whether such errors or omissions result from accident, negligence, or any other cause.

All rights reserved. No part of this publication may be reproduced, distributed, or transmitted in any form or by any means, including photocopying, recording, or other electronic or mechanical methods, without the prior written permission of the publisher, except in the case of brief quotations embodied in critical reviews and certain other noncommercial uses permitted by copyright law. For permission requests, write to the publisher, addressed "Attention: Permissions Coordinator," at the address below.

Design Community College Inc.
PO Box 1153
Topanga CA 90290 USA
info@curedale.com
Designed and illustrated by Robert Curedale
ISBN-10: 1-940805-21-X
ISBN-13: 978-1-940805-21-4

EXPERIENCE MAPS
JOURNEY MAPS
SERVICE BLUEPRINTS
EMPATHY MAPS

Robert Curedale

PUBLISHED BY DESIGN COMMUNITY COLLEGE LOS ANGELES
https://dcc-online.selz.com

Contents

01	INTRODUCTION	04
02	SEGMENTATION & PERSONAS	40
03	RESEARCH AND OPPORTUNITY EXPLORATION	62
04	AFFINITY DIAGRAMS	192
05	EMPATHY MAPS	212
06	EXPERIENCE & JOURNEY MAPS	252
07	SERVICE BLUEPRINTS	298
08	GLOSSARY	342
09	INDEX	358
10	ONLINE CLASSES	376
11	ABOUT THE AUTHOR	379
12	BOOKS IN THIS SERIES	380

Introduction

In this book are described the most powerful tools available to craft a superior experiences for your customers and end users.

In 2007 I established some on-line groups in core design areas including Industrial Design, Interior Design Graphic Design, Architecture and Design Management that have grown to around 1.2 million working designers and managers at the time of publication. It is estimated that there are around 4 chairs in existence for each person in the world today. A total of around 30 billion chairs. We are moving from a design culture built on using marketing and advertising to make people want designed things to a culture of understanding and creating what people need. This is a more efficient and a more responsible way of designing and as well as a way of designing that has a better business case. A McKinsey study provides evidence that businesses that focus on these mapping techniques do dramatically better than those that do not. Through the many discussions that I have had with designers I have put together this series of books to document and communicate methods that can help designers and managers make this important transition.

These powerful and flexible methods are collectively known as experience maps. In the 20th-century product styling like advertising was about making people want things. These maps are a response to the realization that it is more efficient and successful to make products, services, and experiences that people want and need. They can be used to optimize the design of goods, services, architecture, spaces and interactions and to plan business strategy.

The service sector makes up nearly 70% of most western economies and more than 50% of the Chinese economy, yet customers are often frustrated by their service experiences. Customers choose products and services that deliver the best experiences. Designing your customer's entire experience is key to differentiating your designs from competitors in an increasingly crowded competitive marketplace.

Through applying these methods organizations can deliver a more compelling and valuable experience. Mapping builds consensus across your organization with stakeholders, to positively impact your entire organization and your bottom line. These methods are core strategic tools and I believe will become required skills for every working designer and manager.

Why new products fail

Inadequate market understanding	**32%**
Bad product	23%
Higher costs	14%
Weak marketing	13%
Poor Timing	10%
Competition	8%

Many studies have found that the failure rate of new product releases is in the range of 80 to 95%. Most studies conclude that the greatest single reason for the failure of new product and service releases is a lack of understanding of customers. The techniques described in this book are some of the most powerful and proven ways of systematically ensuring that your new product and service development efforts will be successful. Over time, the proven benefits of these methods will lead to widespread adoption.

Organizations that focus on journey optimization perform dramatically better than those that do not

10 to 15%
Greater revenue growth

15 to 20%
Lower cost to serve

20%
Greater customer satisfaction

20 to 30%
More engaged employees

Source: McKinsey

"

80% of service companies believe they provide superior services

8% of their customers agree

Why use Mapping Methods?

CRAFT A BETTER CUSTOMER EXPERIENCE
Understand your customer's point of view Deliver a seamless, useful experience. Bring more humanity to your business.

STRATEGIC AND TACTICAL INNOVATION
Maps provide the best standard platform for all your employees and external stakeholders to contribute to the innovation process.

BUILDING AND SHARING KNOWLEDGE
Maps can be shared via email, in meetings and in other ways to build a common understanding both internally and externally.

DESIGNING THE MOMENTS OF TRUTH
Identify those moments of a user experience that leave a lasting impression both positive or negative.

UNDERSTAND COMPETITIVE POSITIONING
Compare what your customers want with what your competitors are providing.

UNDERSTANDING THE IDEAL EXPERIENCE
If you are repositioning your brand, maps can help you understand where it could be more successful.

REVEAL THE TRUTH THROUGH YOUR CUSTOMER'S EYES
Maps help you understand what customers think about your products and services rather than what you think they think. One study suggested that 80% of businesses believe that they are delivering superior services to their customers, but only 8% of their customers agree.

IDENTIFY OPPORTUNITIES
When you understand where a customer experience is poor, it is an opportunity to improve your competitiveness and make your business more profitable. Evolve and stay competitive. Adapt to changing customer needs and expectations.

EMPATHIZE WITH YOUR CUSTOMERS
Lack of understanding your customer's point of view is the

number one reason new products and services fail. More than 50% of new goods and services fail in the market.

GET CONNECTED TO YOUR CUSTOMERS OR END USERS
80% of service companies believe they offer superior services. Only 8% of their customers agree.

DEVELOP MORE RELEVANT PRODUCTS SERVICES AND EXPERIENCES FOR YOUR CUSTOMERS OR END USERS

DEVELOP A BETTER PRODUCT ROAD MAP
Maps can help you decide where you should be going with your business, what products and services you can and should be delivering and when it is best to introduce them. They can help you build strategic advantage against competitors.

DESIGNING AND IMPROVING SYSTEMS
Ensure systems are efficient, and customer-focused.

TAKE COST & COMPLEXITY OUT OF THE SYSTEM
Identify duplicated touchpoints and position people and other resources where they are most needed.

PRIORITIZE COMPETING DELIVERABLES
Plan how to allocate resources. Maps can help you decide what should be the top priorities for your business to grow and generate the best returns on investment. Your decisions can be guided by real customer data and feedback.

PLAN FOR HIRING
Maps can help you plan strategically and select the best employees and skills for long-term expansion of your business.

BRING YOUR WHOLE ORGANIZATION TOGETHER AROUND THE COMMON GOAL OF CUSTOMER EXPERIENCE

Understand the role that each department plays in a customer-focused strategy. Overcome silo thinking. Help different groups identify common ground. The entire company can focus on the vision of creating an exceptional customer experience.

KNOWLEDGE OF CUSTOMER BEHAVIORS AND NEEDS ACROSS CHANNELS

Customers commonly access a number of different channels when engaging an organization. Maps are a good way to understand complex processes across channels.

DRIVE IDEATION AND INNOVATION

Diagnose experience problems. Maps help an organization decide how to allocate resources to improve best current offerings or to build whole new sets of deliverables based on what customers need and want rather than what your employees think that they want. Maps help you benchmark your current performance against competitors and help you plan future initiatives.

MAKE INTANGIBLE SERVICES TANGIBLE

Elements of services such as human interactions are intangible and changing. Maps provide a focus for common understanding and decision making.

UNDERSTAND WHERE FRICTION EXISTS BETWEEN THE NEEDS OF DIFFERENT MARKET SEGMENTS

Various interested parties commonly have conflicting needs and desires. Maps can help you balance the needs of stakeholders more efficiently.

TAILOR YOUR EXPERIENCES MORE EFFECTIVELY TO DIFFERENT SEGMENT'S NEEDS

Map each segment to understand the differences

in their expectations and experience.

INTRODUCE METRICS FOR WHAT MATTERS MOST FOR YOUR CUSTOMERS

Maps help you plan strategically to achieve long term organizational goals and to measure progress towards those goals

ALIGN YOUR OFFERINGS TO BRAND PROMISE

Maps can help you understand where your current business supports or conflicts with your brand promise.

ELIMINATE POTENTIAL FAILURE POINTS

Maps help you see where your service or customer experience is most likely to fail and to plan to reduce the risk and cost of failure.

IMPROVE EFFICIENCY

Break down organizational silos Reduce duplication. Prioritize between competing requirements. Identify cheapest 'cost to serve', and set performance indicators that you can measure.

IMAGINE FUTURE PRODUCT AND SERVICE EXPERIENCES

Maps are one of the best tools available for planning and implementing future product and service offerings.

HOLISTIC THINKING

Maps help you balance the competing needs of your customers, your business, and technology.

IMPROVE YOUR WHOLE ORGANIZATION'S PERFORMANCE

The mapping process helps your organization work towards one goal of the best possible customer experience rather than multiple departmental goals

A LIVING DOCUMENT

A map is a living document. Update it improve and evolve it as your business changes and your customer needs and expectations.

13

Empathy

Empathy is sometimes defined as 'standing in someone else's shoes' or 'seeing through someone else's eyes'. It is The ability to identify and understand another's situation, feelings and motives. In design it may be defined as: identifying with others and, adopting their perspective. Empathy is different to sympathy. Empathy does not necessarily imply compassion. Empathy is a respectful understanding of what others are experiencing and their point of view.

E.B. Titchener invented the word in 1909 in an attempt to translate the German word "Einfühlungsvermögen".

WHY EMPATHY IS IMPORTANT?

1. Empathy is a core skill for designers to design successfully for other people.
2. Empathy is needed for business success.
3. Empathy is needed for products and services to be adopted by the people we design for.
4. Empathy builds trust.

HOW TO PRACTICE EMPATHY

1. Put yourself in contact and the context of people who you are designing for.
2. Ask questions and listen to the answers.
3. Read between the lines
4. Observe.
5. Listen
6. Restating what you think you heard.
7. Recognize that people are individuals.
8. Notice body language. Most communication is non verbal
9. Withhold judgment when you hear views different to your own.
10. Take a personal interest in people

Thinking styles

ABDUCTIVE THINKING
With abductive reasoning, unlike deductive reasoning, the premises do not guarantee the conclusion. Abductive reasoning can be understood as "inference to the best explanation" Abductive reasoning typically begins with an incomplete set of observations and proceeds to the likeliest possible explanation for the set. It's goal is to explore what could possibly be true.

"A person or organization instilled with that discipline is constantly seeking a fruitful balance between reliability and validity, between art and science, between intuition and analytics, and between exploration and exploitation. The design-thinking organization applies the designer's most crucial tool to the problems of business. That tool is abductive reasoning." Roger Martin

Charles Sanders Peirce originated the term and argued that no new idea could come from inductive or deductive logic.

DEDUCTIVE THINKING
The process of reasoning from one or more general statements (premises) to reach a logically certain conclusion. Deductive reasoning is one of the two basic forms of valid reasoning. It begins with a general hypothesis or known fact and creates a specific conclusion from that generalization.

Described by Aristotle 384-322bce, Plato 428-347bce, and Pythagoras 582-500 BCE

INDUCTIVE THINKING
Inductive thinking is a kind of reasoning that constructs or evaluates general propositions that are derived from specific examples. Inductive reasoning contrasts with deductive reasoning, in which specific examples are derived from general propositions.
Described by Aristotle 384-322bce,

CRITICAL THINKING
"The process of actively and skillfully conceptualizing, applying, analyzing, synthesizing, and evaluating information to reach an answer or conclusion. disciplined thinking that is clear, rational, open-minded,

and informed by evidence, willingness to integrate new or revised perspectives into our ways of thinking and acting" Critical thinking is an important element of all professional fields and academic disciplines

DESIGN THINKING

Design Thinking is a formal method for practical, creative resolution of problems and creation of solutions, with the intent of an improved future result. In this regard it is a form of solution-based, or solution-focused thinking

DIVERGENT THINKING

Convergent thinking is a tool for problem solving in which the brain is applies a mechanized system or formula to some problem, where the solution is a number of steps from the problem. This kind of thinking is particularly appropriate in science, engineering, maths and technology.

Convergent thinking is opposite from divergent thinking in which a person generates many unique, design solutions to a design problem. Divergent thinking is followed by convergent thinking, in which a designer assesses, judges, and strengthens those options. Divergent thinking is what we do when we do not know the answer, when we do not know

CONVERGENT THINKING

The design process is a series of divergent and convergent phases. During the divergent phase of design the designer creates a number of choices. The goal of this approach is to analyze alternative approaches to test for the most stable solution. Divergent thinking is what we do when we do not know the answer, when we do not know the next step. Divergent thinking is followed by convergent thinking, in which a designer assesses, judges, and strengthens those options.

Design Thinking

WHAT IS IT?

Design Thinking is or approach to designing that supports innovation and intelligent change. Design Thinking is a human-centered approach which is driven by creative and analytical thinking, customer empathy and iterative learning.

It involves a toolkit of methods that can be applied to different problems by cross disciplinary groups or by individuals. Anyone can use Design Thinking. It can be fun.

WHO INVENTED IT?

The origins of Design Thinking date back to before the 1950s. Design Thinking adopted ideas that came from the creativity methods of the 1950s, the design science and design methods movements of the 1960s, user centered design movement of the 1980s and experience and service design from the 2,000s. In 1987 Peter Rowe, a Professor at the Harvard Graduate School of Design, published "Design Thinking" the first significant usage of the term "Design Thinking" in literature. After 2000 the term became widely used.

EVIDENCE SUPPORTING THE VALUE OF DESIGN THINKING

A study published in September 2015 by the Hasso Plattner Institute at the University of Potsdam in Germany which was the first large-sample survey of Design Thinking adoption in practice. Organizations of all sizes and from different parts of the world participated. 235 organizations of all sizes and from different parts of the world participated.

1. 72.3% answered that Design Thinking is practiced in parts of their organizations.
2. 71% of our respondents report that Design Thinking improved their working culture on a team level.
3. 69% of our respondents perceive the innovation process to be more efficient with Design Thinking.
4. 48% "Since the introduction of Design Thinking we integrate our users"
5. 18% "Design Thinking helps us saving costs"
6. 29% "Design Thinking helps us increasing sales*
7. 18% said "Design Thinking helps us increasing profitability"

Design thinking evolved from a number of historical design movements

Year	Design movement	Design approaches	People
2010s	Design Thinking	Experience design	David Kelley
		Creative class	Tim Brown
			Roger Martin
			Rolf Faste
2000s	Service Design	Human Centered Design	Lucy Kimbell
1990s	Process Methods	Meta Design	Ezio Manzini
			William Rause
			Richard Buchanan
1980s	Cognitive Reflections	User Centered Design	Don Norman
			Donal Schon
			Nigel Cross
			Peter Rowe
			Bryan Lawson
1970s			Robert McKim
1960s	Design Science	Participatory Design	Horst Rittel
		Design Methods	Herbet Simon
			Bruce Archer
1950s	Creativity Methods	Brainstorming	Alex Osborn

Attributes of design thinking

Ambiguity	Being comfortable when things are unclear or when you do not know the answer	Design Thinking addresses wicked ill-defined and tricky problems.
Collaborative	Working together across disciplines	People design in interdisciplinary teams.
Constructive	Creating new ideas based on old ideas, which can also be the most successful ideas	Design Thinking is a solution-based approach that looks for an improved future result.
Curiosity	Being interested in things you do not understand or perceiving things with fresh eyes	Considerable time and effort is spent on clarifying the requirements. A large part of the problem solving activity, then, consists of problem definition and problem shaping.
Empathy	Seeing and understanding things from your customers' point of view	The focus is on user needs (problem context).
Holistic	Looking at the bigger context for the customer	Design Thinking attempts to meet user needs and also drive business success.
Iterative	A cyclical process where improvements are made to a solution or idea regardless of the phase	The Design Thinking process is typically non-sequential and may include feedback loops and cycles (see below).
Non judgmental	Creating ideas with no judgment toward the idea creator or the idea	Particularly in the brainstorming phase, there are no early judgments.
Open mindset	Embracing Design Thinking as an approach for any problem regardless of industry or scope	The method encourages "outside the box thinking" ("wild ideas"); it defies the obvious and embraces a more experimental approach.

Core Attributes of Design Thinking from Baeck & Gremett, 2011

BUSINESS THINKING	DESIGN THINKING	CREATIVE THINKING
Left Brain	Uses whole brain	Right brain
Rational	Both rational and intuitive	Emotional
Structured	Structured and intuitive	Intuitive
Analytical	Analytical and creative	Creative
Likes well defined problems	Works with defined and ill defined problems	Works with ill defined complex problems
Does not tolerate mistakes	Mistakes are inexpensive and a learning opportunity	Tolerates mistakes during exploration
Analyze then decide	Prototype test decide	Ideate then decide
Focuses on parts of a problem	Focuses on parts and on whole iteratively	Holistic diffuse focus
Convergent	Convergent and divergent	Divergent
Vertical	Vertical and Lateral	Lateral
Objective	Objective and subjective	Subjective
Linear	Linear and associative	Associative
Yes but	Yes and yes but	Yes and .....
Verbal and mathematical	Visual, verbal mathematical	Visual
The answer	Explores, tests iterates	One possible answer
Judges	Withholds judgment until tested	Withhold judgment
Probability	Possibility and probability	Possibility
Improve	Improves and innovates	Innovate
Sequential	Sequential and synthesizing	Synthesizing
Analyze and evaluate	Imagines, synthesizes and tests	Imagine
Parts and details	Parts and the whole	Whole and big picture
Observe	Imagines and observes	Imagine
Numeric models	Numeric and experiential	Experiential models
Phases	Phases and dimesions	Dimensions
Sort and separate	Sorts infuses and blends	Infuse and blend
Independent	Independent and interdependent	Interdependent
Successive	Successive and simultaneous	Simultaneous
Safe	takes risk but minimizes the cost of failure	Risk taking
Knows	Believes, tests and knows	Believes

WHY USE DESIGN THINKING?

Design Thinking is useful when you have:
1. A poorly defined problem.
2. A lack of information.
3. A changing context or environment
4. It should result in consistently innovative solutions.

Design Thinking seeks a balance of design considerations including:
1. Business.
2. Appropriate application of technology
3. Empathy with people.
4. Environmental consideration.

Design Thinking seeks to balance two modes of thinking:
1. Analytical thinking
2. Creative Thinking

WHAT CAN IT BE APPLIED TO?
1. Products
2. Services
3. Experiences
4. Interactions
5. Systems of the above

PROCESS

Design Thinking has a particular process

1. Define intent
2. Through ethnographic research develop empathy for the point of view of the user.
3. Synthesize the research
4. Frame insights
5. Explore Concepts
6. Synthesize the concepts generated
7. Prototype the favored ideas
8. Test the prototypes with users
9. Incorporate changes
10. Iterate prototype and testing till a workable design is reached
11. Implement
12. Deliver Offering

RESOURCES

Multidisciplinary team of 4 to 12 people
A project space
Post-it notes
Dry erase markers
Whiteboard
Digital camera
Copy paper
Chairs
Large table

FOCUS ON PEOPLE
Design is about people than it is about things. Stand in those people's shoes, see through their eyes, uncover their stories, share their worlds. Start each design by identifying a problem that real people are experiencing. Use the methods in this book selectively to gain empathy, understanding, and to inform your design. Good process is not a substitute for talented, motivated and skilled people on your design team.

GET PHYSICAL
Make simple physical prototypes of your ideas as early as possible. Constantly test your ideas with people. Do not worry about making prototypes beautiful until you are sure that you have a resolved design direction. Use the prototypes to guide and improve your design. Do several low cost prototypes to test how your Ideas physically work.. using cardboard, paper, markers, adhesive tape, photocopies, string and popsicle sticks. The idea is to test your idea, not to look like the final product. Expect to change it again. Limit your costs to ten or twenty dollars. Iterate, test and iterate. Do not make the prototype jewelry. It can stand in the way of finding the best design solution. In the minds of some a high fidelity prototype is a finished design solution rather than a tool for improving a design. You should make your idea physical as soon as possible. Be the first to get your hands dirty by making the idea real.

BE CURIOUS
Ask why? Explore and experiment. Go outside your comfort zone. Look for inspiration in new ways and places. Christopher Columbus Henry Ford, Thomas Edisonand Albert Einstein followed their curiosity to new places and you can too.

TEAM DIVERSITY
A diverse design team will produce more successful design than a team that lacks diversity. Innovation needs a collision of different ideas and approaches. Your team should have different genders, different ages, be from different cultures, different socioeconomic backgrounds and have different outlooks to be most successful. With diversity expect some conflict. Manage conflict productively and the best ideas will float to the surface. Have team members who have

lived in different countries and cultures and with global awareness. Cross cultural life experience enables people to be more creative.

TAKE CONSIDERED RISKS

Taking considered risks helps create differentiated design. Many designers and organizations do not have the flexibility or courage to create innovative, differentiated design solutions so they create products and services that are like existing products and services and compete on price.

USE THE TOOLS

To understand the point of view of diverse peoples and cultures a designer needs to connect with those people and their context. The tools in this book are an effective way of seeing the world through the eyes of those people.

LEARN TO SEE AND HEAR

Reach out to understand people. Interpret what you see and hear. Read between the lines. Make new connections between the things you see and hear.

COMBINE ANALYTICAL AND CREATIVE THINKING

Effective collaboration is part of effective design. Designers work like members of an orchestra. We need to work with managers, engineers, salespeople and other professions. Human diversity and life experience contribute to better design solutions.

LOOK FOR BALANCE

Design Thinking seeks a balance of design factors including:
1. Business.
2. Empathy with people.
3. Application OF technology.
4. Environmental consideration.

TEAM COLLABORATION

Design today is a more complex activity than it was in the past. Business, technology, global cultural issues, environmental considerations, and human considerations all need careful consideration. Design Thinking recognizes the need for designers to be working as members of multidisciplinary multi skilled teams.

Design thinking process

GOALS?
What are we looking for?
1. Meet with key stakeholders to set vision
2. Assemble a diverse team
3. Develop intent and vision
4. Explore scenarios of user experience
5. Document user performance requirements
6. Define the group of people you are designing for. What is their gender, age, and income range. Where do they live. What is their culture?
7. Define your scope and constraints
8. Identify a need that you are addressing. Identify a problem that you are solving.
9. Identify opportunities
10. Meet stakeholders

DISCOVER EMPATHIZE RESEARCH
What else is out there?
1. Identify what you know and what you need to know.
2. Document a research plan
3. Benchmark competitive products
4. Create a budgeting and plan.
5. Create tasks and deliverables
6. Explore the context of use
7. Understand the risks
8. Observe and interview individuals, groups, experts.
9. Develop design strategy
10. Undertake qualitative, quantitative, primary and secondary research.
11. Talk to vendors

SYNTHESIZE
What have we learned?
1. Review the research.
2. Make sense out of the research
3. Develop insights
4. Cluster insights
5. Create a hierarchy

DEVELOP A UNIQUE POINT OF VIEW
What is the design brief?

IDEATE
How is this for starters?

1. Brainstorm
2. Define the most promising ideas
3. Refine the ideas
4. Establish key differentiation of your ideas
5. Investigate existing intellectual property.

PROTOTYPE TEST AND ITERATE
How could we make it better?

1. Make your favored ideas physical.
2. Create low-fidelity prototypes from inexpensive available materials
3. Develop question guides
4. Develop test plan
5. Test prototypes with stakeholders
6. Get feedback from people.
7. Refine the prototypes
8. Test again
9. Build in the feedback
10. Refine again.
11. Continue iteration until design works.
12. Document the process.
13. When you are confident that your idea works make a prototype that looks and works like a production product.

IMPLEMENT AND DELIVER
Let's make it. Let's sell it.

1. Create your proposed production design
2. Test and evaluate
3. Review objectives
4. Manufacture your first samples
5. Review first production samples and refine.
6. Launch
7. Obtain user feedback
8. Conduct field studies
9. Define the vision for the next product or service.

Diversity in your team

DIVERSITY
Diversity means different genders, different ages, be from different cultures, different socioeconomic backgrounds and have different outlooks to be most successful.

WHY HAVE DIVERSITY?
1. To attract good people
2. It broadens the customer base in a competitive environment.
3. Diversity brings substantial potential benefits such as better decision making and improved problem solving, greater creativity and innovation, which leads to enhanced product development, and more successful marketing to different types of customers. Diversity provides organizations with the ability to compete in global markets

HOW TO PROMOTE DIVERSITY
1. View employees as individuals.
2. Seek commitment from key participants.
3. Be open-minded. Recognize, and encourage employees to recognize, that one's own experience, background, and culture are not the only ones with value to the organization.
4. Articulate the benefits and motivations for becoming a more diverse organization.
5. Develop a definition of diversity that is linked to organizational mission.
6. Identify other organizations, both locally and nationally, that might serve
7. As models for diversity efforts.
8. Develop a realistic action plan for diversity efforts that takes into account ongoing operations and competing priorities.
9. Develop criteria to measure success. In other words, begin to build an evaluation plan.
10. Create a safe environment for candid and honest participation
11. Set relevant, pragmatic and achievable goals for bringing about organizational diversity.
12. Articulate expected outcomes and measures of change.

Smallest design team

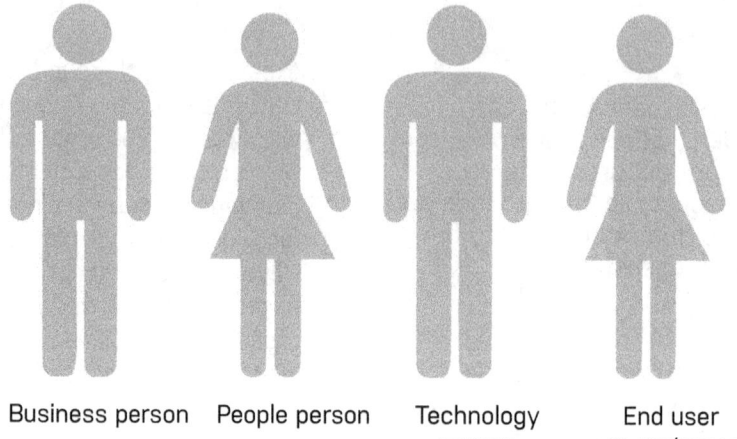

Business person	People person	Technology person	End user or customer
MBA in business Experience in business	Designer Marketer Psychologist Anthropologist	Engineer Factory Manager	Someone with good knowledge of the segment

Select a team with diversity in gender age, and cultural background.
Research suggests 4 or 5 people is the optimum size for group creativity

Keeleys triangle

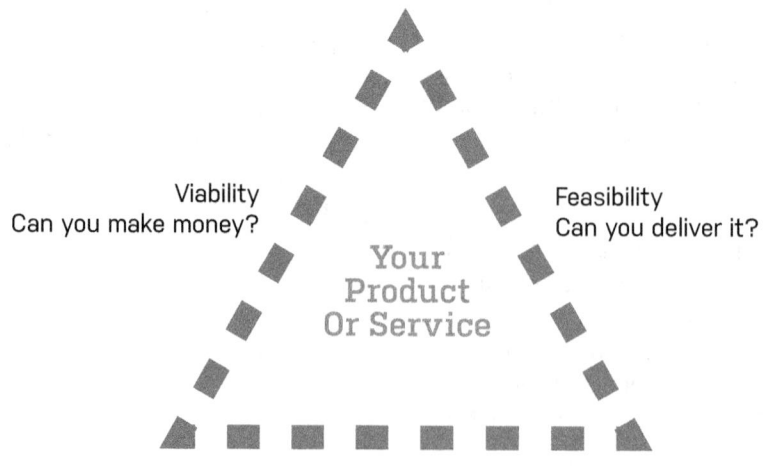

Viability
Can you make money?

Feasibility
Can you deliver it?

Your Product Or Service

Larger design team

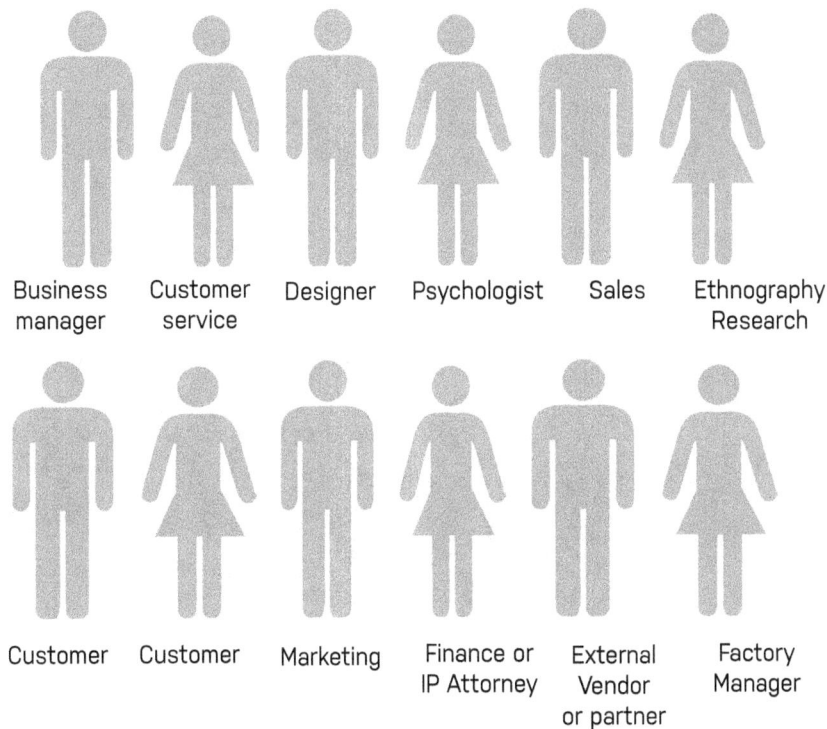

| Business manager | Customer service | Designer | Psychologist | Sales | Ethnography Research |

| Customer | Customer | Marketing | Finance or IP Attorney | External Vendor or partner | Factory Manager |

Teams larger than 12 people may be less productive
Select a team with diversity in gender age, and cultural background.

Keeleys triangle

Viability
Can you make money?

Feasibility
Can you deliver it?

Your Product Or Service

Desirability
Will anyone want it?

Materials

POST-IT NOTES
I allow at least one block poer participant per session.

SHARPIES
A range of different sizes

WHITEBOARD
A whiteboard is a good tool as it allows connections to be drawn between groups of post-it notes

DRY ERASE MARKERS
3 or 4 colors

TAPE
One inch masking tape

CAMERA
A camera with still and video capability. This can be used to record the groups of post-it notes or to create a video of the session for sharing.

FOAM CORE BOARDS
These can be used as an alternative display surface to whiteboards and are portable if you are working with a number of groups

LARGE TABLE
Large enough to seat all the participants

CHAIRS
For all the participants

COFFEE AND REFRESHMENTS
People work better with coffee and snacks.

Spaces

SPACES FOR CREATIVE WORK

1. Lightweight, comfortable, readily movable chairs perhaps on wheels can maximize a relatively small footprint and be arranged in multiple configurations
2. Show your work in progress and let people comment.
3. Surround yourself with the material that your team is working on.
4. Mobile large whiteboards 6 ft x 4 ft and pin boards.
5. Mobile boards can have a magnetic whiteboard on one side and a pin board on the reverse side.
6. A laptop-sized surface for each attendee
7. Walls can be used for projection, writing, or pinning up information in areas visible to everyone
8. Acoustic privacy should be ensured.
9. Large walls can be used as display spaces.
10. Use work tools that are easily accessible
11. Think of every vertical surface as a potential space for displaying work
12. Use flexible technologies such as wi-fi that allow relocation of services such as Internet and power connections.
13. Have a projector and screen
14. Team rooms should offer the flexibility to be arranged to suit the project at hand
15. Seating should allow all participants to see one another and read body language
16. Select furniture with wheels that can be easily moved
17. Small tables can be used for breakouts or grouped into a common surface
18. Ample writing and display areas, as well as surfaces for laying things out, support the need for visual cues and reference materials
19. Provide a large area of vertical displays such as walls whiteboards, pin boards, foam core boards, projection surfaces, that allow users to actively and flexibly interact with the information
20. Build spaces that support different types of collaboration.
21. Consider physical and virtual collaboration.
22. Spaces should be flexible for unplanned collaboration.
23. Position individual works paces around group spaces for flexibility
24. Provide comfortable group areas for informal interactions and information sharing.
25. The spaces need to be large enough to accommodate all the research materials,
26. visuals, and prototypes in order to keep them visible and accessible all of the time.

Source: Haworth

Types of Maps

CURRENT STATE MAPS
With a current-state journey map, you can:
1. Identify pain points and their causes.
2. Identify gaps in what you are offering customers.
3. Improve the efficiency and effectiveness of a current service or customer experience.
4. Craft a better customer experience for a product service or brand.
5. Plan systematically what your organization is delivering to customers.
6. Implement a more efficient system of touchpoints.
7. Understand how customers behave across multiple channels.
8. Identify where your current customer experience or service is most likely to fail.
9. Unite your team with the common goal of a better customer experience.
10. Identify opportunities for feedback or measurement.
11. Develop metrics for progress towards goals.
12. Align your organization with a better customer experience.

FUTURE STATE MAPS
1. With a future-state journey map, you can:
2. Plan a future service or customer experience.
3. Define a new service with better customer experience than your existing service.
4. Implement a new service or customer experience.
5. Develop a product or service roadmap.
6. Envision the ideal customer experience or service.
7. Identify the infrastructure needed to create a new service or customer experience.
8. Plan for hiring new staff
9. Drive positive change in your organization.
10. Develop empathy for customers.

WHAT'S THE DIFFERENCE, BETWEEN A BLUEPRINT AND A JOURNEY OR EXPERIENCE MAP?

A customer journey map captures how your customer is feeling emotionally across touchpoints over time.

A service blueprint captures the

service or experience delivery process across touch points and the elements that make up the service including the things customers see and do not see.

The two types of maps complement each other. The order in which you create them depends on your goals.

SERVICE BLUEPRINT

1. Define employees roles about the customer experience.
2. Identify areas of service improvement.
3. Identify points where moments of truth will occur.
4. Capturing Dynamic Processes
5. Service blueprinting allows the capturing of dynamic processes in a visual manner.
6. A blueprint is one of few methods that allow you to visually convey events that change over time.
7. Relatively few methods allow for this type of dynamic, and at the same time visual, representation.
8. To identify where your customer experience is most likely to fail.
9. Opportunities for improvements
10. To plan and implement a new customer experience.
11. To implement metrics to measure your customer experience.
12. To audit and improve your service evidence or touchpoints.

JOURNEY/EXPERIENCE MAP

1. To identify customer pain points and gaps in your touchpoints
2. To design a new service or experience with a focus on optimizing your customer's experience.
3. To audit the customer experience.
4. To develop new touch points to improve the customer experience.

Segmentation
& Personas

Market segmentation involves subdividing a market into a number of groups where the people in each group have some commonality, or similarity. Members of a market segment share something in common. Segmentation is undertaken to provide design solutions that work for a group of people because it is simpler than developing a different solution for each person.

Personas are a design tool. "A persona is a archetypal character that is meant to represent a group of users in a role who share common goals, attitudes and behaviors when interacting with a particular product or service Personas are user models that are presented as specific individual humans. They are not actual people, but are synthesized directly from observations of real people." (Cooper)

Segmentation

WHAT IS MARKET SEGMENTATION?

Market segmentation involves subdividing a market into a number of groups where the people in each group have some commonality, or similarity. Members of a market segment share something in common. Segmentation is done to provide deign solutions that work for a group of people without the expense of developing a different solution for each person. There are many ways to segment a market. The best way to segment customers depends on your goals. For example if you are entering a new global market one way is to segment your customers by where they live.

GEOGRAPHIC SEGMENTATION

This is one of the more common methods of market segmentation. For example, a company selling products in Europe may segment their customers by the country that they live in. In Europe regional differences in customer preferences exist. You may decide to segment you customers by those who live in a city and those who live in a rural location.

DISTRIBUTION SEGMENTATION

Experience maps and Service blueprints help designers understand a market where most people access multiple channels when purchasing or using a product or service

PRICE SEGMENTATION

Another common way of segmenting a market is by income. Different price-points for a product or service may appeal to people with different incomes. Mass market car companies like ford have models that appeal to people with lower incomes and luxury models that appeal to customers with higher incomes.

DEMOGRAPHIC SEGMENTATION

Demographic segmentation is possibly the most commonly used type of segmentation. There are large number of demographic factors such as gender, age, type of employment and education that are often used for segmentation. Some products and brands are targeted mainly at men. Most people over the age of 40 require glasses to read.

TIME SEGMENTATION

Some products are sold at a particular time of day or year. For example surfboards are sold in summer.

PSYCHOGRAPHIC OR LIFESTYLE SEGMENTATION

Psychographic or lifestyle segmentation, is based on, values, behaviors, emotions, perceptions, beliefs, and interests. For example some customers prefer luxury products. Some customers may follow a particular sporting team.

Markets segments should be large enough to justify creating targeted products and services. Four to six market segments is often a manageable number. Targeting too many segments is sometimes unsuccessful. Products usually do not appeal to everyone.

Consider the income potential of each segment carefully when defining segments.
When defining segments consider:
1. Can you measure the segment?.
2. Is the segment big enough to make a profit?
3. Is the segment changing or evolving?
4. Can you reach the segment?
5. Is there one factor that unites everyone in the segment?
6. Do you have enough data to understand the segment?

Market segmentation involves subdividing a market into a number of groups where the people in each group have some commonality, or similarity. Members of a market segment share something in common. Segmentation is undertaken to provide design solutions that work for a group of people because it is simpler than developing a different solution for each person.

Personas

WHAT IS IT?
"A persona is a archetypal character that is meant to represent a group of users in a role who share common goals, attitudes and behaviors when interacting with a particular product or service Personas are user models that are presented as specific individual humans. They are not actual people, but are synthesized directly from observations of real people."(Cooper)

WHO INVENTED IT?
Alan Cooper 1998

WHY USE THIS METHOD?
1. Helps create empathy for users and reduces self reference.
2. Use as tool to analyze and gain insight into users.
3. Help in gaining buy-in from stakeholders.

HOW TO USE THIS METHOD
1. Inaccurate personas can lead to a false understandings of the end users. Personas need to be created using data from real users.
2. Collect data through observation, interviews, ethnography.
3. Segment the users or customers
4. Create the Personas
5. Avoid Stereotypes
6. Each persona should be different. Avoid fringe characteristics. Personas should each have three to four life goals which are personal aspirations,
7. Personas are given a name, and photograph.
8. Design personas can be followed by building customer journeys

RESOURCES
Raw data on users from interviews or other research
Images of people similar to segmented customers.
Computer
Graphics software

Persona template

PHOTO OF PERSONA   PERSONA NAME

DEMOGRAPHICS
Age   Income
Occupation   Gender
Location   Education

CHARACTERISTICS

GOALS

What does this person want to achieve in life?

MOTIVATIONS
Incentives   Achievement
Fear   Power
Growth   Social

FRUSTRATIONS   QUOTE

What experiences does this person wish to avoid?
                    Characteristic quote

BRANDS

What brands does this persona purchase or wish to purchase?

CHARACTERISTICS

• • • • • • • • • • • • • • • • •   • • • • • • • • • • • • • • • • •

EXTROVERT   **INTROVERT**   FREE TIME

• • • • • • • • • • • • • • • • •   • • • • • • • • • • • • • • • • •

TRAVEL   LUXURY GOODS

• • • • • • • • • • • • • • • • •   • • • • • • • • • • • • • • • • •

TECHNICAL SAVVY   SPORTS

• • • • • • • • • • • • • • • • •   • • • • • • • • • • • • • • • • •

SOCIAL NETWORKING   MOBILE APPS

PHOTO OF PERSONA   PERSONA NAME

image of persona

DEMOGRAPHICS
Occupation   Income
Location   Gender
                    Education

CHARACTERISTIC

GOALS

What does this person want to achieve

demograhic factors

MOTIVATIONS
Incentives   Achievement
Fear   Power
Growth   Social

FRUSTRATIONS   QUOTE

What experiences does this person
wish to avoid?   Characteristic quote

BRANDS

What brands does

CHARACTERIST

········X········   ········X········

sliders show relevant factors

EXTROVERT

············X············   ············X············

TRAVEL   LUXURY GOODS

····X····   ····X····

TECHNICAL SAVVY   SPORTS

············X············   ············X············

SOCIAL NETWORKING   MOBILE APPS

53

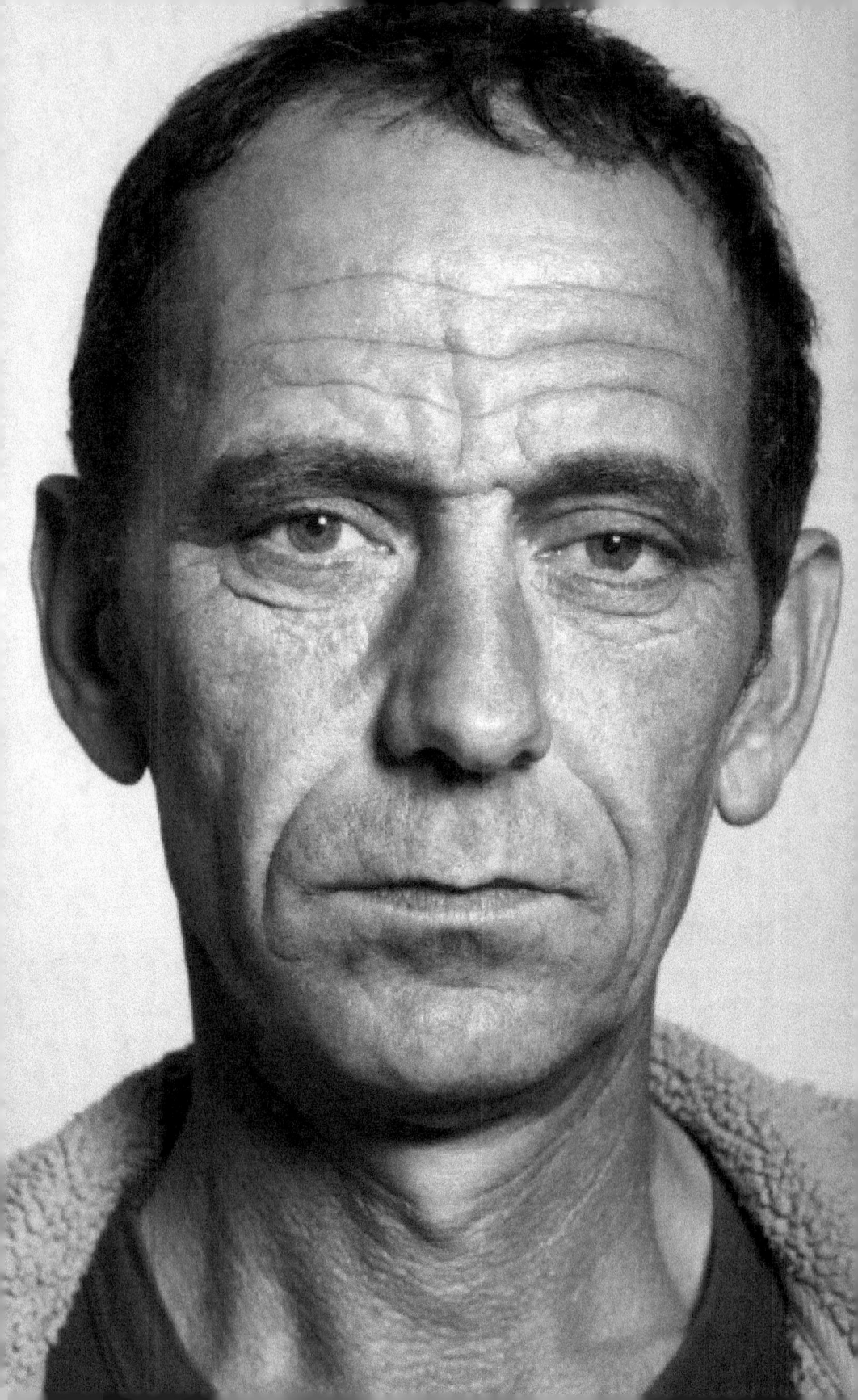

History of personas

The Inmates Are Running the Asylum, written by Alan Cooper published in 1998, introduced the use of personas as a design tool. Alan Cooper describes his first application of the persona technique:

"In 1995 I was working with the three founders of Sagent Technologies, pioneers in the field of what is now called "Business Intelligence" software. It was almost impossible for those brilliant, logical programmers to conceive of a single use of their product when it was obviously capable of so many uses. In frustration I demanded to be introduced to their customers.

The users fell into three distinct groups, clearly differentiated by their goals, tasks, and skill levels. Had I been creating the software myself, I would have role-played those users as I had with Ruby and SuperProject, but in this case I had to describe those user models to the Sagent team. So I created Chuck, Cynthia, and Rob. These three were the first true, Goal-Directed, personas.

At the next group meeting, I presented my designs from the points of view of Chuck, Cynthia, and Rob instead of from my own. The results were dramatic. While there was still resistance to this unfamiliar method, the programmers could clearly see the sense in my designs because they could identify with these hypothetical archetypes. The product was so successful that it defined a new product segment. The company was a success, too, going public four years later.

Over the next few years, we developed and perfected the technique.

Many of my predecessors have employed ethnographic user research and created persona-like constructs to aid their designing. Product marketing professionals have also been using persona-like entities for many years to define demographic segments. But personas are unique and uniquely effective."

Types of personas

PRIMARY
The users who are the main focus of the product or service.

SECONDARY
Secondary users may use the product but are not the primary focus.

STAKEHOLDERS
Stakeholders are people who may be affected by the products or services. A patient may be the primary persona but stakeholders may be doctors, nurses, hospital workers, medical insurance company employees, or relatives of the patient.

Usually persona are not created for each stakeholder. There may be conflicts between the needs of different stakeholders that should be considered.

EXCLUSIONARY
Someone we're not designing for. It is useful to consider non users when defining personas.

Biographical information

NAME
Give each persona a name that may be representative of the user group.

PHOTO
Choose a photograph which represents someone like the persona that you have constructed.

COUNTRY/ REGION
Where within the country does the persona live?

CITY/METROPOLITAN SIZE
1. Under 5,000,
2. 5,000-10,000,
3. 10,000 -20.000
4. 20,000-50,000,
5. 50,000- 250,000,
6. 250,000-500,000,
7. 500,000-1 million,
8. 1 million-4 million,
9. More than 4 million

URBAN OR RURAL?
Do they live in the city or in the country?

Demographic

AGE
Give the persona a precise age. Segments often give age as a range:
1. Under 6
2. 6-11
3. 12-20
4. 20-35
5. 35-50
6. 50-65
7. Over 65

GENDER
Male or female?

FAMILY SIZE
1. 1-2
2. 3-4
3. More than 5

SINGLE OR MARRIED?
Single married or divorced?

LIFE STAGE
1. Child
2. Teenager
3. Young
4. Middle aged
5. Elderly

INCOME
1. Under $10,000;
2. $10,000-20,000,
3. $20,000-30,000,
4. $30,000-50,000,
5. $50,000-100,000,
6. $100,000-150,000
7. Over 150.000

HOUSING
Renter or owner?
Type of dwelling?

OCCUPATION
1. Sales
2. Office worker
3. Nurse
4. Waiter
5. Administration
6. Building
7. Professional
8. Other

EDUCATION
1. Grade school
2. High school
3. College
4. Post Graduate

ETHNICITY
Consider with nationality

NATIONALITY
Many different groups are represented with nationality.

Psychographic

SELF-IMAGE
Outgoing, leader, shy

BELIEFS
Focus on those beliefs that may be most relevant to your product or service.

ATTITUDES
Favorable and unfavorable attitudes relevant to the product or service.

TECH STATUS
1. Innovator
2. Early adopter
3. Fast followers
4. Early mainstream
5. Late mainstream
6. Lagger

INTERESTS
1. Music
2. Sport
3. Food
4. Others

MEDIA
1. Web sites
2. TV shows
3. Magazines
4. Other

Web

TENURE
How long has the persona been using the web?

TIME ONLINE
Hours per week or month

TYPE OF USAGE
1. Email
2. Social networking
3. News
4. Other

BANDWIDTH
How fast is their connection?

INTERNET DEVICE
1. Desk
2. Tablet
3. Phone
4. Other

BROWSER
Type of browser

Sources: "Principles of Marketing" 8th Edition, Phillip Kotler and Gary Armstrong, "The People Who Make Organization Go – Or Stop," Rob Cross and Laurence Prusak, Havard Business Review, June Persona Creation and Usage Toolkit, George Olsen 2004

Research & Opportunity Exploration

Only 10-20% of new products and services succeed. The greatest reasons for failure according to many studies are related to an organization having an inadequate understanding of the changing needs and desires of customers.

Innovation carries risk, but the biggest risk is not to innovate.
One of the best ways to reduce risk is to give your customers a voice through practical research.

Customer journeys that are not based on research can lead to making wrong decisions. To be useful tools, maps should be based on engaging your customers in understanding their point of view. In this chapter, I have recommended some research methods that you can use to figure out what is most important to your customers, where their pain points are and what they experience as they interact with your organization.

1. B
2. C
3. B
4. A
5. C
6. D
7. B
8. B
9. A
10. C
11. D
12. A
13. B
14. D
18. A
19. D
20. C
21. A
22. B
23. A
24. D
25. B
26. —
27. A
28. —
29. B
30. A
31. C

Primary research

WHAT IS IT?
Primary research also called as field research involves collecting data first hand created during the time of the study. Primary research methods can include, including questionnaires and interviews and direct observations.

WHO INVENTED IT?
Robert W. Bruere of the Bureau of Industrial Research 1921 may have been the first to use the term

WHY USE THIS METHOD?
You can collect this information yourself. There may be no secondary research available. It may be more reliable than secondary research.
It may be more up to date than secondary research

CHALLENGES
1. May be more expensive than secondary research.
2. Information may become obsolete
3. Large sample can be time-consuming

HOW TO USE THIS METHOD
Methods such as:
1. Diaries
2. E-mail
3. Interviews
4. News footage
5. Photographs
6. Raw research data
7. Questionnaires
8. Observation

RESOURCES
Camera
Notebook
Pens
Digital Voice recorder
Diaries
E-mail

Secondary research

WHAT IS IT?
Research data that conveys the opinions and experiences of others. Secondary research is as the most widely used method of data collection. Secondary research accesses information that is already gathered from primary research.

WHO INVENTED IT?
Robert W. Bruere of the US Bureau of Industrial Research 1921 may have been the first to use the term secondary research.

WHY USE THIS METHOD?
1. Ease of access
2. Low cost
3. May be the only resource, for example historical documents
4. Only way to examine large scale trends

CHALLENGES
1. Possible bias in sources
2. May be out of date
3. May not be aligned with research goals
4. Lack of consistency of perspective
5. Biases and inaccuracies
6. Data affected by context of its collection

HOW TO USE THIS METHOD
1. Define goals.
2. Define the context of the problem to be researched.
3. Frame research questions.
4. Develop procedure.
5. Select and retrieve appropriate data.
6. Proceed with analysis and interpretation
7. Compare your findings and interpretations with other relevant studies.
8. Draw conclusions.

RESOURCES
Books
Internet
Online search engines
Magazines
E-books
Bibliographies
Biographical works
Commentaries, criticisms
Dictionaries, Encyclopedias
Histories;
Newspaper articles
Web site

Qualitative research

WHAT IS IT?
Seeks to understand people in the context of their daily experiences. Uses ethnographic methods including observation and interviews. Aims to understand questions like why and how. Obtains insights about attitudes and emotions. Often uses small sample sizes. Seeks to see the world through the eyes of research subjects. Methods are flexible. Used to develop an initial understanding.

WHO INVENTED IT?
Bronisław Malinowski 1922., with perhaps six other pioneers working in the first quarter of the 20th century.

WHY USE THIS METHOD?
Methods commonly used by designers to gain empathy for the people they are designing for.

CHALLENGES
1. Concerned with validity
2. Subjective
3. Hard to recreate results
4. People may behave differently to the way they say they behave
5. Experiences can not be generalized.

HOW TO USE THIS METHOD
1. Define research question
2. Select research subjects and context to study.
3. Collect data
4. Interpret data.
5. Study data for insights
6. Collect more data
7. Analyze data

RESOURCES
Camera
Video camera
Note pad
Pens
Digital voice recorder
Whiteboard
Post-it-notes
Blank cards

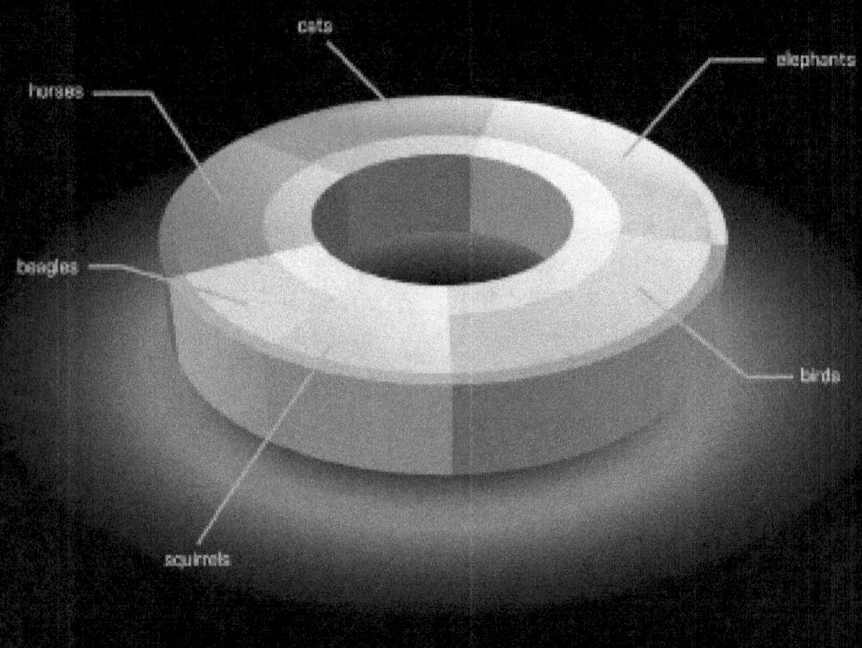
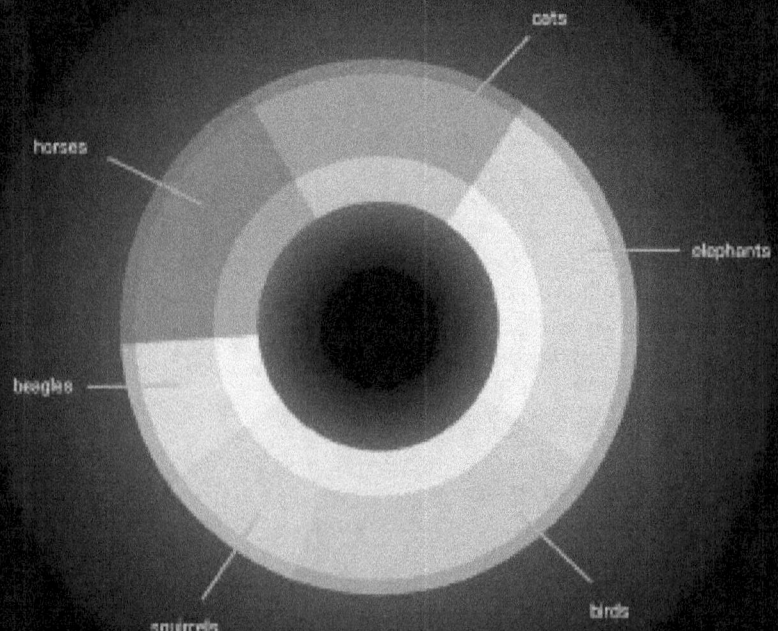

Quantitative research

WHAT IS IT?
Research that uses statistical or mathematical methods. Sample sizes are often large. Findings may be expressed as numbers or percentages. Quantitative research uses methods such as surveys and questionnaires. Asks questions like "How many?" Used to recommend a final course of action.

WHO INVENTED IT?
The Royal Statistical Society founded in 1834 pioneered the use of quantitative methods.

WHY USE THIS METHOD?
1. High level of reliability
2. Minimum personal judgment.
3. It is objective.

CHALLENGES
1. Methods are static. Real world changes.
2. Structured methods
3. Difficult to control the environment
4. Can be expensive if studying a large numb Er of people.

HOW TO USE THIS METHOD
1. Research design
2. Devise ways to measure hypothesis
3. Select subjects and context
4. Undertake research
5. Process data
6. Analyze data
7. Conclusions

Some questions to ask as part of your research

PEOPLE
1. What user group does this product, service or experience target?
2. What problems or needs does our product help with for this group?
3. When and how and where is our product, service or experience used?
4. What features are most important to end users?
5. How should our product, service or experience look and work?
6. Who should we employ?
7. What external partners do we need?
8. What does the customer need?

9. What does the customer want?
10. How does the customer learn to use this product or service?
11. What is the experience when the customer enters this experience?
12. How does the customer purchase or initiate this experience?
13. How does the customer interact with each touchpoint?
14. How are customers retained?
15. What are the barriers to a customer returning?
16. What is the process if a customer has an unsatisfactory experience?
17. This product or service feature or experience will achieve what for which segment or persona?
18. We will know this assumption is true when we see:
- What market feedback?
- What quantitative measure?
- What qualitative insight?

BUSINESS
1. We will make money by:
2. Our customers will find our product service or experience valuable because:
3. We will acquire customers through:
4. It will cost how much to establish these products or services.
5. It will cost how much per month/year to offer these products or services and maintain our business.
6. Establishing these products or services will be funded by:
7. My primary competition of brand and products in the market will be:
8. We will eat them because:
9. Our biggest business risk is:
10. We will reduce this risk by:
11. What could cause our business to fail?

TECHNOLOGY
We are using these technologies/ materials/ processes/ finishes
These offer strategic advantage because

Brainstorming

WHAT IS IT?
Brainstorming is a group creativity technique involving the exploration of a problem by the group where each member proposes possible solutions to the problem.

WHO INVENTED IT?
Popularized by Alex Osborn. The method was first presented in 1948 by Osborn in the book called "Your creative power". He was frustrated by employees' inability to develop creative ideas individually for ad campaigns.
It is now used by an estimated 75% of US corporations

WHY USE THIS METHOD?
This method can generate a lot of good ideas.
This method draws upon the expertise of a group of people. It is democratic. Have a team of 4 to 12 people.
This is a relatively efficient and fast way to generate ideas.

HOW TO USE THIS METHOD
1. Define problem statement.
2. Select a room and moderate
3. The facilitator asks the question or states the brainstorming challenge.
4. Generated as many ideas as possible We recommend aiming to generate 75 to 120 ideas in a session.
5. Stay focused on the topic.
6. Encourage adventurous ideas.
7. One conversation at a time.
8. Build on ideas of others.
Defer judgment. No negative criticism. Consider all ideas.
9. Be visual.
10. Make each explanation short and sweet.
11. Ideas can be recorded on post-it notes and placed by the moderator on a wall or they can be called out and written on a whiteboard or black board by the moderator or an assistant.
12. Allow 30 to 45 minutes.
13. Cluster the ideas into similar groups.
14. Photograph the post-it notes.

RESOURCES
Paper
Pens
Whiteboard
Dry-erase markers
Post-it-notes.

PREPARING FOR BRAINSTORMING

Come to the brainstorm session prepared.

1. Bring a lot of paper and markers.
2. Pens
3. Post-it-notes
4. Index cards
5. A flip chart
6. Whiteboard or wall
7. Video camera
8. Camera
9. One clear goal per brainstorming session.
10. Determine who will write things down and document the proceedings?
11. Allow one to two hours for a brainstorming session.
12. Recruit good people.
13. 8 to 12 people is a good number
14. Prepare brainstorm questions that you think will help guide the group.

CREATE A STRATEGY

1. What do you want to achieve?
2. What problem do you want solved?
3. Define the goal
4. How will you define the problem to the participants?
5. How long will the session be?
6. How many people will be involved?
7. What will be the mix of people?
8. Will there be a follow up session?
9. Will you send out information before the session?
10. Do the participants have the information that they need?
11. Who should you invite?
12. Assemble a diverse team.
13. Do the participants have the right skills and knowledge for the task?
14. Where will the brainstorm be held?
15. Who owns the intellectual property?
16. Will the session be free of interruptions?
17. How will you record the ideas?
18. What will you do with the information?
19. Be mindful of the scope brainstorm questions. Neither too broad nor too narrow.
20. 45-60 minutes for brainstorm time. Warm up 15-30 minutes.
21. Wrap up 15-30 minutes.

CHOOSING A TECHNIQUE

1. There are many different brainstorming methods.
2. Choose a method that suits your task and participants
3. Try different methods over time to find which ones work best for you.

REFRESHMENTS
1. An army marches on its stomach
2. Offer tea, coffee water, soda.

FACILITATING
1. Encourage everyone to contribute.
2. Review the rules and ask the group to enforce them.
3. Ask participants to turn phones off or onto vibrate mode.
4. A facilitator isn't a leader.
5. Do not steer the discussion
6. Do not let particular people dominate the conversation.
7. Keep the conversations on topic.
8. Set realistic time limits for each stage and be sure that you keep on time.
9. Have a brainstorm plan and stick to it.
10. The facilitator should create an environment where it is safe to suggest wild ideas.
11. Provide clear directions at the beginning of the meeting.
12. Clearly define the problem to be discussed.
13. Write the problem on the whiteboard where everyone can see it.
14. Provide next steps at the end of the meeting.
15. Select final ideas by voting.
16. Use your camera or phone to take digital pictures of the idea output at the end of your meeting.
17. Good facilitation requires good listening skills
18. The facilitator should run the whiteboard, writing down ideas as people come up with them,
19. Prevent people from interrupting others
20. Invite quieter people to contribute.
21. Hire a facilitator if necessary.
22. Start on time.
23. End on time.
24. Keep things moving
25. You can filter the best ideas after the session or get the team to vote on their preferred ideas during the session.
26. Listen
27. Write fast & be visual
28. Use humor and be playful
29. Thank the group after the session.
30. Provide next steps to the group after the meeting.
31. Keep participants engaged
32. Encourage interactivity
33. 100 ideas per hour.
34. Avoid social hierarchy
35. Organize small break-out sessions that cut across traditional office boundaries to establish teams.
36. Encourage passion.

RULES FOR BRAINSTORMING

1. "Defer judgment Separating idea generation from idea selection strengthens both activities. For now, suspend critique. Know that you'll have plenty of time to evaluate the ideas after the brainstorm.
2. Encourage wild ideas
3. One conversation at a time Maintain momentum as a group. Save the side conversations for later.
4. Headline Capture the essence quickly "
5. Focus on quantity not on quality."

POST-IT VOTING

1. Give every participant 4 stickers and have everyone put stickers next to their favorite ideas.
2. Each person tags three favorite ideas
3. Cluster favorite ideas
4. Clustering of stickers indicates possible strong design directions.

GROUP REVIEW

Ask everyone to review the boards of ideas, and discuss the specific ideas or directions they like and why.

Source adapted from Hasso Plattner Institute of Design

THE ENVIRONMENT

1. Select a space not usually used by your team.
2. Refreshments
3. Find a quiet comfortable room
4. Comfortable chairs
5. No interruptions
6. Turn phones off
7. Go off-site. A new environment might spur creativity and innovation by providing new stimuli. Helps participants mentally distance themselves from ordinary perceptions and ways of thinking.
8. Use big visible materials for writing on
9. Keep the temperature comfortable
10. Adequate lighting
11. Suitable external noise levels
12. Seats should be not too far apart
13. Have a space with a lot of vertical writing space.

METHODS OF SYNTHESIZING IDEAS

1. 2X2 matrix
2. Clustering
3. Continuum
4. Concentric circles
5. Time-line
6. Prioritization
7. Adoption curve

635 brainstorming process

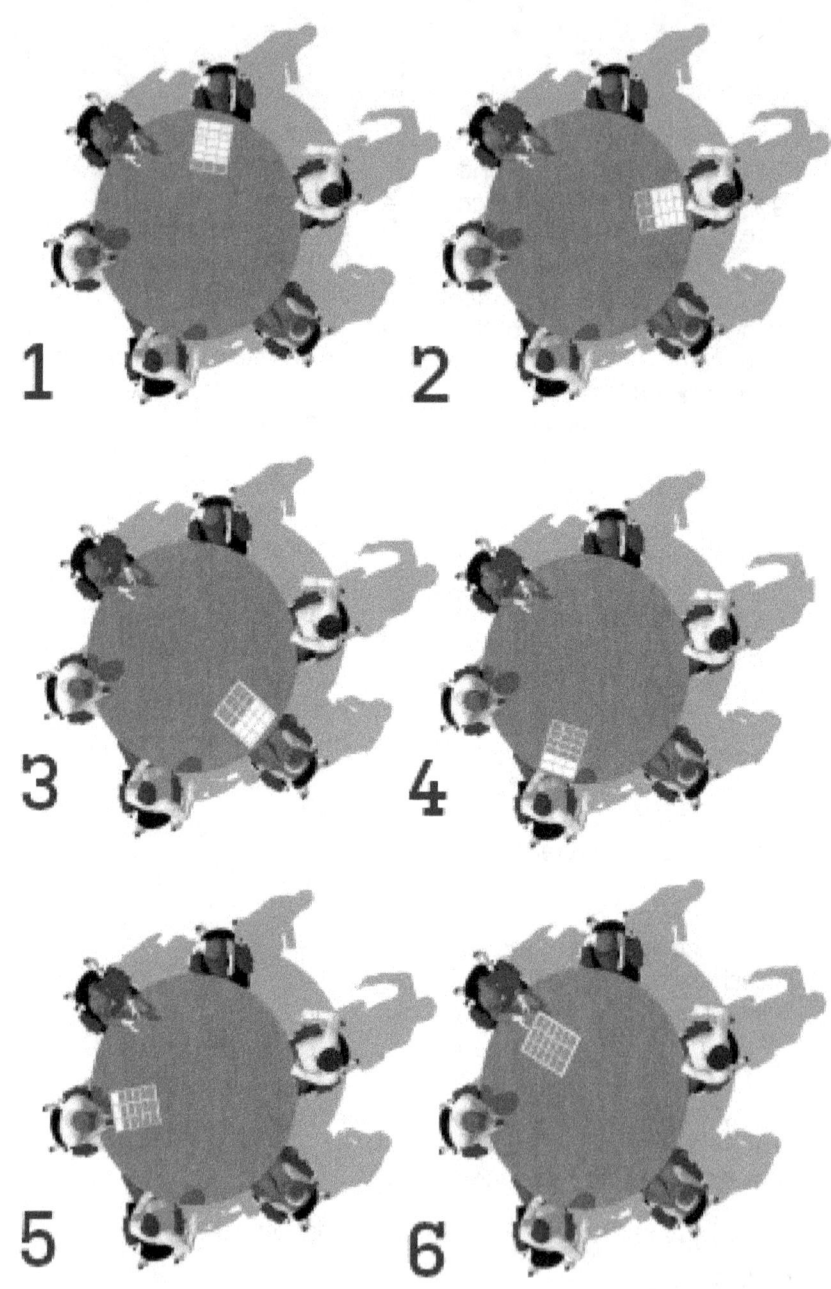

635 brainstorming

WHAT IS IT?
Method 635 is a structured form of brainstorming.

The outcome of each session is 108 ideas in 18 minutes.

WHO INVENTED IT?
Professor Bernd Rohrbach 1968

WHY USE THIS METHOD?
1. Can generate a lot of ideas quickly
2. Participants can build on each others ideas
3. The participants record ideas
4. Democratic process.
5. Ideas are contributed privately.
6. Ideas are iteratively refined five times.
7. Does not need a moderator

HOW TO USE THIS METHOD
1. Your team should sit around a table.
2. Each team member is given a sheet of paper with the design objective written at the top.
3. The sheet can be divided into six rows of three boxes.
4. Each team member is given three minutes to generate three ideas.
5. Your participants then pass the sheet of paper to the person sitting on their left.
6. Each participant must come up with three new ideas.
7. The process can stop when sheets come around the table.
8. Repeat until ideas are exhausted. No discussion during the idea generating period.
9. Ideas can be sketches or written or a combination.
10. You can use an egg timer
11. You can also use post-it notes. One per box. This makes it easier to process the ideas after the session.
12. Analyze ideas as a group,
13. Put the ideas on a whiteboard or wall cluster and vote for the preferred ideas.

RESOURCES
Large room
Large table
Paper
Pens
Post-it notes

Experiences that deliver benefits to customers are far more likely to succeed

Does the experience:
- Have unique features?
- Meet customer needs better?
- Is it the highest quality?
- Solve a problem for the customer?
- Reduce the customer's costs?
- Is it the first of its kind?

TOM HOPKINS
Innovation Director Experian

Backcasting

WHAT IS IT?
Backcasting is a method for planning the actions necessary to reach desired future goals. This approach is often applied in a workshop format with stakeholders participating. The scenarios are developed for periods of between 1 and 20 years in the future.

The participants first identify their goals and then work backward to determine the necessary actions to reach these objectives.

WHO INVENTED IT?
AT&T 1950s, Shel 1970s

WHY USE THIS METHOD?
1. It is inexpensive and fast
2. Backcasting is a tool for identifying, planning and reaching future goals.
3. Backcasting provides a strategy to reach future goals.

CHALLENGES
1. Need a good moderator
2. Needs good preparation

HOW TO USE THIS METHOD
A typical backcasting question is "How would you define success for yourself in 2015?

1. Define a framework
2. Analyze the present situation in relation to the framework
3. Prepare a vision and a number of desirable future scenarios.
4. Back-casting: Identify the steps to achieve this goal.
5. Further elaboration, detailing
6. Step by step strategies towards achieving the outcomes desired.
7. Ask do the strategies move us in the right direction? Are they flexible strategies?. Do the strategies represent a good return on investment?
8. Implementation, policy, organization embedding, follow-up

RESOURCES
Post-it-notes
Whiteboard
Pens
Dry-erase markers

C-box

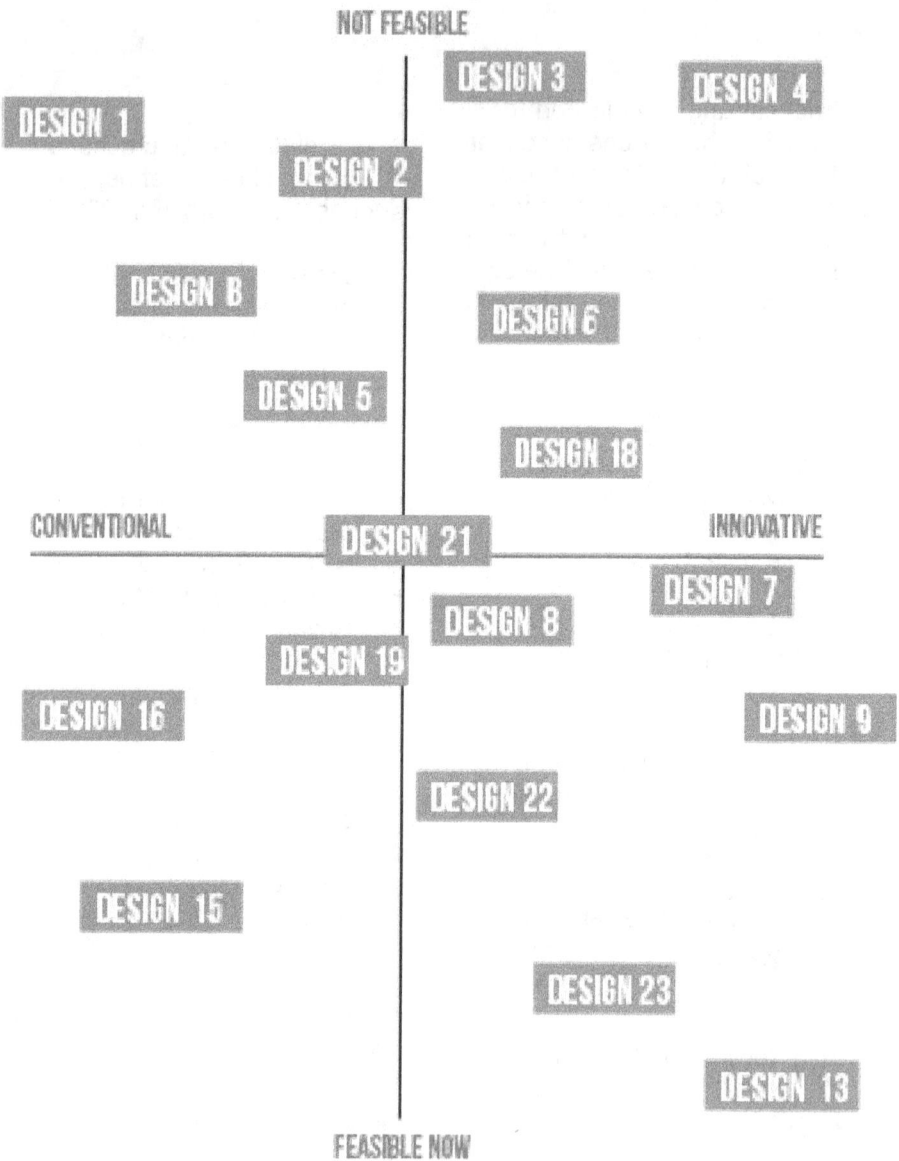

C-box

WHAT IS IT?
A C-box is a type of perceptual map that allows comparison and evaluation of a large number of ideas generated in a brainstorming session by a design team. The method allows everyone to contribute in a democratic way. It can be used to identify the most feasible and innovative ideas. It is up to your team to decide the level of innovation that they would like to carry forward from the idea generation or divergent phase of the project to the convergent or refinement and implementation phases.

WHO INVENTED IT?
Marc Tassoul, Delft 2009

WHY USE THIS METHOD?
1. It is democratic
2. It is quick and productive
3. It is inexpensive

WHEN TO USE THIS METHOD
1. Frame insights
2. Explore Concepts

HOW TO USE THIS METHOD
1. The moderator defines the design problem
2. You group can be optimally from 4 to 20 people.
3. On a whiteboard or large sheet of paper create two axes. You can also use tape on a large wall.
4. Innovation on the horizontal and feasibility on the vertical axes creating 4 quadrants
5. The scale on the innovation ranges from not innovative at the left hand to highly innovative on the right hand end.
6. Alternative axes are attractiveness and functionality.
7. Brainstorm concepts. Each team member to generate 5 to 10 concepts over 30 minutes. One idea per post-it note. Hand out more post-it notes if required.
8. Each team member then presents each idea taking one to three minutes per idea depending on time available.
9. With the group's input discuss the ideas and precise position on the map.
10. Position each post-it-note according to the group consensus.

Context

WHAT IS IT?
Context is the environment situation or circumstances that surround a product or service in use.
The 5 Ws of context
1. Who – the user and other people in the environment
2. What – human activity perception and interpretation
3. Where – location and the perceived path of the user
4. When – time as an index and elapsed time
5. Why – reason a person is doing something

Abowd & Mynatt 2000

WHO INVENTED IT?
The word first appeared in Late Middle English around 1375 to 1425 and meant a joining together, scheme, structure or to join by weaving.

WHY USE THIS METHOD?
Every design is intended to accomplish goals, in a particular environment or context. understanding the context is necessary in order to create a successful design.

CHALLENGES
1. A product or service may be used in diverse contexts.
2. A design can effect the context.
3. A designer needs to experience the context to create a successful design. This may be difficult, time consuming or expensive.

WHEN TO CONSIDER CONTEXT
4. Define goals
1. Know Context
2. Know User
3. Frame insights
4. Generate Concepts
5. Create Solutions

HOW TO USE THIS METHOD
1. Define contextual problem to address
2. Contextual inquiry
3. Discover insights
4. Create possible solutions
5. Create vision and scenarios
6. Prototype and test in context
7. Refine
8. Prototype and test in context
9. Deliver

Experience design

WHAT IS IT?
Experience design is the practice of designing products, processes, services, events, and environments with a focus placed on the quality of the user experience. Experience design is concerned with moments of engagement, or touchpoints, between people and brand. Experience design requires a cross-disciplinary approach.

WHO INVENTED IT?
Donald Norman 1990s

WHY USE THIS METHOD?
1. A user experience can be more valuable than an individual product or service.

CHALLENGES
1. Research methods are necessary to understand another person's experiences
2. Observations can be subjective.

HOW TO USE THIS METHOD
1. Experience evaluation methods include:
2. Diary Methods
3. Experience sampling method
4. Day reconstruction method
5. Laddering interviews.

RESOURCES
Cameras
Video cameras
Note pad
Digital voice recorder
Cell phones
Tablets

"

When you have two coffee shops right next to each other and each sells the exact same coffee at the exact same price, service design is what makes you walk into one and not the other

MARK FONTEIJN
Service designer

Design charette

WHAT IS IT?
A design charette is a collaborative design workshop usually held over one day or several days. Charettes are a fast way of generating ideas while involving diverse stakeholders in your decision process. Charettes have many different structures and often require multiple sessions. The group divides into smaller groups. The smaller groups present to the larger group.

WHO INVENTED IT?
The French word, "charette" spelled with two r's means "cart" This use of the term is said to originate from the École des Beaux Arts in Paris during the 19th century, where a cart, collected final drawings while students finished their work.

WHY USE THIS METHOD?
1. Fast and inexpensive.
2. Increased probability of implementation.
3. Stakeholders can share information.
4. Promotes trust.

CHALLENGES
1. Managing workflow can be challenging.
2. Stakeholders may have conflicting visions.

WHEN TO USE THIS METHOD
1. Define intent
2. Know context and user
3. Frame insights
4. Explore concepts
5. Make Plans

RESOURCES
Large space
Tables
Chairs
Whiteboards
Dry-erase markers
Camera
Post-it-notes

Design ethnography

WHAT IS IT?
Design ethnography is a collection of methods that helps create better more compelling and meaningful design. It helps a designer understand the points of view of people who will use the designs. Ethnographers study and interpret culture, through fieldwork.

WHO INVENTED IT?
Bronisław Malinowski 1922

WHY USE THIS METHOD?
1. To inform the design and innovation processes rather than basing your designs on intuition.
2. To ensure that your design solutions resonate with the people that you are designing for,
3. Ethnography helps designers see beyond their own preconceptions.

CHALLENGES
1. People may behave differently when they are in groups or alone.
2. Researchers need to be aware of the potential impacts of the research on the people and animals they study.

HOW TO USE THIS METHOD
There are many different ethnographic techniques. Some of the general guidelines are:
1. Listen
2. Observe.
3. Be empathetic and honest.
4. Do research in context, in the environments that the people you are studying live or work.
5. Influence your subject's behavior as little as possible with your presence.
6. Beware of bias.
7. Take photos and notes.
8. Have clear goals related to understanding and prediction.
9. Study representative people

RESOURCES
Note pad
Pens
Post-it-notes
Video camera
Camera
Voice recorder
Whiteboard
Dry-erase pens.

Dot voting

Concept 1

● ● ● ● ● ●

Concept 2

● ●

Concept 3

● ● ● ●

Concept 4

● ● ●

Concept 5

●

Concept 6

● ● ● ● ●

Dot voting

WHAT IS IT?
This is a way of efficiently selecting from a large number of ideas the preferred ideas to carry forward in the design process.

WHY USE THIS METHOD?
It is a method of selecting a favored idea by collective rather than individual judgment. It is a fast method that allows a design to progress. It leverages the strengths of diverse team member viewpoints and experiences.

CHALLENGES
1. The assessment is subjective.
2. Groupthink
3. Not enough good ideas
4. Inhibition
5. Lack of critical thinking

RESOURCES
Large wall
Adhesive dots

HOW TO USE THIS METHOD
1. Gather your team of 4 to 12 participants.
2. Brainstorm ideas for example ask each team member to generate ten ideas as sketches.
3. Each idea should be presented on one post-it-note or page.
4. Each designer should quickly explain each idea to the group before the group votes.
5. Spread the ideas over a wall or table.
6. Ask the team to vote on their two or three favorite ideas and total the votes. You can use sticky dots or colored pins to indicate a vote or a moderator can tally the scores.
7. Rearrange the ideas so that the ideas with the dots are ranked from most dots to least.
8. Refine the preferred ideas.

Empathy

WHAT IS IT?
Empathy is sometimes defined as 'standing in someone else's shoes' or 'seeing through someone else's eyes'. It is The ability to identify and understand another's situation, feelings and motives. In design it may be defined as: identify with others and, adopting his or her perspective. It is different to sympathy. Empathy does not necessarily imply compassion. Empathy is a respectful understanding of what others are experiencing.

WHO INVENTED IT?
The English word was coined in 1909 by E.B. Titchener in an attempt to translate the German word "Einfühlungsvermögen". It was later re-translated into the German language as "Empathie".

WHY USE THIS METHOD?
1. Empathy is a core skill for designers to design successfully for other people.
2. Empathy is needed for business success and for designs to be accepted and used by those people we are designing for..
3. Empathy builds trust.

CHALLENGES
1. Increasing use of teams
2. Rapid pace of globalization
3. Global need to retain talent

HOW TO USE THIS METHOD
1. Put yourself in contact and the context of people who you are designing for.
2. Ask questions and listen to the answers.
3. Read between the lines
4. Observe.
5. Don't interrupt
6. Listen
7. Ask clarifying questions.
8. Restating what you think you heard.
9. Recognize that people are individuals.
10. Notice body language. Most communication is non verbal
11. Withhold judgment when you hear views different to your own.
12. Take a personal interest in people

I keep six honest serving men. They taught me all I knew Their names are what and why and when and how and where and who

RUDYARD KIPLING

Five whys

WHAT IS IT
Five whys is an iterative question method used to discover the underlying cause of a problem. For every effect, there is a cause. The primary goal of the technique is to determine the root cause of a problem by repeating the question "Why?"

WHO INVENTED IT
The technique was originally developed by Sachichi Toyoda Sakichi Toyoda was a Japanese inventor and industrialist. He was born in Kosai, Shizuoka. The son of a poor carpenter, Toyoda is referred to as the "King of Japanese Inventors". He was the founder of the Toyota Motor company. The method is still an important part of Toyota training, culture and success.

WHY USE THIS METHOD
When we fix the root cause the problem does not reoccur

HOW TO USE THIS METHOD
1. Five whys could be taken further to a sixth, seventh, or higher level, but five is generally sufficient to get to a root cause.
2. Gather a team and develop the problem statement in agreement
3. Establish the time and place that the problem is occurring
4. Ask the first "why" of the team: why is this problem taking place?
5. Ask four more successive "whys," repeating the process
6. You will have identified the root cause when asking "why" yields no further useful information.
7. Discuss the last answers and settle on the most likely systemic cause.
8. Fix the root problem

Low-fidelity prototyping

WHAT IS IT?
Low-fi prototyping is a quick and cheap way of gaining insight and informing decision-making without the need for costly investment. Simulates function but not aesthetics of proposed design. Prototypes help compare alternatives and help answer questions about interactions or experiences.

WHY USE THIS METHOD?
1. May provide the proof of concept
2. It is physical and visible
3. Inexpensive and fast.
4. Useful for refining functional and perceptual interactions.
5. Assists to identify any problems with the design.
6. Helps to reduce the risks
7. Helps members of team to be in alignment on an idea.
8. Helps make abstract ideas concrete.
9. Feedback can be gained from the user

CHALLENGES
A beautiful prototype completed too early can stand in the way of finding the best design solution.

HOW TO USE THIS METHOD
1. Construct models, not illustrations
2. Select the important tasks, interactions or experiences to be prototyped.
3. Build to understand problems.
4. If it is beautiful you have invested too much.
5. Make it simple
6. Assemble a kit of inexpensive materials
7. Preparing for a test
8. Select users
9. Conduct test
10. Record notes on the 8x5 cards.
11. Evaluate the results
12. Iterate

RESOURCES
Paper
Cardboard
Wire
Foam board,
Post-it-notes
Hot melt glue

Storytelling

WHAT IS IT?
A compelling story can help ensure the success of a new product, service or experience. Storytelling is a uniquely powerful form of persuasion. Research methods can uncover meaningful stories from end users that illustrate needs or desires. These stories can become the basis of new designs and be used to support design decisions. Research shows that our attitudes, fears, hopes, and values are strongly influenced by story. Stories are more effective than traditional fact-based methods at communicating complex ideas and inspiring people to want to change.

WHO INVENTED IT?
1. Storytelling is one of the most ancient forms of human communication.

WHY USE THIS METHOD?
1. The stories help to get buy-in from stakeholders early in the design process and may be used to help sell a final design.
2. They are different to advertising because they are able to influence a design if uncovered from users during the early research phases and provide authenticity.

CHALLENGES
A story with too much jargon will lose an audience

HOW TO USE THIS METHOD
Answer in your story: What, why, when, who, where, how?

An appropriate story
1. Is honest
2. Is real
3. Builds trust
4. Transmits values
5. Shares a vision
6. Shares knowledge
7. Helps Collaboration
8. Must differentiate you.
9. Uses humor
10. Engages the audience
11. Pose a problem and offer a resolution
12. Use striking imagery
13. Fit the audience
14. The audience must be able to act on it.

Tacit knowledge

WHAT IS IT?
Tacit knowledge is knowledge that is gained through personal experience. Examples of tacit knowledge are the ability to ride a bicycle or recognizing someone's face. Tacit knowledge is difficult to pass on to another person by writing it down or describing it. Tacit knowledge is a form of intellectual property. Tacit knowledge includes best practices, stories, experience, wisdom, and insights.

WHO INVENTED IT?
Michael Polanyi 1958

WHY USE THIS METHOD?
1. Tacit knowledge is valuable to any organization.

CHALLENGES
1. Mapping tacit knowledge needs immersion in context.
2. A researcher can map behavior and perceptions.

HOW TO USE THIS METHOD
The methods of capturing tacit knowledge include:
1. Interviews
2. Observation

RESOURCES
Camera
Note pad
Digital voice recorder

Overt observation

WHAT IS IT?
A method of observation where the subjects are aware that they are being observed

WHO INVENTED IT?
Radcliff-Brown 1910
Bronisław Malinowski 1922
Margaret Mead 1928

WHY USE THIS METHOD?
1. To capture behavior as it happens.

CHALLENGES
1. Observation does not explain the cause of behavior.
2. Analysis can be time consuming.
3. Observer bias can cause the researcher to look only where they think they will see useful information.

HOW TO USE THIS METHOD
1. Define objectives.
2. Define participants and obtain their cooperation.
3. Define The context of the observation: time and place.
4. In some countries the law requires that you obtain written consent to video people.
5. Define the method of observation and the method of recording information. Common methods are taking written notes, video or audio recording.
6. Run a test session.
7. Hypothesize an explanation for the phenomenon.
8. Predict a logical consequence of the hypothesis.
9. Test your hypothesis by observation
10. Analyze the data gathered and create a list of insights derived from the observations.

RESOURCES
Note pad
Pens
Camera
Video Camera
Digital voice recorder

Cultural probes

WHAT IS IT?
A cultural probe is a method of collecting information about people, their context, and their culture. The aim of this approach is to record events, behaviors, and interactions in their context. This process involves the participants to record and collect the data themselves.

WHO INVENTED IT?
Bill Gaver Royal College of Art London 1969

WHY USE THIS METHOD?
1. This is a useful method when the participants that are being studied are hard to reach for example if they are traveling.
2. It is a useful technique if the activities being studied take place over an extended period or at irregular intervals.
3. The information collected can be used to build personas.

CHALLENGES
It is important with this method to select the participants carefully and give them support during the study.

HOW TO USE THIS METHOD
1. Define the objective of your study.
2. Recruit your participants.
3. Brief the participants
4. Supply participants with kit. The items in the kit are selected to collect the type of information you want to gather and can include items such as notebooks, diary, camera, voice recorder or post cards.
5. You can use an affinity diagram to analyze the data collected

RESOURCES
Diary
Notebooks
Pens
Post-it notes
Voice recorder
Post cards
Digital Camera

Camera journal

WHAT IS IT?
The research subjects record their activities with a camera and notes. The researcher reviews the images and discusses them with the participants.

WHY USE THIS METHOD?
1. Helps develop empathy for the participants.
2. Participants are involved in the research process.
3. Helps establish rapport with participants.
4. May reveal aspects of life that are seldom seen by outsiders.

CHALLENGES
1. Should obtain informed consent.
2. May not be ideal for research among particularly vulnerable people.
3. May be a relatively expensive research method.
4. May be time consuming.
5. Best used with other methods.
6. Technology may be unreliable.
7. Method may be unpredictable'.
8. Has to be carefully analyzed

HOW TO USE THIS METHOD
1. Define subject of study
2. Define participants
3. Gather data images and insight statements.
4. Analyze data.
5. Identify insights
6. Rank insights
7. Produce criteria for concept generation from insights.
8. Generate concepts to meet needs of users.

RESOURCES
Cameras
Voice recorder
Video camera
Note pad
Pens

Day in the life

WHAT IS IT?
A study in which the designer observes the participant in the location and context of their usual activities, observing and recording events to understand the activities from the participant's point of view. Mapping a 'Day in the Life' as a storyboard can provide a focus for discussion.

WHO INVENTED IT?
ALex Bavelas 1944

WHY USE THIS METHOD?
1. This method informs the design process by observation of real activities and behaviors.
2. This method provides insights with relatively little cost and time.

CHALLENGES
1. Choose the participants carefully
2. Document everything. Something that seems insignificant may become significant later.

HOW TO USE THIS METHOD
1. Define activities to study
2. Recruit participants
3. Prepare
4. Observe subjects in context.
5. Capture data,
6. Create storyboard with text and timeline.
7. Analyze data
8. Create insights.
9. Identify issues
10. Identify needs
11. Add new/more requirements to concept development

RESOURCES
Camera
Notebook
Video camera
Voice recorder
Pens

Diary study

WHAT IS IT?
This method involves participants recording particular events, feelings or interactions, in a diary supplied by the researcher. User Diaries help provide insight into behavior. Participants record their behavior and thoughts. Diaries can uncover behavior that may not be articulated in an interview or readily visible to outsiders.

WHO INVENTED IT?
Gordon Allport, may have been the first to describe diary studies in 1942.

WHY USE THIS METHOD?
1. Can capture data that is difficult to capture using other methods.
2. Useful when you wish to gather information and minimize your influence on research subjects.
3. When the process or event you're exploring takes place intermittently or
4. When the process or event you're exploring takes place over a long period.

CHALLENGES
1. Process can be expensive and time consuming.
2. Needs participant monitoring.
3. It is difficult to get materials back.

HOW TO USE THIS METHOD
1. A diary can be kept over a period of one week or longer.
2. Define focus for the study.
3. Recruit participants carefully.
4. Decide method: preprinted, diary notebook or on line.
5. Prepare diary packs. Can be preprinted sheets or blank 20 page notebooks with prepared questions or on line web based diary.
6. Brief participants.
7. Distribute diaries directly or by mail.
8. Conduct study. Keep in touch with participants.
9. Conduct debrief interview.
10. Look for insights.

RESOURCES
Diary
Preprinted diary sheets
Online diary
Pens
Disposable cameras
Digital camera
Self addressed envelopes

Focus groups

WHAT IS IT?
Focus groups are discussions usually with 6 to 12 participants led by a moderator. Focus groups are used during the the design of products, services and experiences to get feedback from people

They are often conducted in the evening and take on average two hours. 8 to 12 questions are commonly explored in discussion.

WHO INVENTED IT?
Robert K. Merton 1940 Bureau of Applied Social Research.

WHY USE THIS METHOD?
1. Low cost per participant compared to other research methods.
2. Easier than some other methods to manage

CHALLENGES
1. Removes participants from their context
2. Requires a skilled moderator
3. Focus group study results may not be not be generalizable.
4. Focus group participants can influence each other.

HOW TO USE THIS METHOD
1. Select a good moderator.
2. Prepare a screening questionnaire.
3. Decide incentives for participants.
4. Select facility.
5. Recruit participants. Invite participants to your session well in advance and get firm commitments to attend. Remind participants the date of the event.
6. Participants should sit around a large table. Follow discussion guide.
7. Describe rules. Provide refreshments.
8. First question should encourage talking and participation.
9. The moderator manages responses and asks important questions
10. Moderator collects forms and debriefs focus group.
11. Analyze results while still fresh.
12. Summarize key points.
13. Run additional focus groups to deepen analysis.

Fly-on-the-wall

WHAT IS IT?
Observation method where the observer remains as unobtrusive as possible and observes and collects data relevant to a research study in context with no interaction with the participants being observed. The name derived from the documentary film technique of the same name.

WHO INVENTED IT?
ALex Bavelas 1944
Lucy Vernile, Robert A. Monteiro 1991

WHY USE THIS METHOD?
1. Low cost
2. No setup necessary
3. Can observe a large number of participants.
4. Objective observations
5. Compared to other methods such as focus groups, setup, data collection, and processing are much faster.

CHALLENGES
1. No interaction by the observer.
2. Observer cannot delve deeper during a session.
3. No interruption allowed
4. Observer cannot obtain details on customer comments during a session

HOW TO USE THIS METHOD
1. Define activity to study
2. Select participants thoughtfully
3. Choose a context for the observation
4. Carefully observe the interaction or experience. This is best done by members of your design team.
5. It is important to influence the participants as little as possible by your presence.
6. Observe but do not interact with participants while observing them in context.
7. Capture Data
8. Identify issues
9. Identify needs
10. Create design solutions based on observed and experienced human needs.

RESOURCES
Digital camera
Video camera
Notebook
Pens
Voice recorder

Innovation diagnostic

WHAT IS IT?
An innovation diagnostic is an evaluation of an organization's innovation capabilities.
It reviews practices by stakeholders which may help or hinder innovation. An innovation diagnostic is the first step in preparing an implementing a strategy to create an organizational culture that supports innovation.

WHY USE THIS METHOD?
1. It helps organizations develop sustainable competitive advantage.
2. Helps identify innovation opportunities
3. Helps develop innovation strategy.

WHEN TO USE THIS METHOD
1. Know Context
2. Know User
3. Frame insights
4. Explore Concepts
5. Make Plans

HOW TO USE THIS METHOD
An innovation diagnostic reviews organizational and stakeholder practices using both qualitative and quantitative methods including
1. The design and development process
2. Strategic practices and planning.
3. The ability of an organization to monitor and respond to relevant trends.
4. Technologies
5. Organizational flexibility
6. Ability to innovate repeatedly and consistently

Innovation Diagnostic Test

DOES MANAGEMENT COMMUNICATE THE NEED FOR INNOVATION?
1. There is no innovation in our organization
2. Innovation is not a high priority
3. Our managers sometimes talk about innovation
4. Our managers discuss innovation but not why it is needed
5. Managers regularly state the compelling need for innovation

WHAT IS YOUR ORGANIZATIONAL STRATEGY?
1. We make low cost goods or services
2. Efficient operations
3. We are a customer focused organization
4. Fast Follower
5. Market leaders

IS THE BUSINESS THAT YOU ARE IN UNDERSTOOD BY EMPLOYEES?
1. We are not sure
2. We may get different answers from different managers
3. The definition changes in
4. We have some clarity
5. We are very clear about what business we are in

IS YOUR ORGANIZATION INNOVATIVE?
1. No
2. Probably not
3. We would like to be
4. There is some innovation
5. We are clearly an innovative organization

HOW DOES YOUR COMPANY INNOVATE?
1. We react to market forces without innovation
2. There is little innovation
3. We do some incremental innovation
4. We do mainly incremental innovation but would like to do some breakthrough innovation
5. We manage a portfolio of incremental and more substantial innovation and manage risks

DOES YOUR MANAGEMENT SUPPORT INNOVATION?
1. No
2. No resources are allocated to

innovation
3. Some resources are allocated
4. We have some resources and some involvement from managers in innovation
5. We have clearly defined resources allocated and senior management is actively involved in planning and managing innovation

DO YOU HAVE CROSS DISCIPLINARY DESIGN TEAMS?
1. Never
2. Rarely
3. Sometimes
4. Usually
5. Always

DO YOU USE OUTSIDE EXPERTS TO ASSIST IN YOUR INNOVATION PROCESS?
1. Never
2. Rarely
3. Sometimes
4. Usually
5. Always

HOW OFTEN DOES YOUR ORGANIZATION ENGAGE CUSTOMERS TO IDENTIFY THEIR UNMET NEEDS?
1. Never
2. Rarely
3. Sometimes
4. Usually
5. Always

HOW WOULD YOU DEFINE THE RISK TOLERANCE AT YOUR COMPANY?
1. We don't take any risks
2. We rarely take risks
3. Sometimes we take substantial risks
4. We manage our risk portfolio actively and take big risks when appropriate.

HOW ARE NEW IDEAS RECEIVED IN YOUR ORGANIZATION?
1. We fire people with new ideas
2. We rarely adopt new ideas
3. We sometimes adopt new ideas but they are mostly not considered
4. We regularly consider new ideas
5. We actively generate and adopt new ide

How well did you score?

Add up the numbers of each answer that you selected and calculate a total for all the questions

Score 35 to 45
HIGHLY INNOVATIVE ORGANIZATION

The highest level of innovation is where companies can create innovations that change how people live. The maximum level of innovation also brings the highest level of risk, as many times this level of innovation involves products or services that no one has thought of and customers do not know they want.

Score 25 to 35
INNOVATIVE ORGANIZATION

The third level is the beginning of large financial and product risk, but it is also where the rewards are potentially greater. This level also requires that the business devotes resources to monitoring progress and actively assessing risk throughout the development process. Evolutionary products, significant investment, medium risk, some payoff

Score 15 to 25
SOMEWHAT INNOVATIVE

The second level is a higher level of changes. Level Two changes include integrating new features into existing products on the market or creating differentiated versions of the same new product to sell to various demographic groups. These new features require what can be considered a medium level of investment and risk. Advancement of existing products medium investment and risk medium payoff

Score 0 to 15
LOW INNOVATION

The first level emphasizes minimal changes to existing products, a low amount of new investment, and very small risk. Examples at this level would be modifying the color of a product or putting a new logo design on a label. Essentially all companies are capable of achieving this level, as it does not require unique skills. Few new features on existing products, low investment and risk low payoff.

Interviewing

WHAT IS IT?
Interviewing is a method of ethnographic research that has been described as a conversation with a purpose.

WHY USE THIS METHOD?
1. Contextual interviews uncover tacit knowledge about people's context.
2. The information gathered can be detailed.
3. The information produced by contextual inquiry is relatively reliable

CHALLENGES
1. End users may not have the answers
2. Contextual inquiry may be difficult to challenge even if it is misleading.
3. Keep control
4. Be prepared
5. Be aware of bias
6. Be neutral
7. Select location carefully

WHEN TO USE THIS METHOD
1. Know Context
2. Know User
3. Frame insights

HOW TO USE THIS METHOD
1. Contextual inquiry may be structured as 2 hour one on one interviews.
2. The researcher does not usually impose tasks on the user.
3. Go to the user's context. Talk, watch listen and observe.
4. Understand likes and dislikes.
5. Collect stories and insights.
6. See the world from the user's point of view.
7. Take permission to conduct interviews.
8. Do one-on-one interviews.
9. The researcher listens to the user.
10. 2 to 3 researchers conduct an interview.
11. Understand relationship between people, product and context.
12. Document with video, audio and notes.

RESOURCES
Computer
Notebook
Pens
Video camera
Release forms
Interview plan or structure
Questions, tasks and discussion items
Confidentiality agreement

Writing an interview guide

HOW TO CREATE AN INTERVIEW GUIDE

1. Plan in advance what you want to achieve
2. Research the topic
3. Select a person to interview.
4. Meet them in their location if possible.
5. Set a place, date, and time.
6. Be sure he or she understands how long the interview should take and that you plan to record the session.
7. Start with an open-ended question. It is a good way to put the candidate at ease,
8. Tape record the interview if possible.
9. Decide what information you need
10. Write down the information you'd like to collect through the interview. Now frame your interview questions around this information.
11. Prepare follow-up questions to ask.
12. Research the person that you are interviewing
13. Check your equipment and run through your questions.
14. Use neutral wording
15. Do not ask leading questions or questions that show bias.
16. Leave time for a General Question in the End
17. The last question should allow the interviewee to share any thoughts or opinions that they might want to share, such as "Thank you for all that valuable information, is there anything else you'd like to add before we end?"
18. Bring your questions to the interview
19. Explore the answers but return to your list of questions to follow your guide.
20. Record details such as the subject's name contact and details
21. Take detailed notes
22. Use empathy tools to encourage your participant to share information.
23. Final question: "Is there anything you think I should have asked that I didn't?"
24. Transcribe the interview
25. Write out both sides of the conversation, both question and answer.
26. Never change what the interviewee said or how they said it.
27. Outline the important points.
28. Edit the transcript for clarity, flow, and length.
29. Tell a story Now that you've gathered all of this great information and have accurately recorded it. It is important that you find a way to effectively document and share the story in a way that celebrates and accurately describes the story you were told.
30. Add details from your notes appearance and personality of your subject, ambient sounds, smells, visuals.
31. Check the facts.

Source: adapted from The Art of Interview" by Anne Williams

Contextual inquiry

WHAT IS IT?
Contextual inquiry involves one-on-one observations and interviews of activities in the context. Contextual inquiry has four guiding principles:
1. Context
2. Partnership with users.
3. Interpretation
4. Focus on particular goals.

WHO INVENTED IT?
Whiteside, Bennet, and Holtzblatt 1988

WHY USE THIS METHOD
1. Contextual interviews uncover tacit knowledge about people's context.
2. The information gathered can be detailed.
3. The information produced by contextual inquiry is relatively reliable

CHALLENGES
1. End users may not have the answers
2. Contextual inquiry may be difficult to challenge even if it is misleading.

HOW TO USE THIS METHOD
1. Contextual inquiry may be structured as 2 hour one on one interviews.
2. The researcher does not usually impose tasks on the user.
3. Go to the user's context. Talk, watch listen and observe.
4. Understand likes and dislikes.
5. Collect stories and insights.
6. See the world from the user's point of view.
7. Take permission to conduct interviews.
8. Do one-on-one interviews.
9. The researcher listens to the user.
10. 2 to 3 researchers conduct an interview.
11. Understand relationship between people, product and context.
12. Document with video, audio and notes.

Contextual laddering

WHAT IS IT?
Contextual laddering is a one-on-one interviewing technique done in context. Answers are further explored by the researcher to uncover root causes or core values.

WHO INVENTED IT?
Gutman 1982, Olsen and Reynolds 2001.

WHY USE THIS METHOD?
1. Laddering can uncover underlying reasons for particular behaviors.
2. Laddering may uncover information not revealed by other methods.
3. Complement other methods
4. Link features and product attributes with user/customer values

CHALLENGES
1. Analysis of data is sometimes difficult.
2. Requires a skilled interviewer who can keep the participants engaged.
3. Laddering may be repetitive
4. Sometimes information may not be represented hierarchically.

HOW TO USE THIS METHOD
1. Interviews typically take 60 to 90 minutes.
2. The introduction. The researcher gives information about the length of the interview, content, confidentiality and method of recording.
3. The body of the interview. The researcher investigates the user in context and documents the information gathered.
4. Ask participants to describe what kinds of features would be useful in or distinguish different products.
5. Ask why.
6. If this answer doesn't describe the root motivation ask why again.
7. Repeat step 3. until you have reached the root motivation.
8. Wrap up. Verification and clarification

E-mail interview

WHAT IS IT?
With this method an interview is conducted via an e-mail exchange.

WHY USE THIS METHOD?
1. Extended access to people.
2. Background noises are not recorded.
3. Interviewee can answer the questions at his or her own convenience
4. It is not necessary to take notes
5. It is possible to use on-line translators.
6. Interviewees do not have to identify a convenient time to talk.

CHALLENGES
1. Interviewer may have to wait for answers.
2. Interviewer is disconnected from context.
3. Lack of communication of body language.

HOW TO USE THIS METHOD
1. Choose a topic
2. Identify a subject.
3. Contact subject and obtain approval.
4. Prepare interview questions.
5. Conduct interview
6. Analyze data.

RESOURCES
Computer
Internet connection
Notebook
Pens
Interview plan or structure
Questions, tasks and discussion items
Confidentiality agreement

Extreme user interview

WHAT IS IT?
Interview experienced or inexperienced users of a product or service in order to discover useful insights that can be applied to the general users.

WHY USE THIS METHOD?
Extreme user's solutions to problems can inspire solutions for general users. Their behavior can be more exaggerated than general users so it is sometimes easier to develop useful insights from these groups.

CHALLENGES
1. Keep control
2. Be prepared
3. Be aware of bias
4. Be neutral
5. Select location carefully

HOW TO USE THIS METHOD
1. Do a time line of your activity and break it into main activities
2. Identify very experienced or very inexperienced users of a product or service in an activity area.
3. Explore their experiences through interview.
4. Discover insights that can inspire design.
5. Refine design based on insights.

RESOURCES
Computer
Notebook
Pens
Video camera
Release forms
Interview plan or structure
Questions, tasks and discussion items
Confidentiality agreement

Group interview

WHAT IS IT?
This method involves interviewing a group of people.

WHY USE THIS METHOD?
People will often give different answers to questions if interviewed on=on=-one and in groups. If resources are available it is useful to interview people in both situations.

CHALLENGES
1. Group interview process is longer than an individual interview

RESOURCES
Computer
Notebook
Pens
Video camera
Release forms
Interview plan or structure
Questions, tasks and discussion items
Confidentiality agreement

HOW TO USE THIS METHOD
1. Welcome everyone and introduce yourself
2. Describe the process.
3. Ask everyone to introduce themselves.
4. Conduct a group activity or warming-up exercise.
5. Break the larger group into smaller groups of 4 or 5 people and give them a question to answer. Ask each participant to present their response to the larger group.
6. Allow about 25 minutes.
7. Ask each interviewee to write a summary
8. Collect the summaries.
9. Ask if have any further comments.
10. Thank everyone and explain the next steps.
11. Give them your contact details.

Guided storytelling

WHAT IS IT?
Guided storytelling is interview technique, where the designer asks a participant to walk you through a scenario of use for a concept. Directed storytelling guides participants to describe their experiences and thoughts on a particular topic.

WHO INVENTED IT?
Whiteside, Bennet, and Holtzblatt 1988

WHY USE THIS METHOD?
1. Guided storytelling uncovers tacit knowledge.

CHALLENGES
1. Keep control
2. Be prepared
3. Be aware of bias
4. Be neutral
5. Select location carefully

HOW TO USE THIS METHOD
1. Contextual inquiry may be structured as 2 hour one on one interviews.
2. The researcher does not usually impose tasks on the user.
3. Go to the user's context. Talk, watch listen and observe.
4. Understand likes and dislikes.
5. Collect stories and insights.
6. See the world from the user's point of view.
7. Take permission to conduct interviews.
8. Do one-on-one interviews.
9. The researcher listens to the user.
10. 2 to 3 researchers conduct an interview.
11. Understand relationship between people, product and context.

RESOURCES
Computer
Notebook
Pens
Video camera
Release forms
Interview plan or structure
Questions, tasks and discussion items
Confidentiality agreement

Man in the street interview

WHAT IS IT?
Man in the street interviews are impromptu interviews recorded on video. They are usually conducted by two people, a researcher and a cameraman.

WHY USE THIS METHOD?
1. Contextual interviews uncover tacit knowledge.
2. The information gathered can be detailed.

CHALLENGES
1. Keep control
2. Be prepared
3. Be aware of bias
4. Be neutral
5. Ask appropriate questions
6. Select location carefully
7. Create a friendly atmosphere, interviewee to feel relaxed.
8. Clearly convey the purpose of the interview.
9. This method results in accidental sampling which may not be representative of larger groups.

HOW TO USE THIS METHOD
1. Decide on goal for research.
2. Formulate about 10 questions related to topic
3. Use release form if required.
4. Conduct a preliminary interview.
5. Select location. It should not be too noisy or have other distracting influences
6. Approach people, be polite. Say, "Excuse me, I work for [your organization] and I was wondering if you could share your opinion about [your topic]."
7. If someone does not wish to respond, select another subject to interview.
8. Limit your time. Each interview should be no be longer than about 10 minutes.
9. Conduct 6 to 10 interviews

RESOURCES
Notebook
Pens
Video camera
Digital voice recorder
Release forms
Interview plan
Questions, and tasks

Naturalistic group interview

WHAT IS IT?
Naturalistic group interview is an interview method where the participants know each other prior to the interview and so have conversations that are more natural than participants who do not know each other.

WHY USE THIS METHOD?
1. This method has been applied in research in Asia where beliefs are informed by group interaction.
2. Can help gain useful data in cultures where people are less willing to share their feelings.

CHALLENGES
1. Familiarity of participants can lead to Group-think.

HOW TO USE THIS METHOD
1. The interview context should support natural conversation.
2. Select participants who have existing social relationships.
3. Group the participants in natural ways so that the conversation is as close as possible to the type of discussion they would have in their everyday life.
4. Groups should be no larger than four people for best results.

RESOURCES
Notebook
Pens
Video camera
Digital voice recorder
Release forms
Interview plan
Questions, and tasks
Use local moderator

One-on-one interview

WHAT IS IT?
The one-on-one interview is an interview that is between a researcher and one participant in a face-to-face situation.

WHY USE THIS METHOD?
1. The best method for personal information
2. Works well with other methods in obtaining information to inform design.
3. Can be used to exchange ideas or to gather information to inform design

CHALLENGES
1. Keep control
2. Be prepared
3. Be aware of bias
4. Be neutral
5. Select location carefully
6. Record everything
7. Combine one on one interviews with group interviews.

HOW TO USE THIS METHOD
1. May be structured as 2 hour one on one interviews.
2. Select the questions and the subjects carefully.
3. Create interview guide,
4. Conduct a preinterview to refine the guide.
5. The researcher does not usually impose tasks on the user.
6. Go to the user's context. Talk, watch listen and observe.
7. Understand likes and dislikes.
8. Collect stories and insights.
9. See the world from the user's point of view.
10. Take permission to conduct interviews.
11. Understand relationship between person, product and context.
12. Document with video, audio and notes.

RESOURCES
Notebook
Pens
Video camera
Digital voice recorder
Release forms
Interview plan
Questions, and tasks

Structured interview

WHAT IS IT?
In a structured interview the researcher prepares a list of questions, script or an interview guide that they follow during the interview. Most interviews use a structured method.

WHY USE THIS METHOD?
1. A structured interview is often used for phone interviews.
2. It is easy to analyze the results.
3. Structured interviews are often used by quantitative researchers.

CHALLENGES
1. Respondents may be less likely to discuss sensitive experiences.

HOW TO USE THIS METHOD
1. The researcher should follow the script exactly.
2. The interviewer is required to show consistency in behavior across all interviews

RESOURCES
Computer
Notebook
Pens
Video camera
Release forms
Interview plan
Questions, and tasks
Confidentiality agreement

Photo elicitation interview

WHAT IS IT?
Photos are used by a researcher as a focus to discuss the experiences, thoughts and feelings of participants.

WHY USE THIS METHOD?
1. A method sometimes used to interview children.
2. Photos can make staring a conversation with a participant easier.
3. Photos can uncover meaning which is not uncovered in a face to face interview.

CHALLENGES
1. Photos can create ethical questions for the researcher.
2. A researcher may show bias in selecting subject of photos.

HOW TO USE THIS METHOD
1. Define the context.
2. Select the participants
3. Either researcher or participant may take the photos.
4. Researcher analyses photos and plans the interview process
5. Researcher shows the photos to the participant and discusses their thoughts in relation to the photographs.
6. The interview is analyzed by the researcher.
7. The researcher creates a list of insights.

RESOURCES
Notebook
Pens
Video camera
Release forms
Interview plan
Questions, and tasks
Digital voice recorder
Photographs

Unstructured interview

WHAT IS IT?
Unstructured interviews are interviews where questions can be modified as needed by the researcher during the interview.

WHY USE THIS METHOD?
1. A useful technique for understanding how a subject may perform under pressure.
2. Unstructured interviews are used in ethnographic case studies
3. Respondents may be more likely to discuss sensitive experiences.

CHALLENGES
1. Interviewer bias is unavoidable

HOW TO USE THIS METHOD
Researchers need a list of topics to be covered during the interview

RESOURCES
Computer
Notebook
Pens
Video camera
Release forms
Interview plan
Questions, and tasks
Confidentiality agreement

Telephone interview

WHAT IS IT?
With this method an interview is conducted via telephone.

WHY USE THIS METHOD?
Wide geographical access
1. Allows researcher to reach hard to reach people.
2. Allows researcher to access closed locations.
3. Access to dangerous or politically sensitive sites

CHALLENGES
1. Lack of communication of body language.
2. Interviewer is disconnected from context.

HOW TO USE THIS METHOD
1. Choose a topic
2. Identify a subject.
3. Contact subject and obtain approval.
4. Prepare interview questions.
5. Conduct interview
6. Analyze data.

RESOURCES
Computer
Notebook
Pens

Method bank

WHAT IS IT?
A method bank is a central bank where design methods are documented by an organization's employees and can be accessed and applied by other employees.

WHO INVENTED IT?
1. Lego have compiled a Design Practice and emerging methods bank.
2. Microsoft have a methods bank in their Online User Experience best practice intra-net.
3. Starbucks have a methods bank in their on-line work flow management tool

WHY USE THIS METHOD?
1. This approaches helps document tacit knowledge within an organization.

HOW TO USE THIS METHOD
1. Methods are uploaded to the intra-net bank.
2. The bank may include descriptions, video, images charts or sketches.

RESOURCES
Intra-net
Camera
Video camera
Templates
Data base.
Computers

Design thinking mind map

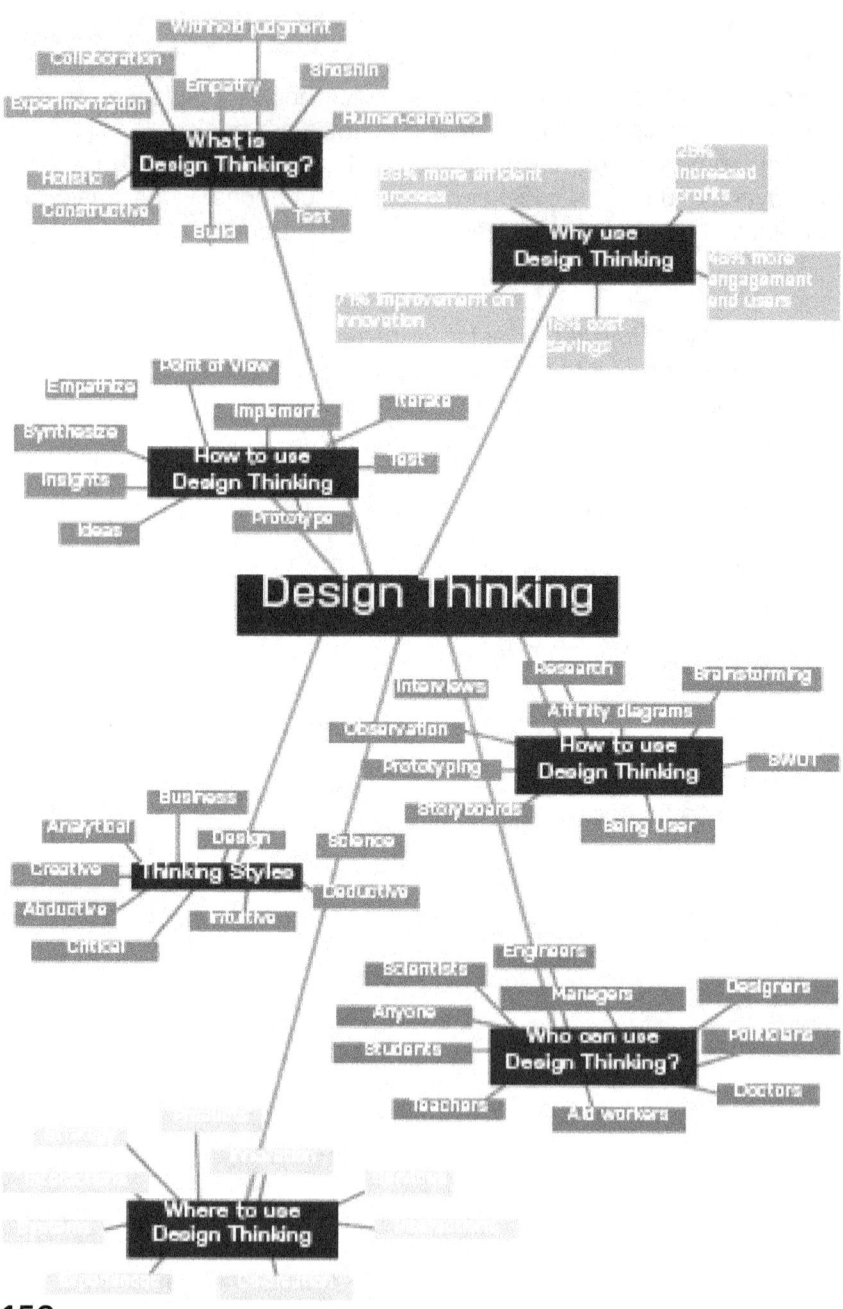

Mind maps

WHAT IS IT?
A mind map is a diagram used to represent the affinities or connections between many ideas or things. Understanding relationships is the starting point for design. Mind maps are a method of analyzing information and relationships.

WHO INVENTED IT?
Porphry of Tyros 3rd century BC. Allan Collins, Northwestern University 1960, USA

WHY USE THIS METHOD?
1. The method helps identify relationships.
2. There is no right or wrong with mind maps. They help with they help with memory and organization.
3. Problem solving and brainstorming
4. Relationship discovery
5. Summarizing information
6. Memorizing information

CHALLENGES
Print words clearly, use color and images for visual impact.

HOW TO USE THIS METHOD
1. Start in the center with a key word or idea. Put box around this node.
2. Use images, symbols, or words for nodes.
3. Select key words.
4. Keep the key word names of nodes s simple and short as possible.
5. Associated nodes should be connected with lines to show affinities.
6. Make the lines the same length as the word/image they support.
7. Use emphasis such as thicker lines to show the strength of associations in your mind map.
8. Use radial arrangement of nodes.

RESOURCES
Paper
Pens
Whiteboard
Dry-erase markers

Mobile diary study

WHAT IS IT?
A mobile diary studies is a method that uses portable devices to capture a person's experiences in context when and where they happen such as their workplace or home. Participants can create diary entries from their location on mobile phones or tablets.

WHY USE THIS METHOD?
1. Most people carry a mobile phone.
2. It is a convenient method of recording diary entries.
3. It is easier to collect the data than collecting written diaries.
4. Collection of data happens in real time.
5. Mobile devices have camera, voice and written capability.

CHALLENGES
1. Can miss non verbal feedback.
2. Technology may be unreliable

HOW TO USE THIS METHOD
1. Define intent
2. Define audience
3. Define context
4. Define technology
5. Automated text messages are sent to participants to prompt an entry.
6. Analyze data

RESOURCES
Smart phones, Cameras, Laptops and Tablets

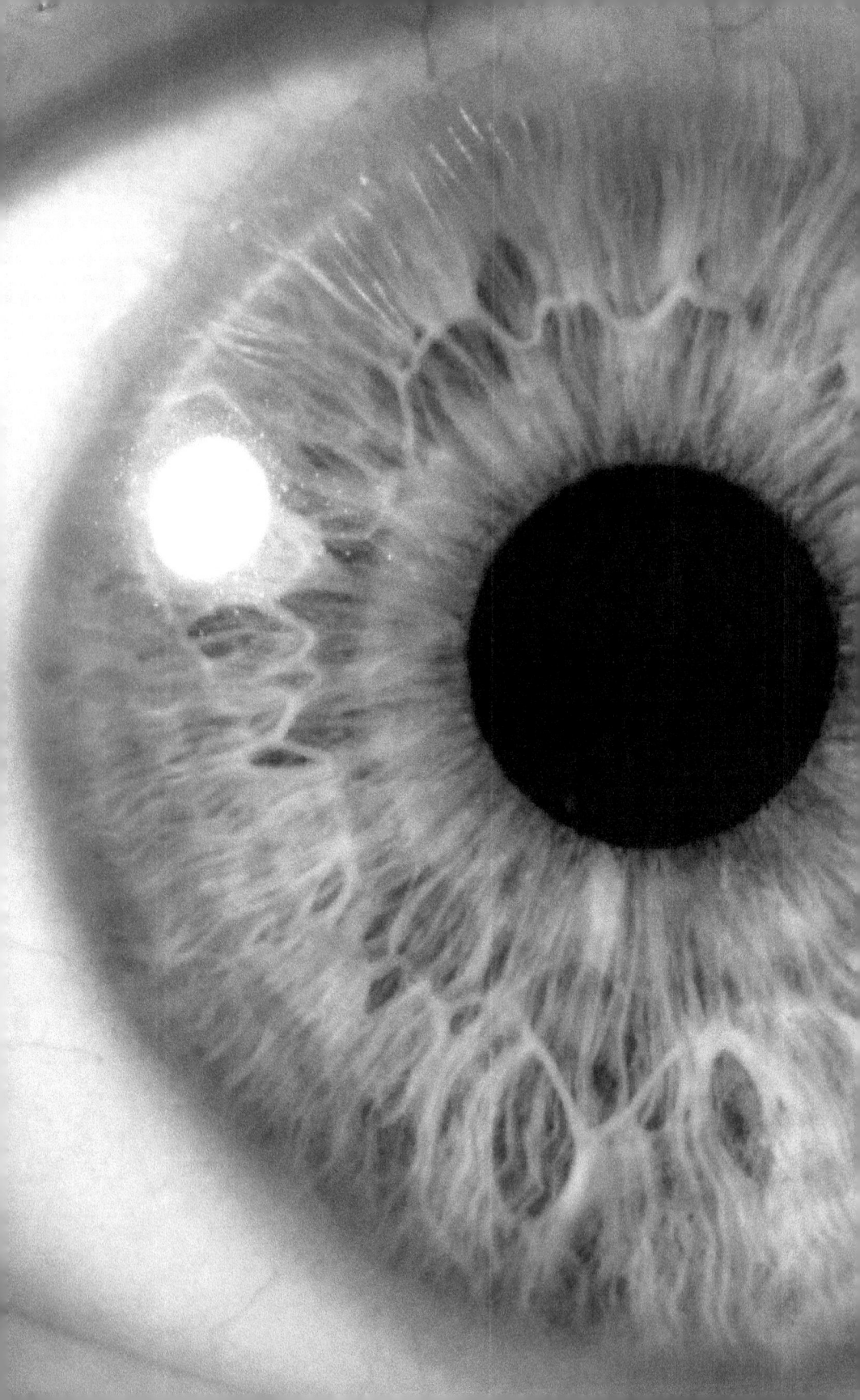

Observation

WHAT IS IT?
This method involves observing people in their natural activities and current context such as work environment. With direct observation the researcher is present and indirect observation the events may be recorded by means such as video or digital voice recording.

WHY USE THIS METHOD?
1. Allows the observer to view what users actually do in context.
2. Indirect observation uncovers activity that may have previously gone unnoticed

CHALLENGES
1. Observation does not explain the cause of behavior.
2. Obtrusive observation may cause participants to alter their behavior.
3. Analysis can be time consuming.
4. Observer bias can cause the researcher to look only where they think they will see useful information.

HOW TO USE THIS METHOD
1. Define objectives
2. Define participants and obtain their cooperation.
3. Define The context of the observation: time and place.
4. In some countries the law requires that you obtain written consent to video people.
5. Define the method of observation and the method of recording information. Common methods are taking written notes, video or audio recording.
6. Run a test session.
7. Hypothesize an explanation for the phenomenon
8. Predict a logical consequence of the hypothesis
9. Test your hypothesis by observation
10. Analyze the data gathered and create a list of insights derived from the observations.

RESOURCES
Note pad
Pens
Camera
Video camera
Digital voice recorder

Covert observation

WHAT IS IT?
Covert observation is to observe people without them knowing. The identity of the researcher and the purpose of the research are hidden from the people being observed.

WHY USE THIS METHOD?
1. This method may be used to reduce the effect of the observer's presence on the behavior of the subjects.
2. To capture behavior as it happens.
3. Researcher is more likely to observe natural behavior

CHALLENGES
1. The method raises serious ethical questions.
2. Observation does not explain the cause of behavior.
3. Can be difficult to gain access and maintain cover
4. Analysis can be time consuming.
5. Observer bias can cause the researcher to look only where they think they will see useful information.

HOW TO USE THIS METHOD
1. Define objectives.
2. Define participants and obtain their cooperation.
3. Define The context of the observation: time and place.
4. In some countries the law requires that you obtain written consent to video people.
5. Define the method of observation and the method of recording information. Common methods are taking written notes, video or audio recording.
6. Run a test session.
7. Hypothesize an explanation for the phenomenon.
8. Predict a logical consequence of the hypothesis.
9. Test your hypothesis by observation
10. Analyze the data gathered and create a list of insights derived from the observations.

RESOURCES
Camera
Video Camera
Digital voice recorder

Direct observation

WHAT IS IT?
Direct Observation is a method in which a researcher observes and records behavior events, activities or tasks while something is happening recording observations as they are made.

WHO INVENTED IT?
Radcliff-Brown 1910
Bronisław Malinowski 1922
Margaret Mead 1928

WHY USE THIS METHOD?
1. To capture behavior as it happens.

CHALLENGES
1. Observation does not explain the cause of behavior.
2. Analysis can be time consuming.
3. Observer bias can cause the researcher to look only where they think they will see useful information.
4. Obtain a proper sample for generalization.
5. Observe average workers during average conditions.
6. The participant may change their behavior because they are being watched.

HOW TO USE THIS METHOD
1. Define objectives.
2. Make direct observation plan
3. Define participants and obtain their cooperation.
4. Define The context of the observation: time and place.
5. In some countries the law requires that you obtain written consent to video people.
6. Define the method of observation and the method of recording information. Common methods are taking written notes, video or audio recording.
7. Run a test session.
8. Hypothesize an explanation for the phenomenon.
9. Predict a logical consequence of the hypothesis.
10. Test your hypothesis by observation
11. Analyze the data gathered and create a list of insights derived from the observations.

RESOURCES
Note pad
Pens
Camera
Video Camera
Digital voice recorder

Indirect observation

WHAT IS IT?
Indirect Observation is an observational technique whereby some record of past behavior is used than observing behavior in real time. Humans cannot directly sense some things. We must rely on indirect observations with tools such as thermometers, microscopes, telescopes or X-rays

WHY USE THIS METHOD?
1. To capture behavior or an event as it happens in it's natural setting.
2. Indirect observation uncovers activity that may have previously gone unnoticed
3. May be inexpensive
4. Can collect a wide range of data

CHALLENGES
1. Observation does not explain the cause of behavior.
2. Analysis can be time consuming.
3. Obtain a proper sample for generalization.
4. Observe average workers during average conditions.
5. The participant may change their behavior because they are being watched.

HOW TO USE THIS METHOD
1. Define objectives.
2. Make direct observation plan
3. Define participants and obtain their cooperation.
4. Define The context of the observation: time and place.
5. In some countries the law requires that you obtain written consent to video people.
6. Define the method of observation and the method of recording information.
7. Run a test session.
8. Hypothesize an explanation for the phenomenon.
9. Predict a logical consequence of the hypothesis.
10. Test your hypothesis by observation
11. Analyze the data gathered and create a list of insights derived from the observations.

RESOURCES
Note pad
Pens
Camera
Video Camera
Digital voice recorder

Non participant observation

WHAT IS IT?
The observer does not become part of the situation being observed or intervene in the behavior of the subjects. Used when a researcher wants the participants to behave normally. Usually this type of observation occurs in places where people normally work or live

WHY USE THIS METHOD?
1. To capture behavior as it happens.

CHALLENGES
1. Observation does not explain the cause of behavior.
2. Analysis can be time consuming.
3. Observer bias can cause the researcher to look only where they think they will see useful information.
4. Obtain a proper sample for generalization.
5. Observe average workers during average conditions.
6. The participant may change their behavior because they are being watched.

HOW TO USE THIS METHOD
1. Determine research goals.
2. Select a research context
3. The site should allow clear observation and be accessible.
4. Select participants
5. Seek permission.
6. Gain access
7. Gather research data.
8. Analyze data
9. Find common themes
10. Create insights

RESOURCES
Note pad
Pens
Camera
Video Camera
Digital voice recorder

Participant observation

WHAT IS IT?
Participant observation is an observation method where the researcher participates. The researcher becomes part of the situation being studied. The researcher may live or work in the context of the participant and may become a regular member of the participant's community. This method was used extensively by the pioneers of field research.

WHO INVENTED IT?
Radcliff-Brown 1910
Bronisław Malinowski 1922
Margaret Mead 1928

WHY USE THIS METHOD?
1. The goal of this method is to become close and familiar with the behavior of the participants.
2. To capture behavior as it happens.

CHALLENGES?
1. My be time consuming
2. May be costly
3. The researcher may influence the behavior of the participants.
4. The participants may not show the same behavior if the observer was not present.
5. May be language barriers
6. May be cultural barriers
7. May be risks for the researcher.
8. Be sensitive to privacy, and confidentiality.

HOW TO USE THIS METHOD
1. Determine research goals.
2. Select a research context
3. The site should allow clear observation and be accessible.
4. Select participants
5. Seek permission.
6. Gain access
7. Gather research data.
8. Analyze data
9. Find common themes
10. Create insights

RESOURCES
Note pad
Pens
Camera
Video Camera
Digital voice recorder

Structured observation

WHAT IS IT?
Particular types of behavior are observed and counted in a survey. The observer may create an event so that the behavior can be more easily studied. This approach is systematically planned and executed..

WHY USE THIS METHOD?
1. Allows stronger generalizations than unstructured observation.
2. May allow an observer to study behavior that may be difficult to study in unstructured observation.
3. To capture behavior as it happens.
4. A procedure is used which can be replicated.

CHALLENGES
1. Observation does not explain the cause of behavior.
2. Analysis can be time consuming.
3. Observer bias can cause the researcher to look only where they think they will see useful information.

HOW TO USE THIS METHOD
1. Define objectives.
2. Define participants and obtain their cooperation.
3. Define The context of the observation: time and place.
4. In some countries the law requires that you obtain written consent to video people.
5. Define the method of observation and the method of recording information. Common methods are taking written notes, video or audio recording.
6. Run a test session.
7. Hypothesize an explanation for the phenomenon.
8. Predict a logical consequence of the hypothesis.
9. Test your hypothesis by observation
10. Analyze the data gathered and create a list of insights derived from the observations.

RESOURCES
Note pad
Pens
Camera
Video Camera
Digital voice recorder

Unstructured observation

WHAT IS IT?
This method is used when a researcher wants to see what is naturally occurring without predetermined ideas. We use have an open-ended approach to observation and record all that we observe.

WHY USE THIS METHOD?
1. To capture behavior as it happens.
2. Observation is the most direct measure of behavior

CHALLENGES
1. Replication may be difficult.
2. Observation does not explain the cause of behavior.
3. Analysis can be time consuming.
4. Observer bias can cause the researcher to look only where they think they will see useful information.
5. Data cannot be quantified
6. In this form of observation there is a higher probability of observer's bias.

HOW TO USE THIS METHOD
1. Select a context to explore
2. Take a camera, note pad and pen
3. Record things and questions that you find interesting
4. Record ideas as you form them
5. Do not reach conclusions.
6. Ask people questions and try to understand the meaning in their replies.

RESOURCES
Note pad
Pens
Camera
Video Camera
Digital voice recorder

Personal inventory

WHAT IS IT?
This method involves studying the contents of a research subject's purse, or wallet. Study the things that they carry every day.

WHO INVENTED IT?
Rachel Strickland and Doreen Nelson 1998

WHY USE THIS METHOD?
1. To provide insights into the user's lifestyle, activities, perceptions, and values.
2. to understand the needs priorities and interests

HOW TO USE THIS METHOD
1. Formulate aims of research
2. Recruit participants carefully.
3. "The participant is asked to bring their 'most often carried bag' and lay the objects they carry on a flat surface, talking through the purpose and last-use of each item. Things to look out for where the bag is kept in the home and what is clustered around it, what is packed/repacked on arrival/departure, and the use of different bags for different activities." *Jan Chipchase*
4. Document the contents with photographs and notes
5. ask your research subject to talk about the objects and their meaning.
6. Analyze the data.

RESOURCES
Camera
Note pad

SCAMPER

WHAT IS IT?
SCAMPER is a brainstorming technique and creativity method that uses seven words as prompts.
1. Substitute.
2. Combine.
3. Adapt.
4. Modify.
5. Put to another use.
6. Eliminate.
7. Reverse.

WHO INVENTED IT?
Alex Osborne

WHY USE THIS METHOD?
1. Scamper is a method that can help generate innovative solutions to a problem.
2. Leverages the diverse experiences of a team.
3. Makes group problem solving fun.
4. Helps get buy in from all team members for solution chosen.
5. Helps build team cohesion.
6. Everyone can participate.

CHALLENGES
1. Some ideas that you generate using the tool may be impractical.
2. Best used with other creativity methods

WHEN TO USE THIS METHOD
Generate concepts

HOW TO USE THIS METHOD
1. Select a product or service to apply the method.
2. Select a diverse design team of 4 to 12 people and a moderator.
3. Ask questions about the product you identified, using the SCAMPER mnemonic to guide you.
4. Create as many ideas as you can.
5. Analyze
6. Prioritize.
7. Select the best single or several ideas to further brainstorm.

RESOURCES
Pens
Post-it-notes
A flip chart
Whiteboard or wall
Refreshments

SCAMPER questions

SUBSTITUTE
1. What materials or resources can you substitute or swap to improve the product?
2. What other product or process could you substitute?
3. What rules could you use?
4. Can you use this product in another situation?

COMBINE
1. Could you combine this product with another product?
2. Could you combine several goals?
3. Could you combine the use of the product with another use?
4. Could you join resources with someone else?

ADAPT
1. How could you adapt or readjust this product to serve another purpose or use?
2. What else is the product like?
3. What could you imitate to adapt this product?
4. What exists that is like the product?
5. Could the product adapt to another context?

MODIFY
1. How could you change the appearance of the product?
2. What could you change?
3. What could you focus on to create more return on investment?
4. Could you change part of the product?

PUT TO ANOTHER USE
1. Can you use this product in another situation?
2. Who would find this product useful?
3. How would this product function in a new context?
4. Could you recycle parts of this product to create a new product?

ELIMINATE
1. How could you make the product simpler?
2. What features, parts, could you eliminate?
3. What could you understate or tone down?
4. Could you make the product smaller or more efficient?
5. What components could you substitute to change the order of this product?

Scenarios

WHAT IS IT?
A scenario is a narrative or story about how people may experience a design in a particular future context of use. They can be used to predict or explore future interactions with concept products or services. Scenarios can be presented by media such as storyboards or video or be written. They can feature single or multiple actors participating in product or service interactions.

WHO INVENTED IT?
Herman Kahn, Rand Corporation
1950, USA

WHY USE THIS METHOD?
1. Scenarios become a focus for discussion which helps evaluate and refine concepts.
2. Usability issues can be explored at a very early stage in the design process.
3. The are useful tool to align a team vision.
4. Scenarios help us create an end to end experience.
5. Interactive experiences involve the dimension of time.
6. Personas give us a framework to evaluate possible solutions.

CHALLENGES
1. Generate scenarios for a range of situations.
2. Include problem situations
3. Hard to envision misuse scenarios.

WHEN TO USE THIS METHOD
1. Frame insights
2. Generate Concepts
3. Create Solutions

HOW TO USE THIS METHOD
1. Identify the question to investigate.
2. Decide time and scope for the scenario process.
3. Identify stakeholders and uncertainties.
4. Define the scenarios.
5. Create storyboards of users goals, activities, motivations and tasks.
6. Act out the scenarios.
7. The session can be videotaped.
8. Analyze the scenarios through discussion.
9. Summarize insights

RESOURCES
Storyboard templates
Pens
Video cameras
Props
Whiteboard
Dry-erase markers

Shadowing

WHAT IS IT?
Shadowing is observing people in context.
The researcher accompanies the user and observes user experiences and activities.
It allows the researcher and designer to develop design insights through observation and shared experiences with users.

WHO INVENTED IT?
Alex Bavelas 1944
Lucy Vernile, Robert A. Monteiro 1991

WHY USE THIS METHOD?
1. This method can help determine the difference between what subjects say they do and what they really do.
2. It helps in understanding the point of view of people. Successful design results from knowing the users.
3. Define intent
4. Can be used to evaluate concepts.

CHALLENGES
1. Selecting the wrong people to shadow.
2. Hawthorne Effect, The observer can influence the daily activities under being studied.

HOW TO USE THIS METHOD
1. Prepare
2. Select carefully who to shadow.
3. Observe people in context by members of your design team.
4. Capture behaviors that relate to product function.
5. Identify issues and user needs.
6. Create design solutions based on observed and experienced user needs.
7. Typical periods can be one day to one week.

RESOURCES
Video camera
Digital still camera
Note pad
Laptop Computer

Storyboard template

PROJECT	NAME	DATE

DIALOGUE

ACTION

PROJECT	NAME	DATE

DIALOGUE

ACTION

PROJECT	NAME	DATE

DIALOGUE

ACTION

Storyboards

WHAT IS IT?
A storyboard is a narrative tool derived from cinema. A storyboard is a form of prototyping which communicates each step of activity, experience or interaction. Used in films and multimedia as well as product and UX design. Storyboards consist of some 'frames' that communicate a sequence of events in context.

WHO INVENTED IT?
Invented by Walt Disney in 1927. Disney credited animator Webb Smith with creating the first storyboard. By 1937-38 all studios were using storyboards.

WHY USE THIS METHOD?
1. Can help gain insightful user feedback.
2. Conveys an experience.
3. Can use a storyboard to communicate a complex task as a series of steps.
4. Allows the proposed activities to be discussed and refined.
5. Storyboards can be used to help designers identify opportunities or use problems.

HOW TO USE THIS METHOD
1. Decide what story you want to describe.
2. Choose a story and a message: what do you want the storyboard to express?
3. Create your characters
4. Think about the whole story first rather than one panel at a time.
5. Create the drafts and refine them through an iterative process. Refine.
6. Illustrations can be sketches or photographs.
7. Consider: Visual elements, level of detail, text, experiences and emotions, number of frames, and flow of time.
8. Keep text short and informative.
9. 6 to 12 frames.
10. Tell your story efficiently and effectively.
11. Brainstorm your ideas.

RESOURCES
1. Pens
2. Digital camera
3. Storyboard templates
4. Comic books for inspiration

Patient stakeholder map

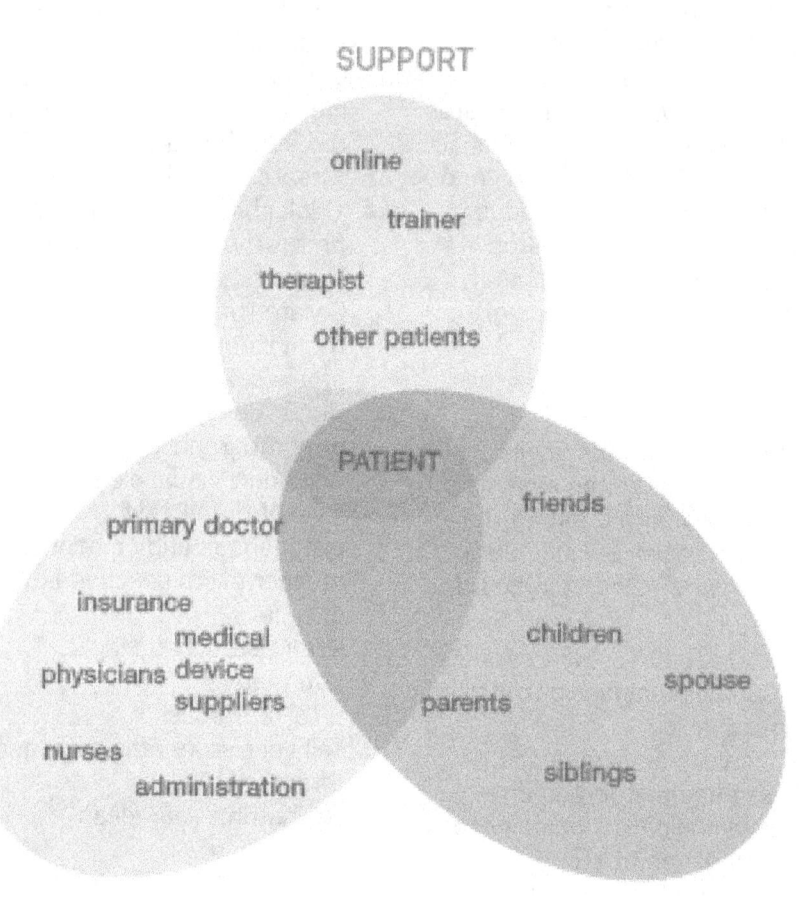

Stakeholder maps

WHAT IS IT
Stakeholders maps are used to document the key stakeholders and their relationship.

At the beginning of a design project it is important to identify the key stakeholders and their relationships. The map serves as a reference for the design team.

WHO INVENTED IT
Mitchell 1997

WHY USE THIS METHOD
1. Stakeholder mapping helps discover ways to influence other stakeholders.
2. Stakeholder mapping helps discover risks.
3. Stakeholder mapping helps discover positive stakeholders to involve in the design process.

CHALLENGES?
Stakeholder mapping helps discover negative stakeholders and their associated risks.

HOW TO USE THIS METHOD
1. Invite six known stakeholders to a meeting.
2. Give each stakeholder a block of post-it notes.
3. Brainstorm with the group additional stakeholders
4. Cluster stockholders into relevant groups
5. Assign priorities for individual stakeholders based on the value of their potential feedback during the design process,
6. Map the stakeholders.
7. Can initially be documented on a whiteboard, cards, post-it-notes and consolidated as a diagram through several iterations showing hierarchy and relationships.

SWOT template

STRENGTHS

WEAKNESSES

OPPORTUNITIES

THREATS

SWOT analysis

WHAT IS IT?
SWOT Analysis is a useful technique for understanding your strengths and weaknesses, and for identifying both the opportunities open to you and the threats you face.

WHO INVENTED IT?
Albert Humphrey 1965 Stanford University

WHY USE THIS METHOD?
1. SWOT analysis can help you uncover opportunities that you can exploit.
2. You can analysis both your own organization, product or service as well as those of competitors.
3. Helps develop a strategy of differentiation.
4. It is inexpensive

CHALLENGES
1. Use only verifiable information.
2. Have system for implementation.

HOW TO USE THIS METHOD
1. Explain basic rules of brainstorming.
2. Ask questions related to the SWOT categories.
3. Record answers on a whiteboard or video
4. Categorize ideas into groups
5. Consider when evaluating "What will the institution gain or lose?"

RESOURCES
Post-it-notes
SWOT template
Pens
Whiteboard
Video camera
Dry-erase markers

Sample SWOT questions

STRENGTHS
1. Advantages of proposition
2. Capabilities
3. Competitive advantages
4. Marketing - reach, distribution
5. Innovative aspects
6. Location and geographical
7. Price, value, quality?
8. Accreditation, certifications
9. Unique selling proposition
10. Human resources
11. Experience,
12. Assets
13. Return on investment
14. Processes, IT, communications
15. Cultural, attitudinal, behavioral
16. Management cover, succession

WEAKNESSES
1. Value of proposition
2. Things we cannot do.
3. Things we are not good at
4. Perceptions of brand
5. Financial
6. Own known vulnerabilities
7. Time scales, deadlines and pressures
8. Reliability of data, plan predictability
9. Morale, commitment, leadership
10. Cash flow, start-up cash-drain

OPPORTUNITIES
1. Market developments
2. Competitors' vulnerabilities
3. New USP's
4. Tactics - surprise, major contracts
5. Business and product development
6. Information and research
7. Partnerships, agencies, distribution
8. Industrial trends
9. Technologies
10. Innovations
11. Global changes
12. Market opportunities
13. Specialized market niches
14. New exports or imports
15. Volumes, production, economies
16. Seasonal, weather, fashion influences

THREATS
1. Political effects
2. Legislative effects
3. Obstacles faced
4. Insurmountable weaknesses
5. Environmental effects
6. IT developments
7. Competitor intentions
8. Loss of key staff
9. Sustainable financial backing
10. Market demand
11. New technologies, services, ideas

Video prototyping

WHAT IS IT?
Video prototypes use video to illustrate how users will interact with a new system. Video prototypes can be thought of as sketches that illustrate what the interaction with the new system will be like.

WHY USE THIS METHOD?
1. Capturing an experience over time requires a linear medium like video
2. Video prototypes are a good way of communicating a complex system of interactions in an easy to access way that can be shared with a large number of people.

RESOURCES
1. Video camera
2. Smartphone camera
3. Card for titles
4. Simple props
5. Actors
6. Lights
7. Post-it-notes

HOW TO USE THIS METHOD
1. Choose a director and a camera person.
2. Decide who the actors are and who will create the storyboard and props.
3. Decide how you will communicate the story: title-cards only, an off-camera voice-over or through dialog.
4. Storyboard the sequence of shots.
5. Begin by shooting the initial title card 4 seconds with the name of the project, group, date, time and version number.
6. Shoot a title card 6 seconds that identifies the personas and the context.
7. Shoot an establishing shot that shows the user(s) in context.
8. Shoot the series of interaction points that tell the story and communicate the interaction.
9. Use mid shots to show conversation and close-ups to show devices.
10. "editing-in-the-camera" involves shooting each sequence of the video prototype in the order that it will be viewed,so that it does not need to be edited afterward.
11. Some video prototypes use a narrator or voice over, others use only title cards others rely on the actors to explain interactions.

WWWWWH

WHAT IS IT?
'Who, What, Where, When, Why, and How'? is a method for getting a thorough understanding of the problem, It is used to obtain basic information in police investigations. A well-known golden rule of journalism is that if you want to know the full story about something you have to answer all the five W's. Journalists argue your story isn't complete until you answer all six questions.
1. Who is involved?
2. What occurred?
3. When did it happen?
4. Where did it happen?
5. Why did it occur?

WHO INVENTED IT?
Hermagoras of Temnos, Greece 1st century BC.

WHY USE THIS METHOD?
This method helps create a story that communicates clearly the nature of an activity or event to stakeholders.

HOW TO USE THIS METHOD
1. Ask the questions starting with the 5 w's and 1 h question words.
2. Identify the people involved
3. Identify the activities and make a list of them.
4. Identify all the places and make a list of them.
5. Identify all the time factors and make a list of them.
6. Identify causes for events of actions and make a list of them.
7. Identify the way events took place and make a list of them.
8. Study the relationships between the information.

RESOURCES
Computer
Notebook
Pens
Video camera
Digital camera
Digital voice recorder
Release forms
Interview plan or structure
Questions, tasks and discussion items

Some WWWWWH questions

WHO
1. Is affected?
2. Who believes that the problem affects them?
3. Needs the problem solved?
4. Does not want the problem to be solved?
5. Could stand in the way of a solution?

WHEN
1. Does it happen
2. Doesn't it happen?
3. Did it start?
4. Will it end?
5. Is the solution needed?
6. Might it happen in the future?
7. Will it be a bigger problem?
8. Will it improve?

WHERE
1. Does it happen?
2. Doesn't it happen
3. Else does it happen?
4. Is the best place to solve the problem

WHY
1. Is this situation a problem?
2. Do you want to solve it?
3. Do you not want to solve it?
4. Does it not go away?
5. Would someone else want to solve it?
6. Can it be solved?
7. Is it difficult to solve?

WHAT
1. May be different in the future
2. Are its weaknesses?
3. Do you like?
4. Makes you unhappy about it?
5. Is flexible?
6. Is not flexible?
7. Do you know?
8. Do you not understand?
9. How have you solved similar problems?
10. Are the underlying ideas?
11. Are the values involved?
12. Are the elements of the problem and how are they related?
13. What can you assume to be correct
14. Is most important
15. Is least important
16. Are your goals?
17. Do you need to discover?

Affinity Diagrams

Traditional design methods struggle when dealing with complex or chaotic problems or with large amounts of data. The affinity diagram organizes a large quantity of information by natural relationships. This method taps a team's analytical thinking as well as creativity and intuition. It was invented in the 1960s by Japanese anthropologist Jiro Kawakita and is sometimes referred to as the KJ Method.

For around 50 years affinity diagrams have been an essential pillar of what is known as the Seven Management and Planning Tools, used in Japan.
The seven management and planning tools are used in leading global organizations for making and implementing better team decisions.

You can use an affinity diagram to:
- Understand what is most important from ambiguous data
- Tame complexity
- Identify connections in data
- Create hierarchies
- Identifying themes
- Identify what factors to focus on that will support the most successful design possible from a customer's perspective.

"Most groups that use this technique are amazed at how powerful and valuable a tool it is. Try it once with an open mind and you'll be another convert."

Nancy R. Tague

What are affinity diagrams?

WHAT ARE AFFINITY DIAGRAMS?

An affinity diagram is a method used to organize many ideas into groups with common themes or relationships. Affinity diagrams are tools for analyzing large amounts of data and discovering relationships which allow a design direction to be established based on the associations. This method may uncover significant hidden relationships.

Jiro Kawakita developed the method, and so it was sometimes referred to as the K-J method.

The affinity diagram is a method that an individual or team can use for problem-solving. Affinity diagrams encourage creative input by everyone on the team.

The tool is used in project management to sort brainstorming ideas into groups, based on their natural relationships and for synthesis and analysis. It is also used in design research to synthesize insights from field research. Affinity diagrams are built through consensus of a design team on how the information should be grouped in logical ways.

WHY USE THIS AFFINITY DIAGRAMS?

1. Traditional design methods do not work when dealing with complex or chaotic problems with large amounts of data. This tool helps to establish relationships or similarities between many pieces of information. From these relationships, insights can be determined which are the starting point of design solutions. It is possible using this method to reach consensus faster than many other methods.

You can use an affinity diagram to:
1. Understand what is most important from a large amount of complex or ambiguous data.
2. Tame complexity.
3. Understand connections between ideas.
4. Identify relationships in data.
5. Create hierarchies.

6. Exercise team decision making.
7. Make sense from brainstorming ideas.
8. Support design and data workshops.
9. Identifying themes from data
10. Identify patterns from data.
11. It helps to reduce "team paralysis," from too many options and lack of consensus.

HISTORY

Affinity diagrams were created in the 1950s by Japanese anthropologist Jiro Kawakita It is sometimes called the K-J Method. Jiro Kawakita worked in remote Nepalese villages researching problems, related to water supplies and transportation. He was awarded the Ramon Magsaysay Award in 1984.

Affinity diagrams were part of the Seven Management and Planning Tools, used in Total Quality Control in Japan. Jiro Kawakita named the method around 1967 and published a comprehensive description of the KJ method in 1986. Since 1969, Kawakita has presented KJ method workshops in Japan.

WHEN SHOULD WE USE AFFINITY DIAGRAMS?

An Affinity Diagram is useful when you want to:
1. Make sense out of large volumes of chaotic data.
2. Encourage new patterns of thinking. An affinity diagram can break through traditional or entrenched thinking.

STRENGTHS

1. It is a simple method.
2. Supports innovation.
3. Causes breakthroughs to emerge
4. Helps groups come to a consensus about most important issues
5. Multiple people can combine their ideas by on post-it notes and be organizing them.
6. Organizing generates useful discussions.
7. Builds critical thinking skills.
8. Allows for involvement of each team member
9. Helps your team to see the

big picture and where the biggest problems are.
10. Post-it notes are a flexible method to organize ideas into various levels of groups and sub-groups.
11. It is both a creative and analytical method
12. Promotes the emergence of breakthrough thinking
13. Most effective when applied to a team with varied perspectives and open-mindedness.
14. Is useful to make sense of complex apparently unrelated ambiguous or chaotic data
15. It makes your analysis highly visible to others in the company.

WEAKNESSES

1. Good facilitation is required to when there is a lot of data.
2. Affinity diagrams are not portable or mobile.
3. Affinity diagrams occupy a large space for a period.
4. Can be time-consuming when there are a large number of pieces of data.
5. The small size of post-it notes and the effort of writing forces you to be brief,
6. It is an analog or physical activity
7. the rationale behind particular groupings can be lost.
8. Affinity diagrams are temporary and must be photographed to keep a permanent record.
9. It may be difficult find individual pieces of information.

USE AN AFFINITY DIAGRAM WHEN:

1. You have a large body of information in apparent chaos.
2. To uncover hidden connections between pieces of information or ideas
3. When issues seem too broad and complex to grasp.
4. There is no clear solution evident to your team.
5. When group consensus is necessary.
6. You wish to move beyond habitual thinking and preconceived categories.
7. When other solutions to a problem have failed.

8. To rethink how issues are connected.
9. To brainstorm root causes and solutions to problems, especially when little or no data is available
10. Organize qualitative data from stakeholders to uncover insights and themes
11. The solution requires consensus amongst the team members to work effectively
12. Extract requirements from user research
13. To organize ideas from brainstorming.
14. To brainstorm root causes of problems, especially when data is confusing or ambiguous.

DO NOT USE AN AFFINITY DIAGRAM WHEN:
if less than 15 items of data.

Gather your data and spread it over a wall

Affinity diagram process

SELECT YOUR TEAM
Care should be taken in choosing your team. As many groups and diverse points of view involved in design delivery and use of the service as possible should be represented.
1. Keep groups to six people or less.
2. Break large groups into smaller groups of six or fewer people.
3. Have a diverse team with different genders, age, occupations and status represented.
4. Have at least two or three "T" shaped people. That is people with two or more areas of expertise such as technology and management or administration and design. T-shaped team members make the team more flexible and help group collaboration.
5. Involve external and internal stakeholders such as customers, suppliers, internal business management, engineering, design, and sales.
6. Have customer facing people where possible because they better see the client's perspective.

APPOINT YOUR MODERATOR
1. Create handouts with clear instructions
2. Provide copies of research summaries
3. Take breaks every 90 minutes
4. Photograph the map as it is being built.

MODERATOR SKILLS
1. Effective Listening Skills
2. Flexibility
3. Customer empathy
4. Sincerely Interested in People
5. Enthusiasm
6. People management skills
7. Able to establishing common direction and buy-in.
8. Understands Group Dynamics
9. Authority
10. Neutral and Objective
11. Patient and Persistent
12. Guide discussion promptly.

RESOURCES
Whiteboard
Large wall spaces or tables
Dry-erase markers
Sharpies
Post-it notes

Move the data into related groups

Group the post-it-notes by association or affinity

202

There are two ways to use affinity diagrams:

RESEARCH TOOL

To make sense of a large body of research data. This approach can be used to establish connections between different pieces of research, to uncover insights from the data that can then be used to develop design concepts. With this approach, the team can develop a hierarchy of significance of the connections or themes and the insights. This hierarchy helps to establish the levels of focus for different ideas and themes uncovered by the research for the ideation design phase.

BRAINSTORMING TOOL

Affinity diagrams can also be used during the ideation or idea generation phase of a design project. When the technique is used for ideation it helps synthesize a large number of design ideas. The design team can decide which ideas are the best ideas and then combine features of various ideas to develop themes and variations through iterative cycles of brainstorming, affinity diagrams and synthesis.

GATHER YOUR DATA

First gather your data. Break the data down into pieces. For example, if an interview subject has raised several interesting points during an interview transcribe the interview, highlight the interesting points then copy each point onto a separate post it note. Use only one color post-it notes at this stage. The most common color used at this phase for the raw data is yellow.

FIND YOUR SPACE

Once you have selected your team, your moderator, and space to work, spread the ideas randomly across a wall, a whiteboard or large table. A floor in a little traffic area also can work for this stage of the process. You need plenty of space.

Affinity diagrams work best with more than 100 discreet pieces of information and work efficiently up to several thousand pieces of data.

Move the data into related groups

CLUSTERING

Hand a block of blank 2" x 3" yellow post-it notes to each team member.

You can use the "Rule of 7 plus or minus 2". The summary should have no less than 5 and no more than 9 words in it, including a verb and a noun. Use also simple cartoon sketches and a combination of drawings and words. Gather your team around the place where you have placed the post-it notes. Look for ideas that seem to be related.

Go for volume, suspend judgment, build on each other's ideas and set a strict time limit. Allow 30 or 40 minutes for brainstorming ideas.

The moderator then asks the team to take two ideas that seem to belong together and place them together, at least, three feet away from the other post-it notes. Keep moving post-it notes into the groups until all the post-its have been placed into groups. It is OK to replace another person's group if it doesn't make sense to you. Some groups may have only a small number of items.

The type of relationship that you see will depend on your background, your profession your personality and your life experience.

Move related ideas into groups and continue moving the post-it notes until all notes are in groups. Some ideas may not seem to fit a group. Place those ideas into a group. If a note belongs in two groups, make a second note.

It is best that no one speaks at this stage, so different perspectives are represented.
Work silently. Ask the team to move the ideas into groups based on their gut instincts and without talking. This approach encourages unconventional thinking and discourages one person from steering the affinity. It is important to maintain silence at this stage, as it ensures that each member has an equal opportunity to apply their perspective without being influenced to conform to others'

thinking.

Ask your team not to struggle over placing the data into groups, use gut instincts. If consensus is not reached, make a duplicate of the idea and place one copy in two groups. The idea written on each post-it should be a phrase or sentence that clearly conveys the meaning to people who are not on the team. Make the notes large enough to be readable from 10 feet distance.

HEADERS

Hand out a block of blank 2" x 3" blue post-it notes to each team member. Using the second color of post-it notes, ask each participant to assign a name to each group. Write a header above each cluster that describes what connects the data in the group. Use a different color post-it notes for the headers. Blue is a color that is often used for headers. You can use any color, but it should be the same color for all headers and a different color than the color utilized in the previous phase. The most efficient use of space is to position the post-it notes in a group vertically with the header above the group.

To create headers ask for each grouping: "What key words summarize the central idea that this grouping communicates?" Sometimes a post it from within the group can be used as a header.

Create a heading for each group that captures the theme of each group. Place it above the group. A header should capture the association or affinity among the ideas contained in a group. The team develops headers by discussing and agreeing on the wording of the header post-it notes.

Review each group and write down a name that best represents each cluster on the new set of sticky notes. Do not use full sentences for headers but summarize the association with just one or two words.

If a group has two themes, then split the group into two groups. If two groups share the same theme combine the two groups into one or move the two groups

Vote for groups

near to each other and place a header above the headers of the two groups that defines the association of the two groups.

Making a simple title involves abductive thinking, which is the best form of problem solving for complex, changing and ambiguous problems. Some notes will not fit into any group. Put these in a separate group.

When people slow down it is time to break the silence, and start discussing the groups that have emerged. When consensus is reached, move on to the next step.

SUPERHEADERS

If two groups have the same theme then place an additional header in a third color above those two groups. Leave the previous headers in place. Pink is commonly used for a combined header of two groups. This type of header is sometimes called a super header. Repeat the process until the number of groupings is between 5 and 9 groups. Ask each participant to read through the post-it notes in each group.

The moderator should then say "We will now see if we can combine some groups. Please nominate two groups that you think we can combine. Only combine groups that have the same theme but not groups that are subsets of one another"

DOT VOTING

Give each participant 3 adhesive dots and ask them to place the dots next to the header of the three groups that they think are most important in relation to the design goals.
1. What are the user needs?
2. What are the needs of the business?
3. What technologies are most appropriate?

After each person has voted tally the number of votes for each group.

This gives you a hierarchy of importance for the themes in order to address these themes in the next phase of the design process, the ideation phase.

This is a way of efficiently selecting from a large number of ideas the preferred ideas to carry forward in the design process.

WHY USE DOT VOTING?

It is a method of selecting a favored idea by collective rather than individual judgment. It is a fast method that allows a design to progress. It leverages the strengths of diverse team member viewpoints and experiences

CHALLENGES

1. The assessment is subjective.
2. Group-think
3. Not enough good ideas
4. Inhibition
5. Lack of critical thinking

HOW TO USE THIS METHOD

1. Gather your team of 4 to 12 participants.
2. Brainstorm ideas, for example, ask each team member to generate ten ideas as sketches.
3. Each idea should be presented on one post-it-note or page.
4. Each designer should quickly explain each idea to the group before the group votes.
5. Spread the ideas over a wall or table.
6. Ask the team to vote on their two or three favorite ideas and total the votes. You can use sticky dots or colored pins to indicate a vote or a moderator can tally the scores.
7. Rearrange the ideas so that the ideas with the dots are ranked from most dots to least.
8. Refine the preferred ideas.

Think and feel
- What is important to them?
- How are they reacting?
- What are the emotions at each stage?

See
- What are they seeing?
- In the environment?
- Which sights are obstacles?
- What are pleasant sounds?
- Are sights conflicting with their needs?

Persona
- Name
- Age
- Gender
- Occupation
- Other Criteria

Say and do
- What are the activities stage by stage?
- Are their conflicts between thoughts, actions and intentions?

Gain
- What are their goals?
- What are they trying to achieve?
- What are their needs?
- What are their desires?
- How do they measure success?

Hear
- What are they hearing?
- Which sounds are obstacles?
- In the environment?
- From interactions with people?
- What are pleasant sounds?

Pain
- What are the pain points?
- What are the frustrations?
- What are the obstacles?
- What are the fears?
- What are the risks?

Empathy Maps

Empathy maps analyze each part of a user experience to create a high-level view of where an experience is good or bad. It is a relatively fast and efficient technique to consider the main elements of a customer experience systematically. Empathy maps are most useful at the beginning of the design process after user research.

Empathy maps are used to help craft a better customer experience. It reveals the underlying "why" behind users' actions, choices and decisions so we can pro-actively design for customer's real needs.

This method helps draw out the main components of the customer experience so that problems can be identified and fixed.

An empathy map is a tool that helps the design team understand people they are designing for. You can create an empathy map for a group of customers or a persona.
They are a fast way of making user needs tangible for non-designers and because they're quick to create, are a good start to take your team beyond their experiences to immerse themselves in the customer's world and to uncover what drives your customer's behavior. Empathy maps help your team to understand "why" customers do things so that your team can design for their real needs. It lays the foundation for innovative design that fulfills your customer's unmet and unarticulated needs.

Empathy maps

WHAT IS AN EMPATHY MAP?
A mapping method that analyzes each part of a user experience. An Empathy Map gives a high-level view of where an experience is good or bad. Used to improve a customer experience.

The biggest single cause of failure of new products and services in the marketplace is that the organization creating the product or service did not thoroughly understand the customer's perspective. This method helps draw out the main components of the client's experience so that problems can be identified and fixed.

Empathy Map is a tool that helps the design team empathize with the end users. You can create an empathy map for a group of customers or a persona.

WHAT IS EMPATHY?
The identification with the feelings, thoughts, or attitudes of another. Keep in mind, empathy and sympathy are different things

WHO INVENTED THE EM?
Scott Matthews and Dave Gray at XPLANE now Dachis Group.

HOW LONG DOES IT TAKE?
One to three hours per persona.

WHY USE THIS METHOD?
This tool helps a design team understand the customers and their context. It is an outside-in technique.

CHALLENGES
1. Emotions must be inferred by observing clues.
2. This method is not as rigorous as traditional personas but requires less investment.

RESOURCES
Empathy map template
Whiteboard
or chalkboard
or video projector
or Large sheet of paper
Dry-erase markers
Post-it-notes
Pens
Video Camera

On a whiteboard draw a circle then 4 radiating boxes

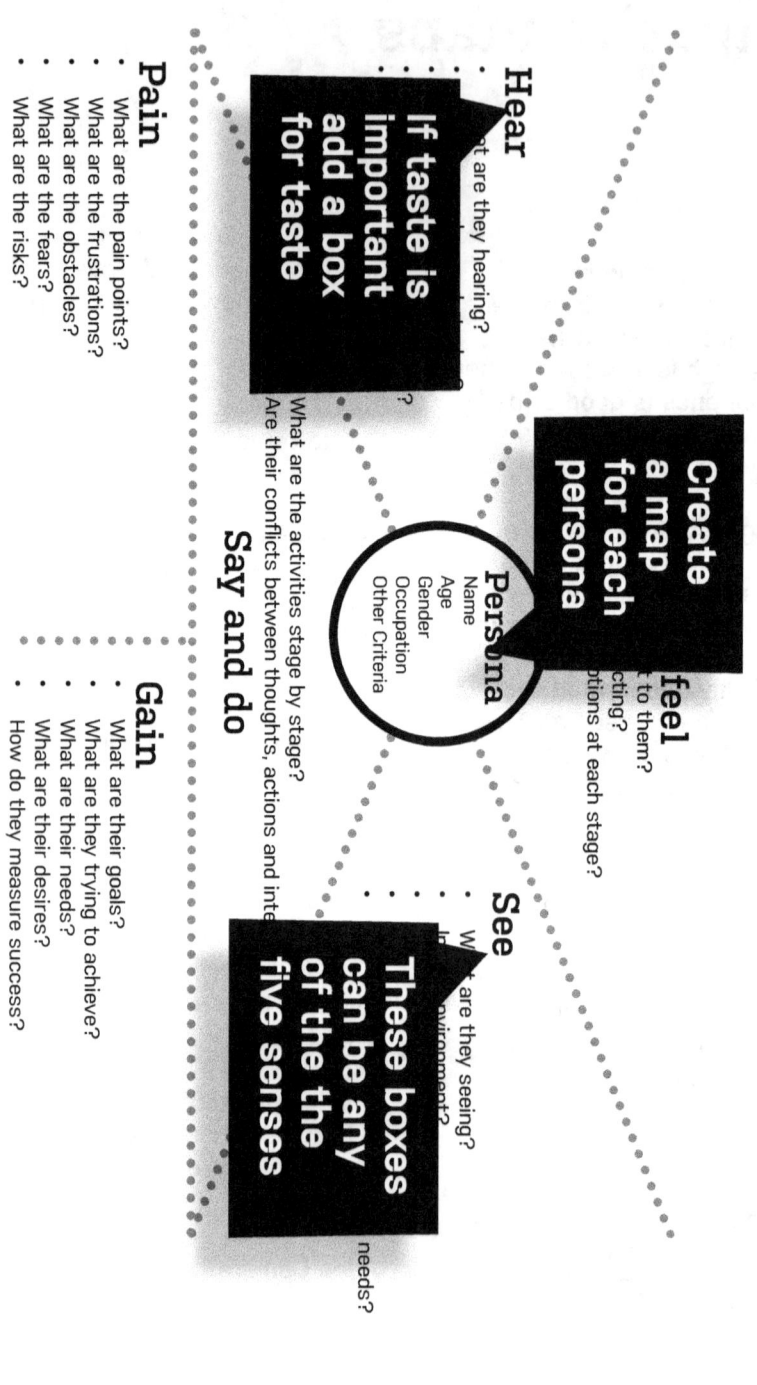

Persona
Name
Age
Gender
Occupation
Other Criteria

Create a map for each persona

- What are they hearing?

Hear

If taste is important add a box for taste

See
- What are they seeing?
- ...environment?
- ...needs?

Say and do
- What are the activities stage by stage?
- Are their conflicts between thoughts, actions and inte...

Pain
- What are the pain points?
- What are the frustrations?
- What are the obstacles?
- What are the fears?
- What are the risks?

Gain
- What are their goals?
- What are they trying to achieve?
- What are their needs?
- What are their desires?
- How do they measure success?

These boxes can be any of the the five senses

SUMMARY HOW TO MAKE AN EMPATHY MAP

1. A team of 4 to 12 people is a good number for this method.
2. The best people to involve are individuals who have direct interaction with customers.
3. The team should represent various functions in your organization such as management, design, marketing, sales, and engineering. It is helpful also to include some stakeholders such as customers and others affected by the end design. The process will help draw out useful information from them.
4. This method can be used with personas.
5. The map should be based on real information from customers. Research can be gathered from sources such as interviews, observation, web analytics, customer service departments and focus groups.
6. Segment your market then create a persona representing an average customer in each segment. Create four to six personas.
7. Draw a circle. The circle will represent your target persona.
8. Create some radial boxes around the circle to represent aspects of that person's sensory experience. It is common to have boxes for seeing and hearing. Some experiences such as drinking coffee could include boxes for other senses such as taste and smell.
9. Place two boxes at the bottom of the map and label them "Pain" and "Gain".
10. Ask your team to describe from the persona's point of view their experience.
11. Populate the map by using the research gathers through your fieldwork: What are they thinking, feeling, saying, doing, hearing, seeing?
12. Once you have filled all of the top boxes move the post-it notes for negative components of the experience into the lower pain box and positive into the gain box.
13. The pain box can serve as a start for identifying the problems to fix in the ideation phase.

Empathy mapping process

Here is a list of stages that you can complete to create an empathy map. Considerer the map to be a living document that will develop and improve so it doesn't have to be perfect first time. Concentrate on your customers and their point of view.

CREATE YOUR GOAL STATEMENT

1. What is the problem, unmet needs or opportunities that the blueprint is to realize?
2. Your customer's goals and needs should be compatible with your goals and with an outcome that satisfies them.
3. Who are the internal and external stakeholders who will be affected in some way by the design?
4. Where will the service or experience be delivered?
5. When will the service or experience be provided?
6. What are the channels?
7. Why is there a need for a design solution?
8. Have you identified problems?
9. Do you want to improve the customer experience?
10. Do you wish to engage your customers effectively? Do you want to create a more efficient process?
11. Define your goals in a statement and return to that statement as you build your map to ensure that your efforts contribute to reaching the goal.

DEFINE YOUR TARGET AUDIENCE SEGMENT AND THEIR NEEDS

The most successful products and services target precise customer segments. Designs that try to please everyone do not please anyone.

1. Identify before starting your empathy map:
2. Your focus
3. Problems that your customers are experiencing.
4. Questions that your customers are asking.
5. What your customers want

VISIT THE PLACE WHERE YOUR CUSTOMER IS ACCESSING YOUR PRODUCT OR SERVICE

Observe what your customer is doing and talk to at least 6 customers.

1. Who are your customers?
2. What are they doing step by step?
3. What are the barriers that stand in the way of your customers being successful?
4. Where are the activities located?
5. When do the activities occur??
6. Why does your customer behave as they do?
7. How do they interact with your organization step by step?
8. What are the touchpoints?

GATHER YOUR EXISTING RESEARCH

Start by auditing internal customer experience data that has been previously gathered. If available review existing user data, including call center logs, customer satisfaction surveys, existing personas, mystery shopping data, web analytics and customer satisfaction data. Examine the data and determine what new research is necessary. to fill in the knowledge gaps. To be useful data should be current. The most significant insights will come directly from engaging the stakeholders located in their natural context concerning the service. Engage stakeholders through a variety of possible research techniques in the physical location of the service such as contextual observation and interviews.

Quantitative data is less useful than qualitative research when trying to understand the feelings and emotions of your customers.

Interviews are amongst the most common methods used to gather data. Ask them to walk you through their experience and talk about their problems, needs, desires and feelings at each stage. Start by talking to between five and twenty people as a minimum sample size. Focus your questions on the areas relevant to the lanes of the service blueprint. If you are creating a journey map ask what are they doing, thinking,

and feeling at each stage of the activity. Ask them what touch points they are engaging at each stage. Ask them where they are experiencing problems or frustrations in achieving their goals. Document your interviews or observations by using video or a digital recorder. Quantitative data with a larger sample size is also useful. Create a survey for existing or prospective customers.

In order to be useful your service blueprint needs to be based on real and truthful information.
Use draft maps in focus group discussions to validate findings directly with customers.

REVIEW YOUR EXISTING RESEARCH
Review Existing Research Identify gaps in data and create a list of recurring customer experience problems.

CREATE A RESEARCH PLAN TO FILL THE GAPS.
Identify gaps in data and create a list of recurring customer experience problems.

1. Create a research plan to fill the gaps.
2. What do you still need to know?
3. What questions do you need to ask?
4. How many people will you involve?
5. What type of people will you research?
6. What will be the context of the study?
7. What methods will you use?
8. When will you select and screen the subjects, conduct the research and report on findings?

SYNTHESIZE YOUR RESEARCH
Place each potentially useful piece of information on a separate post it note. Put the post-it notes on a wall and ask your team to organize the customer's comments into related groups or themes. Which themes are most significant to more customers? Build a hierarchy of themes. Identify themes and patterns from the interviews.
What are your customers needs and goals at each stage of their activity? What touchpoints are

they engaging at each step?

SELECT YOUR TEAM

Care should be taken in selecting your team. As many groups and diverse points of view involved in design delivery and use of the service as possible should be represented.

1. Keep groups to six people or less.
2. If your total group size is larger than twelve people, break the large group into smaller groups of six or less.
3. Have a diverse team with different genders, age, occupations and seniority represented.
4. Have at least two or three "T" shaped people. That is, individuals with two or more areas of expertice such as technology and management or design. This makes the team more flexible and helps group collaboration.
5. Involve external and internal stakeholders such as customers, suppliers, internal business management, engineering, design, and sales.
6. Have customer facing people where possible because they better understand the perspective of the client.

APPOINT YOUR MODERATOR

1. Create handouts with clear instructions
2. Provide copies of research summaries
3. Take breaks every 90 minutes
4. Photograph the map as it is being built

MODERATOR SKILLS

1. Effective Listening Skills
2. Flexibility
3. Customer empathy
4. Sincerely Interested in People
5. Enthusiasm
6. People management skills
7. Able to establishing collective direction and buy-in.
8. Understands Group Dynamics
9. Authority
10. Neutral and Objective
11. Patient and Persistent
12. Curious
13. Guide discussion in a timely manner.

14. Able to draw our quieter group members.
15. Reads between the lines and understand what is not said.
16. Beginner's mind
17. Get Panelists to Talk to Each Other.
18. Get the Audience Involved Early.
19. Able to read body language
20. Able to create an atmosphere where divergent views can be explored
21. Encourage all participants to share their views openly.
22. Keep the conversation focused and relevant
23. Track and record the key themes and ideas expressed by the group.

SELECT AND PREPARE YOUR WORKSPACE

A good space is a large room with plenty of natural light with a large table and sufficient chairs for your team.

USEFUL MATERIALS

1. A large wall
2. Butcher paper
3. Masking tape
4. Mobile dry erase boards
5. Dry erase markers
6. Sharpies
7. Adhesive notes in 5 colors
8. Digital camera
9. Tripod

IDENTIFY YOUR TARGET SEGMENT TO MAP

Identifying customer segments.

CREATE PERSONAS

Create your customer personas. Personas are archetypal characters created to represent the different user types that might use a product or service in a similar way. Create 3 to 6 personas to cover all your customers.

IDENTIFY STAKEHOLDERS

A stakeholder is someone who may be in some way influenced by your design. For example, in a hospital stakeholders may be patients, relatives of patients, hospital workers, doctors, nurses, health insurance workers. Stakeholders are also people who represent various areas within your organization such as technology, design, business management, sales, customer experience.

HOLD STAKEHOLDER

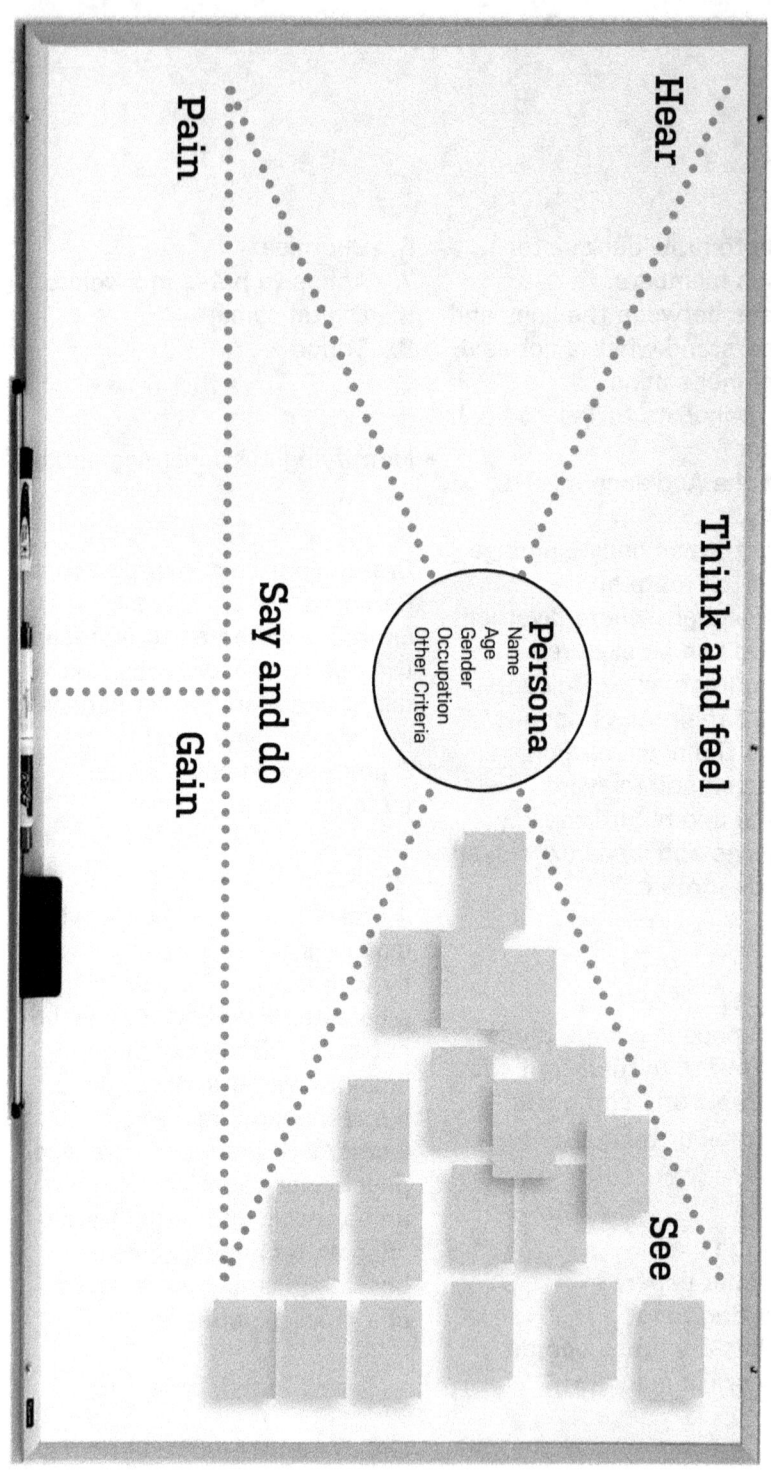

WORKSHOPS
Organize a workshop, and guide internal and external stakeholders through the process of creating the first draft. Go over the user experience in detail and discuss the experience from the perspective of customers and diverse interested parties.

SELECT THE SERVICE TO BE BLUEPRINTED
Choose your journey or experience to map. We suggests starting small with part of an experience that is important or problematic. For example rather than mapping an entire customer journey for air travel from New York to London, map a part of it that is important su8ch as selecting the airline and booking on line. Explore several
challenging sub-journeys before tackling the whole journey.

DECIDE PRESENT OR FUTURE SERVICE TO MAP
It is most usual first to map your existing customer experience. A current state map can help identify ways to make your existing customer experience better or more efficient.

After mapping your current service you may be interested in creating a map as a concept for a future service or customer experience. You may not have a current service in which case go straight to a map of a future service or experience.

SELECT START AND END POINTS OF THE CUSTOMER EXPERIENCE
Define the scope in terms of time ad customer activities.

SELECT CHANNELS TO MAP
Typical examples of channels include
1. In-store experience
2. Print,
3. Web,
4. Mobile

The channel defines the opportunities and constraints of a touchpoint. Here is a list of stages that you can complete to create a Service Blueprint. Considerer the blueprint to be a living document that will develop and improve so

Then populate the box with what your persona hears

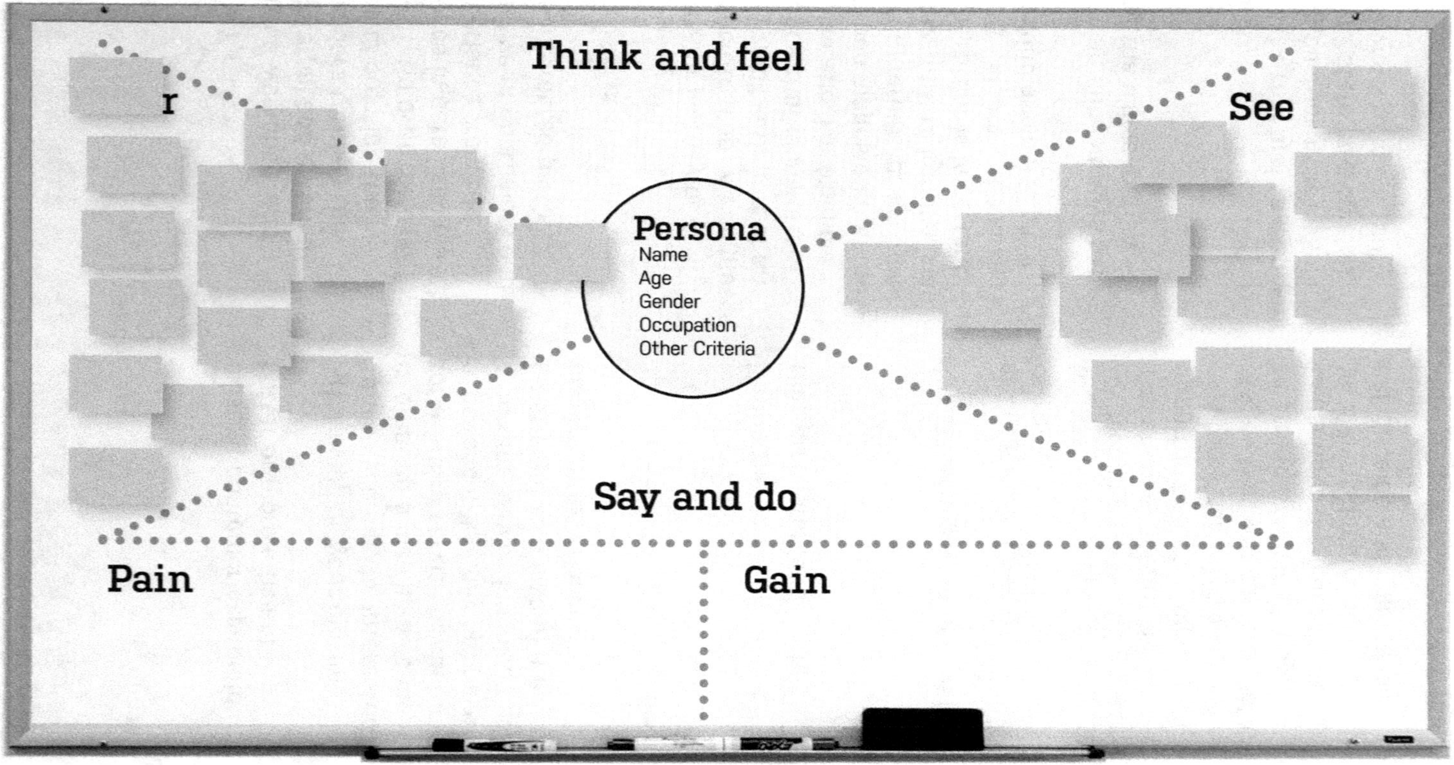

Think and feel

See

Say and do

Gain

Pain

Persona
Name
Age
Gender
Occupation
Other Criteria

it doesn't have to be perfect first time. Concentrate on your customers and their point of view.

CREATE YOUR GOAL STATEMENT

1. What is the problem, unmet needs or opportunities that the blueprint is to realize?
2. A map should be compatible with your goals and with an outcome that satisfies them.
3. Who does this problem or opportunity involve or affect. Who are the stakeholders?
4. Where is the service delivered?
5. When is the service delivered?
6. What are the channels?
7. Why is there a need for a new design solution?
8. Are you looking to address issues already identified?
9. Do you want to enhance the customer experience?
10. Do you want engage your customers more effectively? Do you wish to create a more efficient process? Define your goals in a statement and return to that statement as you build your map to ensure that your efforts contribute to reaching the goal.

DEFINE YOUR TARGET AUDIENCE SEGMENT AND THEIR NEEDS

The most successful products and services target precise customer segments. Designs that try to please everyone sometimes do not satisfy anyone.

GATHER YOUR EXISTING RESEARCH

Start by auditing internal customer experience data that has been previously gathered. If available review existing user data, including call center logs, customer satisfaction surveys, existing personas, mystery shopping data, web analytics and customer satisfaction data. Review the data and determine what new research is necessary. to fill in the knowledge gaps. To be useful data should be current. The most significant insights will come directly from engaging the stakeholders located in their natural context in relation to the service. This

233

Then what your persona thinks and feels

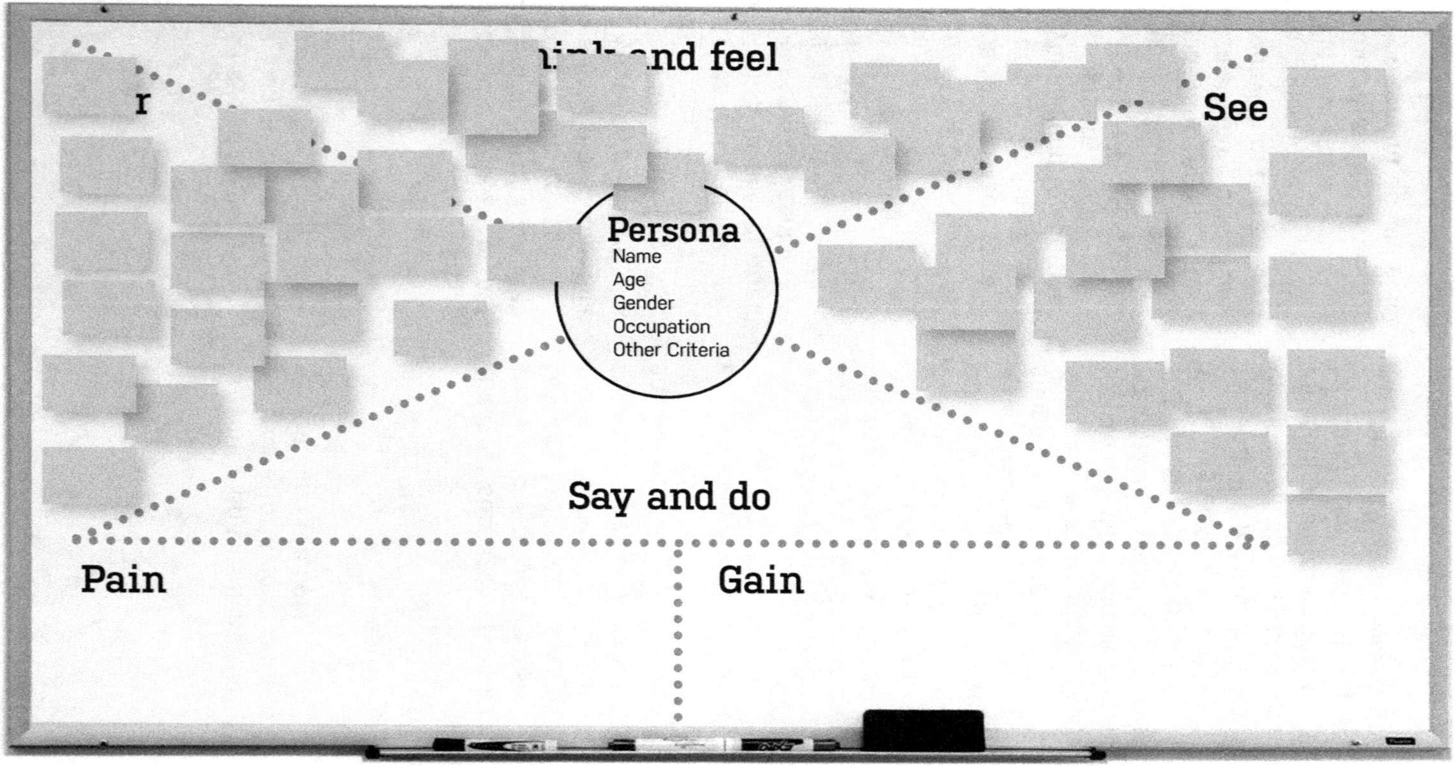

Persona
Name
Age
Gender
Occupation
Other Criteria

Think and feel

See

Say and do

Pain

Gain

means engaging stakeholders through a variety of possible research techniques in the physical location of the service such as contextual observation and interviews.

Quantitative data is less useful than qualitative research when trying to understand the feelings and emotions of your customers.

Interviews are one of the most common methods used to gather data. Ask them to walk you through their experience and talk about their problems, needs, desires and feelings at each stage. Start by talking to between five and twenty people as a minimum sample size. Focus your questions on the areas relevant to the lanes of the service blueprint. If you are creating a journey map ask what are they doing, thinking, and feeling at each stage of the activity. Ask them what touch points they are engaging at each phase. Ask them where they are experiencing problems or frustrations in achieving their goals. Document your interviews or observations by using video or a digital recorder. Quantitative data with a larger sample size is also useful. Create a survey for existing or prospective customers.

Your service blueprint needs to be based on real and truthful information to be useful,.

Use prototype maps in focus group discussions to validate findings directly with customers.

REVIEW YOUR EXISTING RESEARCH

Review Existing Research Identify the gaps in data and create a list of recurring customer experience problems.

CREATE A RESEARCH PLAN TO FILL THE GAPS.

1. What do you still need to know?
2. What questions do you need to ask?
3. How many people will you involve?
4. What type of people will you research?
5. What will be the context of the study?

Then what your persona says and does

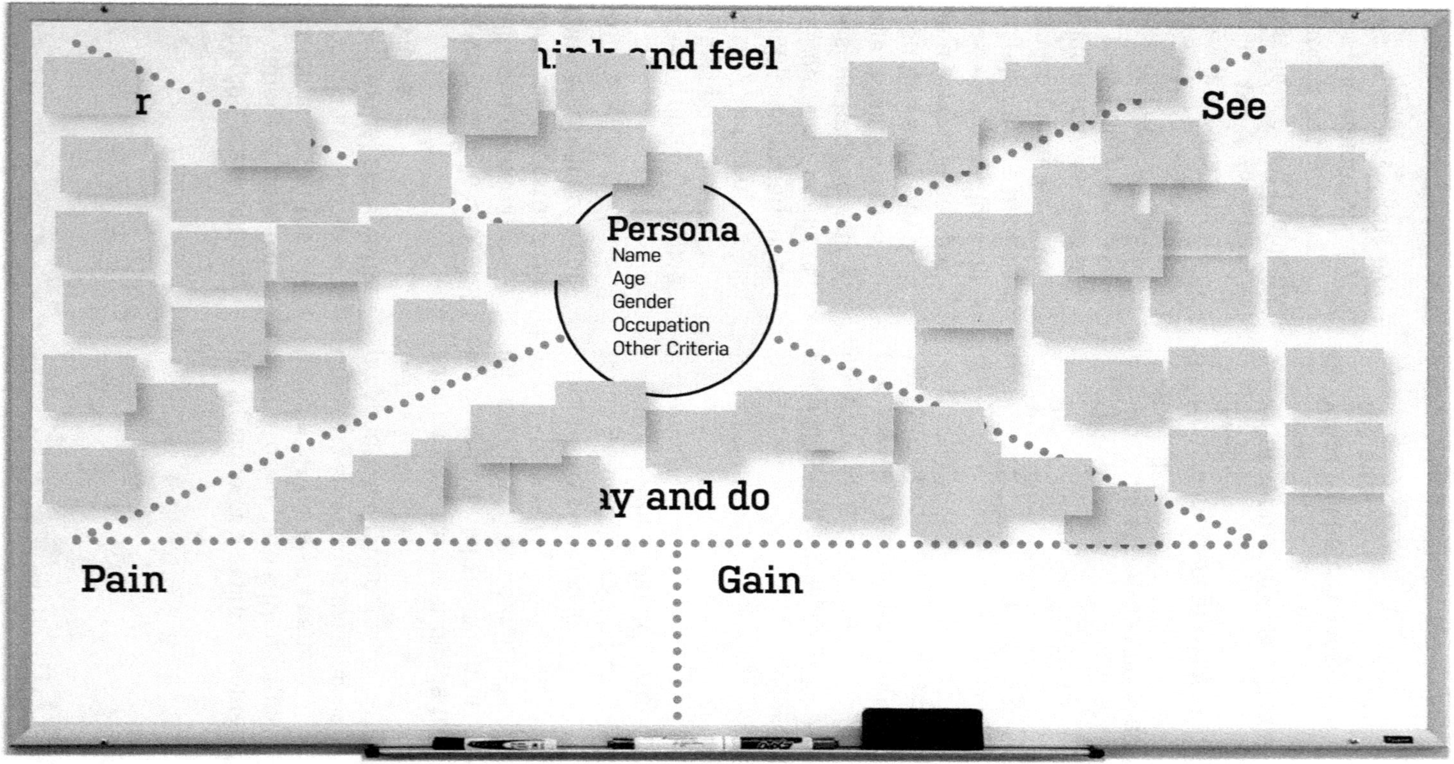

Pain

Gain

...y and do

Persona
Name
Age
Gender
Occupation
Other Criteria

...nd feel

See

6. What methods will you use?
7. When will you select and screen the subjects, conduct the research and report on findings?

SYNTHESIZE YOUR RESEARCH

Put each potentially useful piece of information on a separate post-it note. Put the post-it notes on a wall and ask your team to organize the customer's comments into related groups or themes. Which issues are most significant to more customers? Build a hierarchy of ideas. Identify topics and patterns from the interviews.

What are your customers needs and goals at each stage of their activity? What touchpoints are they engaging at each step?

SELECT YOUR TEAM

Care should be taken in choosing your team. As many groups and diverse points of view involved in design delivery and use of the service as possible should be represented.

1. Keep groups to six people or less.
2. If your group size is larger than 12 people, break the group into smaller groups of six or less.
3. Have a diverse team with different genders, age, occupations and status represented.
4. Have at least two or three "T" shaped people. That is people with two or more areas of expertise such as technology and management or design. "T" shaped team members makes the team more flexible and helps group collaboration.
5. Involve external and internal stakeholders such as customers, suppliers, internal business management, engineering, design, and sales.
6. Have customer facing people where possible because they better understand the perspective of the client

APPOINT YOUR MODERATOR

1. Create handouts with clear instructions
2. Provide copies of research summaries
3. Take breaks every 90

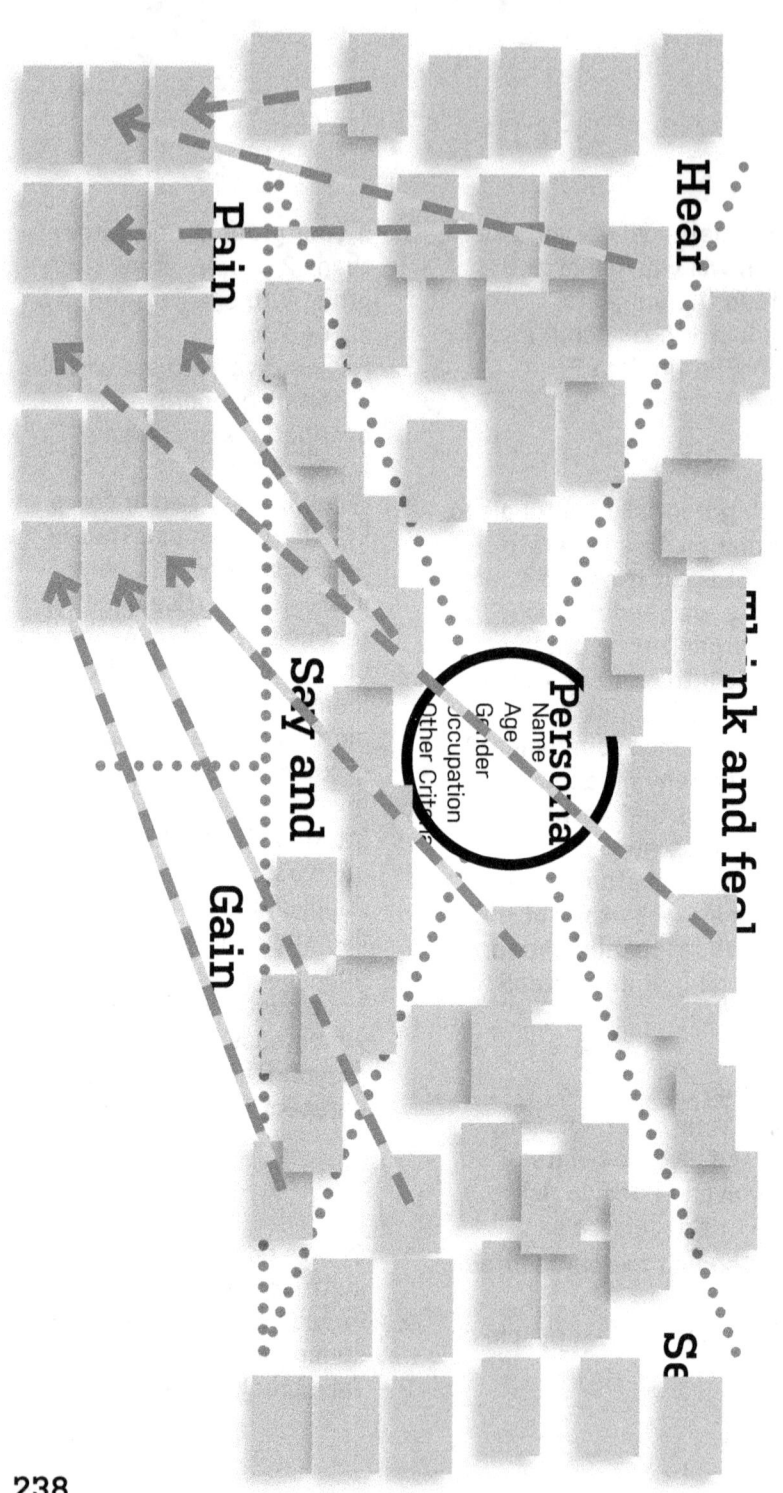

minutes
4. Photograph the map as it is developing.

MODERATOR SKILLS
1. Effective Listening Skills
2. Flexibility
3. Customer empathy
4. Sincerely Interested in People
5. Enthusiasm
6. People management skills
7. Able to establishing common direction and buy-in.
8. Understands Group Dynamics
9. Authority
10. Neutral and Objective
11. Patient and Persistent
12. Curious
13. Guide discussion on time.
14. Able to draw our quieter group members.
15. Able to read between the lines and understand what is not said.
16. Beginner's mind
17. Get panelists to talk to each other.
18. Get the audience involved early.
19. Able to read body language
20. Able to create an atmosphere where divergent views can be explored
21. Encourage all participants to share their opinions openly.
22. Keep the conversation focused and relevant
23. Track and record the key themes and ideas expressed by the group.

SELECT AND PREPARE YOUR WORKSPACE
A safe space is a large room with plenty of natural light with a large table and sufficient chairs for your team.
1. Useful materials
2. A large wall
3. Butcher paper
4. Masking tape
5. Mobile dry erase boards
6. Dry erase markers
7. Sharpies
8. Adhesive notes in 5 colors
9. Digital camera
10. Tripod

IDENTIFY YOUR TARGET SEGMENT TO MAP
Identify customer segments.

CREATE PERSONAS
Create your customer personas. Personas are archetypal characters created to represent the different user types that

might use a product or service in a similar way. Create 3 to 6 personas to cover all your customers.

IDENTIFY STAKEHOLDERS

A stakeholder is someone who may be in some way influenced by your design. For example in a hospital stakeholders may be patients, relatives of patients, hospital workers, doctors, nurses, health insurance workers. Stakeholders are also people who represent various areas within your organization such as technology, design, business management, sales, customer experience.

HOLD STAKEHOLDER WORKSHOPS

Organize a workshop, and guide internal and external stakeholders through the process of creating the first draft. Go over the user experience in detail and discuss the experience from the perspective of customers and diverse interested parties.

SELECT THE SERVICE TO BE MAP

Choose your journey or experience to map. We suggests starting small with part of an experience that is important or problematic. For example rather than mapping an entire customer journey for air travel from New York to London, map a part of it that matters such as selecting the airline and booking online. Explore several challenging sub-journeys before tackling the whole journey.

DECIDE PRESENT OR FUTURE SERVICE TO MAP

It is most usual first to map your existing customer experience. A current state map can help identify ways to make your existing customer experience better or more efficient.

After mapping your current service you may be interested in creating a map as a concept for a future service or customer experience. You may not have a current service in which case go straight to a map of a future service or experience.

SELECT START AND END POINTS OF THE CUSTOMER

EXPERIENCE
Define the scope in terms of time and customer activities.

SELECT CHANNELS TO MAP
Typical examples of channels include
1. In-store experience
2. Print,
3. Web,
4. Mobile

The channel identifies the opportunities and constraints of a touchpoint. Post the Empathy Map on a large whiteboard in your office, where it is accessible to you and your colleagues. Have team members do the research.

On a large whiteboard draw a circle about 6 inches to one foot in diameter near the center of the board.

Inside this circle describe the persona that you are about to map. This persona represents a significant segment of your customers.

Fill in the persona's name, age, gender, occupation, income, location and any other important information.

Write down the answers to the following questions:
• What's their role i.e. how do they spend their day?
• What are their goals?
How do they measure success?
• What are their top hopes and hurdles?
• What's their age, marital status, income and location.
Select an appropriate name for your persona.

For your product or service, what are the most important senory inputs?For example sight sound smell and taste may be essential for a coffee shop. Now divide the top three quarters of the board space into a number of boxes radiating from your persona circle. Name these boxes "Think and Feel", "Say and Do" and the appropriate senses selected from the five senses

1. See
2. Hear
3. Touch
4. Taste
5. Smell

With your team seated around the board populate the boxes one box at a time.

What is the perspective of your customer? Take a walk in her shoes?

What are your customer segments?
1. List all customer segments
2. Pick one to work on
3. Give the customer a name
4. Develop some demographic
5. characteristics
6. Income, marital status, etc.
7. Create Story

SEE
1. What does he see in his Environment that influences him?
2. What is the persona seeing in their surroundings?
3. Who surrounds them?
4. Who are their friends?
5. What visual problems do they encounter?

HEAR
1. What does your customer hear in the context of the experience?
2. What do their friends say?
3. What does their partner say?
4. Which media channels do they access?
5. What friends say
6. What work colleagues say?
7. What news says
8. What influences say

THINK AND FEEL
1. What matters most to your customers?
2. What is your client thinking?
3. Talk to them and ask them what they are thinking.
4. What concerns them most?
5. What are their dreams, desires and aspirations?
6. What doesn't your customer articulate?
7. What things move her?

SAY AND DO
Some questions:
1. What do they say when experiencing your product or service?
2. What do they say when experiencing competitor's goods or services?
3. What do they say to their friends or colleagues?
4. What do they do? What are the activities?
5. How do they behave?
6. •Are there differences

between what they say and do?
7. What is common for her to say?
8. How does she behave?
9. What are her hobbies?
10. What does he like to say?
11. How is the world in which he lives?
12. What do people around him / her do?
13. Who are her friends?
14. What is popular in his daily life?
15. What people and ideas influence her?
16. What do the important people in his life say?
17. What are her favorite brands?
18. Who are his role models?
19. What does he want to achieve?
20. How does she measure success?
21. What would make it a better experience?
22. What are his aspirations?
23. Imagine what the customer
24. might say, or how they
25. might behave in public
26. What is her attitude?
27. What could she be telling
28. others?
29. Pay particular attention to potential conflicts between what a customer might say and what the customer truly thinks and feels.
30. What is his attitude?
31. What could he be telling others?
32. What does he say that normally contradicts to what he thinks and feels?

PAIN

What are the fears, frustrations, and the obstacles that concern your customer most? What obstacles stand in the way of your customer reaching their goals?
1. What are the pain points?
2. What does the persona fear?
3. What is the persona frustrated by in relation to the experiuence?
4. Why doesn't the customer come back?
5. What is standing in the way of your client reaching their goals?
6. What does your customer need?
7. What does your customer desire?
8. What do competitors do better?

9. When is your customer most unhappy?
10. Where is your customer most unhappy?
11. Here are some questions:
12. What are their fears? What do they worry about?
13. What are their aspirations? What do they dream about?
14. What else do they think about during the day?
15. Do they love or hate what they do?
16. What are the differences between what they say/do and think/feel?
17. • How do they feel about using your product or alternative solution?
18. What are the customer's biggest frustrations?
19. What obstacles stand between the customer and what they want or need to achieve?
20. Which risk might she fear taking?
21. What are his biggest frustrations?

GAIN

What are their goals, desires, and needs; how do they work towards these goals?

1. How does your customer measure success?
2. Is the customer satisfied?
3. What short term goals does your customer have?
4. What long term goals does your customer have?
5. When is your customer happy?
6. What do you do better than your competitors?
7. When is your customer happy
8. Where is your customer happy?
9. What is ultimate dream? What are they desperately hoping to achieve?
10. Why is getting that outcome so important? What would that mean for them?
11. What have you learned by building the empathy map? What are the themes and insights? How can you improve your customer's holistic experience?
12. What does the customer want or need to achieve?
13. How does your customer measure success?
14. What are the strategies the customer might use
15. to achieve their goals.

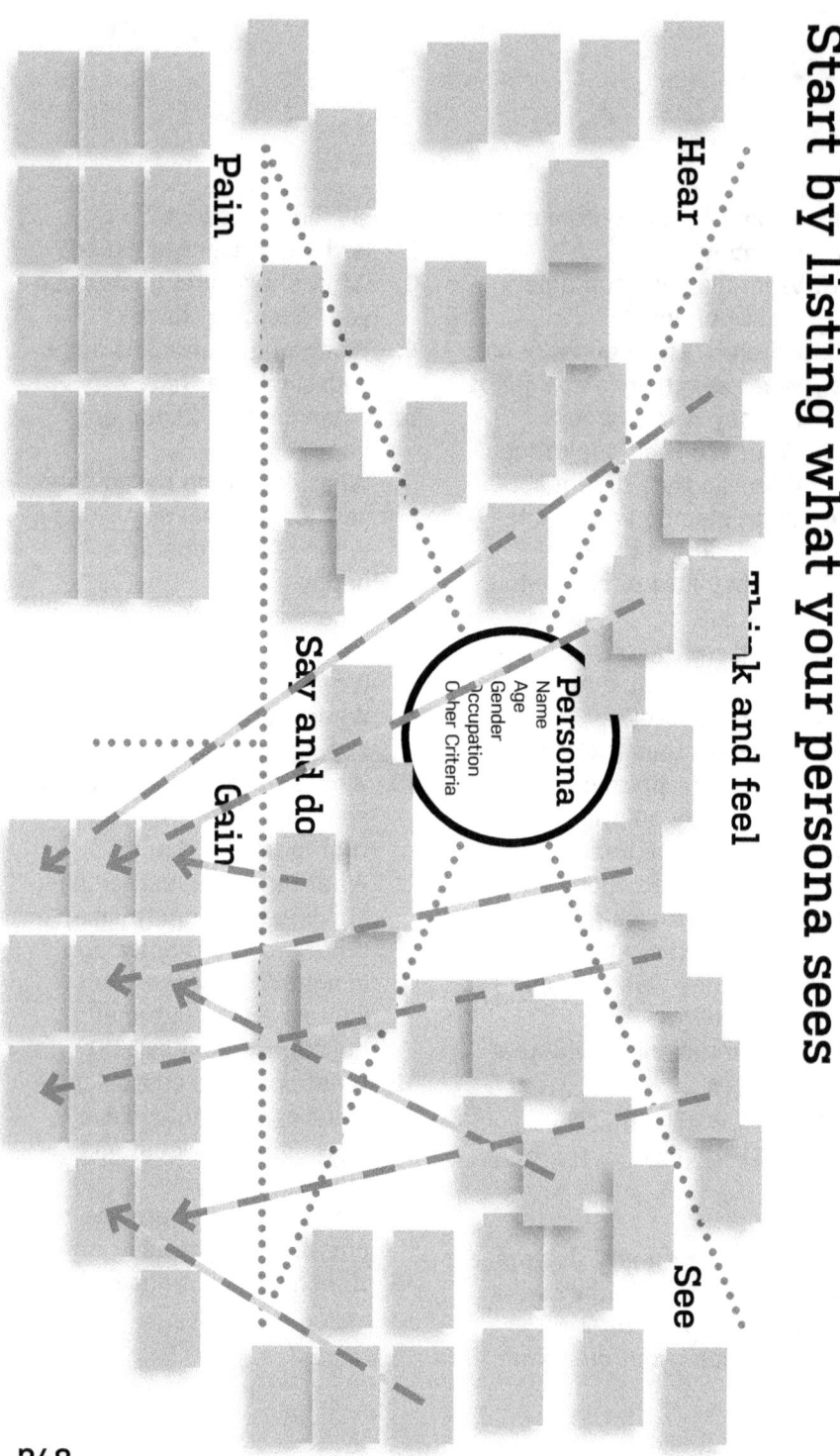

Empathy Canvass

Persona
Name
Age
Job
Residence
Education
Goals
Needs
Frustrations

See · Think
Touch · Hear
Pain · Taste
· Smell
Gain · Do
· Feel
Opportunities · · · · · · · · · · · · · · Say

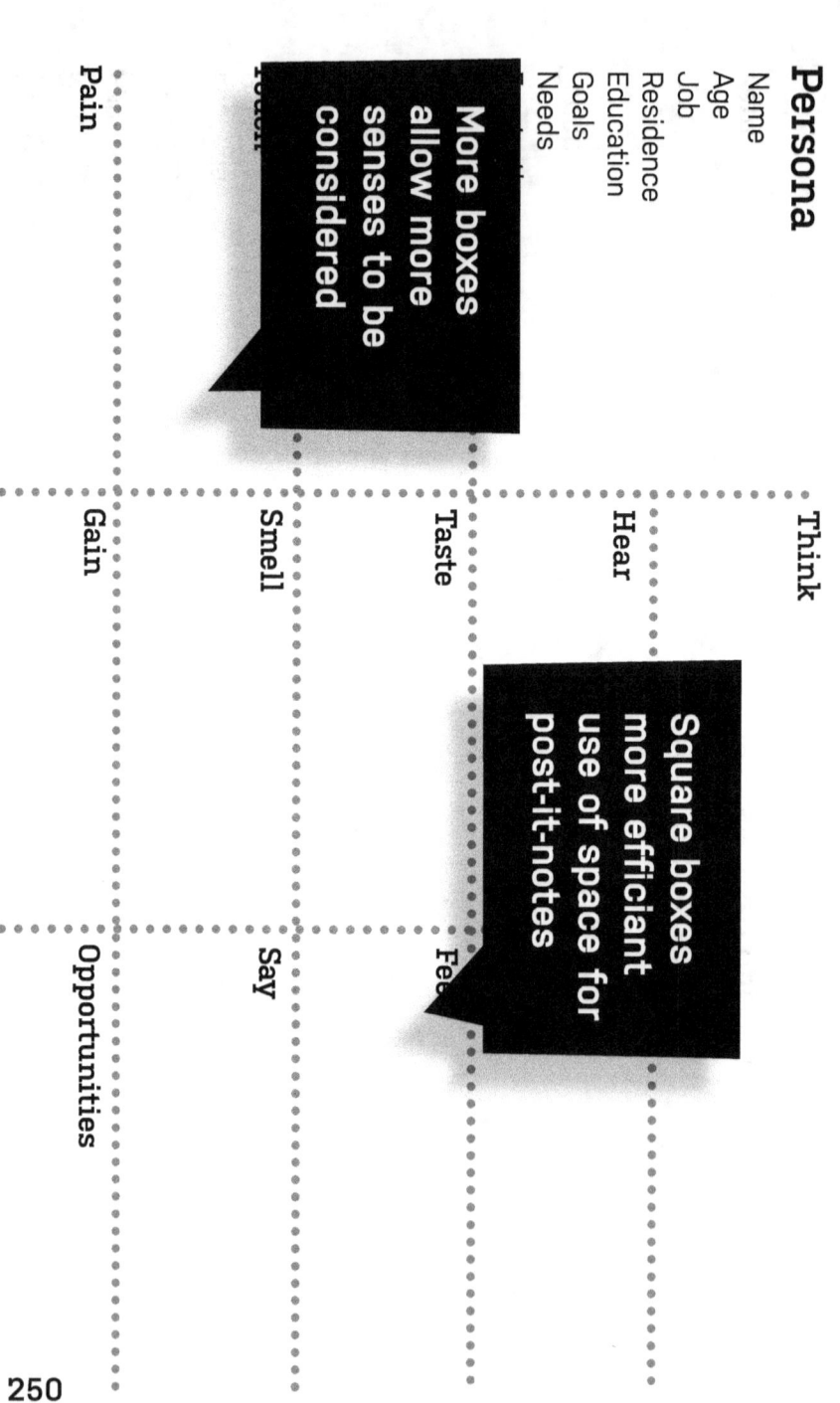

Priority of customer experience improvements

	Value to customer (low → high)	
Value to organization: high	medium priority	high priority
Value to organization: low	low priority	medium priority

STAGES	EVALUATE		ENTER		USE/ENGAGE					EXIT		
TOUCH POINTS	Home Interior	Internet Laptop	Car	Car park Coffee shop exterior	Coffee shop interior Counter	Counter Coffee cup	Coffee shop interior Chair table	Laptop Power socket Internet	Laptop Internet chair table Cup	Cup Trash can coffee shop interior	Car Car park	Car
DOING	Customer at home decides to go out to have a coffee	Checks location of coffee shop on Internet	Drives car to coffee shop	Parks and enters coffee shop	Selects a drink and waits in line to order	Pays and picks up coffee	Finds a table and sits down	Drinks coffee and reviews emails on laptop	Writes and sends some emails. Tops up coffee	Finishes coffee and puts cup in trashcan	Returns to car	Drive back to supermarket
THINKING	Should I call a friend? Will I have a long wait to be served?	Which coffee shop should I go to?	Will be able to park close to the coffee shop?	Will there be a long queue?	Should I have a latte or a drip coffee?	The coffee is more expensive than last time	Is there a spare seat/table at the window?	The coffee is very hot. Is there a plug for my laptop?	Not a plug seat/table. How long will my battery last?	Where is the trashcan?	Will the traffic be heavy?	There was a long queue. I will go to another coffee shop next time.
FEELING	Should I call a friend? Will I have a long wait to be served?	Which coffee shop should I go to?	Will be able to park close to the coffee shop?	Will there be a long queue?	Should I have a table or a drip coffee?	The coffee is more expensive than last time	Is there a seat available at the window?	The coffee is very hot. Is there a plug for my laptop?	Not a plug available. How long will my battery last?	Where is the trashcan?	Will the traffic be heavy?	I will go to another coffee shop next time.
PAIN POINTS	Hard to find part of best coffee shop	No parking place available close to coffee shop	Queue takes 20 minutes	Too many drink/cuisine menu	Price has increased	Needs to wait for a seat/table. Chairs uncomfortable	Coffee too hot to drink. Coffee also cold	No plug available for laptop. Plastic too hard	No visible trashcan	Long walk back to car. Traffic heavy		
OPPORTUNITIES	Improve website	Differentiate coffee shop from other coffee shops	Make more parking available.	Reduce number of options	Offers more lower priced menu items	Replace chairs. Open up second room	Adjust coffee temperature. Re: baby wisdom.	Add power points	Relocate trash cans. Increase number of trashcans.	Make more parking available.		

Experience & Journey Maps

Experience and journey maps are diagrams that allow a designer or manager to understand the elements of a customer experience in concise terms from the customer's point of view.

Many different elements can be part of an experience map depending on your area of interest.

Experience maps focus on the emotional state of the customer. Are they feeling happy with your product or service or are they feeling frustrated or confused? What touchpoints are they interacting within each channel over time? Experience or journey maps have a similar structural approach to service blueprints.

Service blueprints differ from experience maps in that they focus on the structure of a service or experience and what physical, virtual things such as [products, spaces and web sites] and people [employees and actors] they are interacting with at any point in time.

Experience & journey maps

WHAT ARE EXPERIENCE MAPS?
They are diagrams that allow a designer or manager to describe the elements of a customer experience in concise terms.

WHY USE THESE METHODS?
1. Helps develop a consistent, predictable customer experience.
2. Identifies problems in a customer experience and how to fix them.
3. Presents an overview of your customer's experience from their point of view.
4. A tool for developing more loyal customers
5. Can be used with different personas.
6. A focus for discussion between departments of an organization that helps develop a consistent and superior customer experience.
7. Can be used to understand where to place resources most efficiently

HOW TO USE THIS METHOD
1. Identify your team. Use a cross-disciplinary team of 4 to 12 people with stakeholders.
2. Collect research data related to customer experience using ethnographic techniques such as interviews.
3. Identify the customer experience to be analyzed. Identify the context. Identify personas.
4. Break the customer experience down into sub-activities and place each activity in a horizontal time-line
5. Below each activity describe what the customer is doing
6. Do one line of comments for what they are doing, one line for what they are thinking, and feeling.
7. Use post-it-notes to add positive and negative experiences to the relevant parts of the time line.
8. Brainstorm opportunities where customer experiences are negative.
9. When you are complete photograph the map and document it using a program such as Adobe Illustrator.
10. Circulate the map to stakeholders for feedback and refine.

HISTORY OF JOURNEY AND EXPERIENCE MAPPING

The origin of journey and experience mapping is less apparent than Service Blueprints, but they have been used at least since 1991 (Whittle & Foster, 1991).

Several sources mention these methods from 2006 (Parker & Heapy, 2006; Voss & Zomerdijk, 2007). The detailed application is still evolving (Følstad et al., 2013). Følstad defines a customer journey as the process a customer goes through to reach a particular goal. The value of these techniques is greatest when the complexity of the route is higher. Customer journey maps describe not only what a customer experiences but also the customer's response to those experiences.

Wechsler (2012) describes internal workshops for creating customer journey maps. The analysis of customer journeys may also concern quantitative measurement of the customer's experience. In the scientific literature, such analysis is typically conducted as part of the mapping process to quantify changes in experiential quality during the customer journey (Trischler & Zehrer, 2012). Kankainen et al. (2012) describe the use of customer journeys for co-design, where customers formulate "dream journeys". In 2007 the British Government published guidelines on customer journey mapping (HM Government, 2007).

WHY USE EXPERIENCE MAPPING?

Journey and experience mapping can be used for the following purposes:
1. Understand the collective experiences of customer segments
2. To create a more streamlined, consistent, and efficient customer experience.
3. Create a more seamless customer experience across business departments, and channels.
4. Design a new service or product customer experience

5. Allocate people and resources more effectively.
6. Develop alignment across departments of an organization.
7. Craft a better customer experience.
8. Expose places where your service or customer experience may fail.
9. Craft a better customer experience
10. Strategic and tactical innovation
11. Building and sharing knowledge
12. Designing the moments of truth
13. Understand competitive positioning
14. Understanding the ideal experience
15. Reveal the truth from your customer's perspective
16. Identify opportunities
17. Empathize with your custom
18. Designing and improving Systems
19. Develop a better product road map
20. Take cost & complexity out of the system
21. Prioritize competing deliverables
22. Plan for hiring
23. Bring different parts of your business together to work to improve the customer experience
24. Build knowledge of customer behaviors and needs across channels
25. Identify specific areas of opportunity to drive ideation and innovation
26. Make intangible services tangible.
27. Develop customer insights
28. Understand where friction exists between the needs of different market segments
29. Introduce metrics for what matters most for your customers.
30. Align your offerings to brand promise.
31. Identify failure points.
32. Improve efficiency.
33. Imagine future product and service experiences.
34. More Holistic thinking.
35. Making better decisions.
36. A living document that can evolve with your business.
37. Is a holistic view of key touch points and interactions personas have with the brand.
38. Communicate the experience visually.
39. Promotes better coordination of across channels.

Perceptual map of opportunities

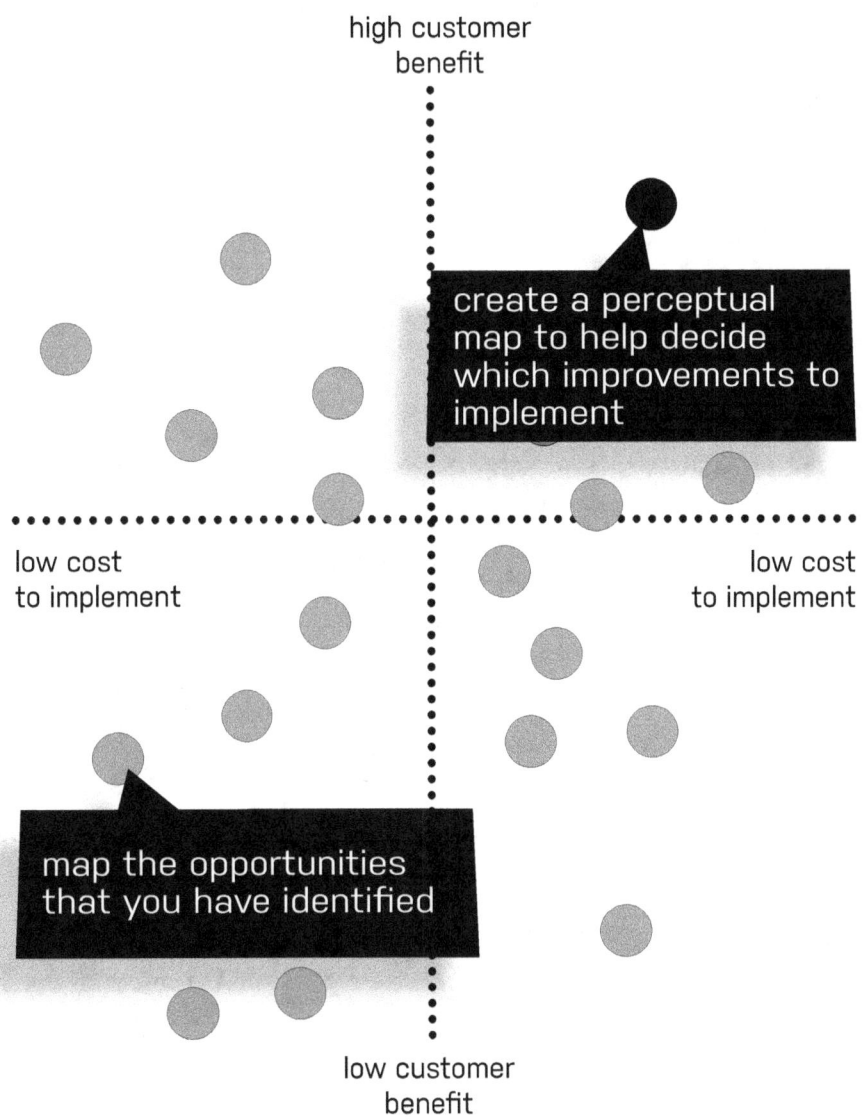

What is an experience map?

A journey map focuses on identifying touch points, An experience map focuses on the emotions your customer experiences. In practice many people use these terms interchangeably. The particular lanes included can be mixed and matched to your goals.

Customer journeys depict what customers really want. These methods help us to understand interactions from users' point of view. They must be developed from your customers' perspective. They are a framework to craft a better customer experience.. With these tools you can identify problem areas and opportunities for improvement.

Maps are usually created to help understand a partricular segment or persona. The more complex your service or customer experience, the more value there is in mapping the customer journey and experience.

A map helps you
1. Plan your product or service offering most efficiently for various customer segments
2. Evaluate customer experience gaps or fail points before they occur.
3. Identify opportunities to improve you customer experience.
4. identify ways to improve your touchpoints and remove duplication.
5. You can create a map as a concept for a customer's ideal future experience.
6. Put all stakeholders on the same page so that you can reach a common understanding and agreement on how to move forward towards your organizational goals.
7. Helps make measures of success clear.
8. From analyzing your map recommendations and a plan to reach your objectives can be put into place.

Creating an experience map

Here is a list of stages that you can complete creating a Service Blueprint. Consider the blueprint to be a living document that will develop and improve, so it doesn't have to be perfect first time. Concentrate on your customers and their point of view.

CREATE YOUR GOAL STATEMENT

1. What is the problem, unmet needs or opportunities that the blueprint is to realize?
2. A clear outline of customer goals and needs should be compatible with your goals and with an outcome that satisfies them.
3. Who does this problem or opportunity involve or affect? Who are the stakeholders?
4. Where is the service or experience delivered?
5. When is the service or experience provided?
6. What are the channels?
7. Why is there a need for a new design solution?
8. Are you looking to address issues already identified?
9. Do you want to enhance the customer experience?
10. Do you wish to engage your customers more effectively? Do you wish to create a more efficient process? Define your goals in a statement and return to that statement as you build your map to ensure that your efforts contribute to reaching the goal.

DEFINE YOUR TARGET AUDIENCE SEGMENT AND THEIR NEEDS

The most successful products services and experiences target precise customer segments.

GATHER YOUR EXISTING RESEARCH

Start by auditing internal customer experience data that has been previously gathered. If available review existing user data, including call center logs, customer satisfaction surveys, existing personas, mystery shopping data, web analytics and customer satisfaction data. Examine the data and determine what new research is necessary to fill in the knowledge gaps. To be useful data should be current. The most significant insights will come directly from engaging the stakeholders located in their natural context concerning the service. This means engaging stakeholders through a variety of possible research techniques in the physical location of the service such as contextual observation and interviews.

Quantitative data is less useful than qualitative research when trying to understand the feelings and emotions of your customers.

Interviews are one of the most usual methods used to gather data. Ask them to walk you through their experience and talk about their problems, needs desires and feelings at each stage. Start by talking to between five and twenty people as a minimum sample size. Focus your questions on the areas relevant to the lanes of the service blueprint. If you are creating a journey map, ask what are they doing, thinking, and feeling at each stage of the activity. Ask them what touch points they are engaging at each phase. Ask them where they are experiencing problems or frustrations in achieving their goals. Document your interviews or observations by using video or a digital recorder. Quantitative data with a larger sample size is also useful. Create a survey for existing or prospective customers.

To be useful, your service blueprint needs to be based on the real and truthful information.
Use prototype maps in focus group discussions to validate findings directly with customers.

REVIEW YOUR EXISTING RESEARCH
Review existing research Identify gaps in data and create a list of recurring customer experience problems.

CREATE A RESEARCH PLAN TO FILL THE GAPS
1. What do you still need to know?
2. What questions do you need to ask?
3. How many people will you involve?

4. What type of people will you research?
5. What will be the context of the research?
6. What methods will you use?
7. When will you select and screen the subjects, conduct the research and report on findings?

SYNTHESIZE YOUR RESEARCH

Put each potentially useful piece of information on a separate post-it note. Put the post-it notes on a wall and ask your team to organize the customer's comments into related groups or themes. Which issues are most significant to more customers? Build a hierarchy of issues. Identify topics and patterns from the interviews. What are your customers needs and goals at each stage of their activity? What touchpoints are they engaging at each step?

SELECT YOUR TEAM

Care should be taken in choosing your team. As many groups and diverse points of view involved in design delivery and use of the service as possible should be represented.

1. Keep groups to six people or less.
2. If your total group size is larger than six break the large group into smaller groups of six or less.
3. Have a diverse team with different genders, age, occupations and seniority represented.
4. Have at least two or three "T" shaped people. That is, people with two or more areas of expertise such as technology and management or management and design. This makes the team more flexible and helps group collaboration. This experience can be gained through education or work. Look for people with at least 10,000 hours of experience in each of two areas. That corresponds to three or four years of work experience in each area.
5. Involve external and internal stakeholders such as customers, suppliers, internal business management, engineering, design, marketing, distribution, IT and sales.

Have customer facing people where possible because they better understand the customer's perspective.

APPOINT YOUR MODERATOR

1. Create handouts with clear instructions
2. Provide copies of research summaries
3. Take breaks every 90 minutes
4. Photograph the map as it is being built

MODERATOR SKILLS

1. Effective Listening Skills
2. Flexibility
3. Customer empathy
4. Sincerely Interested in People
5. Enthusiasm
6. People management skills
7. Able to establishing collective direction and buy-in.
8. Understands Group Dynamics
9. Authority
10. Neutral and Objective
11. Patient and Persistent
12. Curious
13. Guide discussion in a timely manner.
14. Able to draw our quieter group members.
15. Able to read between the lines and understand what is not said.
16. Beginner's mind
17. Get Panelists to Talk to Each Other.
18. Get the Audience Involved Early.
19. Able to read body language
20. Able to create an atmosphere where divergent views can be explored
21. Encourage all participants to share their views openly.
22. Keep the conversation focused and relevant
23. Track and record the key themes and ideas expressed by the group.

SELECT AND PREPARE YOUR WORKSPACE

A safe space is a large room with plenty of natural light with a large table and sufficient chairs for your team.
Some useful materials
1. A large wall
2. Butcher paper
3. Masking tape
4. Mobile dry erase boards
5. Dry erase markers
6. Sharpies
7. Adhesive notes in 5 colors

8. Digital camera
9. Tripod

IDENTIFY YOUR TARGET SEGMENTS TO MAP
Identifying customer segments.

CREATE A PERSONA FOR EACH TARGET SEGMENT
Personas are archetypal characters created to represent the different user types that might use a product or service in a similar way. Create 3 to 6 personas to cover all your customers.

IDENTIFY STAKEHOLDERS
A stakeholder is someone who may be in some way influenced by your design when it is complete and marketed. For example, in a hospital stakeholders may be patients, relatives of patients, hospital workers, doctors, nurses, health insurance workers. Stakeholders are also people who represent various areas within your organization such as technology, design, business management, sales, and customer experience.

HOLD STAKEHOLDER WORKSHOPS
Organize a workshop, and guide internal and external stakeholders through the process of creating the first draft. Go over the user experience in detail and discuss the experience from the perspective of customers and diverse stakeholders,

SELECT THE SERVICE TO BE MAPPED
Select your journey or experience to map. We suggest starting small with part of an experience that is important or problematic. For example rather than mapping an entire customer journey for air travel from New York to London, map a part of it that is important such as selecting the airline and booking the travel on-line. Then explore several challenging sub-journeys before tackling the whole journey.

DECIDE PRESENT OR FUTURE SERVICE TO MAP
It is most usual to first map your existing customer

experience. A current state map can help identify ways to make your existing customer experience better or more efficient.

After mapping your existing service you may be interested in creating a map as a scenario for a future service or customer experience.

SELECT START AND END POINTS OF THE CUSTOMER EXPERIENCE
Define the scope in terms of time and customer activities.

SELECT CHANNELS TO MAP
Some examples of channels include
1. In-store experience
2. Face to face
3. Print
4. Web
5. Call center
6. Tablet app
7. TV
8. Mobile phone

The channel defines the opportunities and constraints of a touchpoint. You can map all channels on one map in parallel lanes. This type of map is called a multichannel map. You can map just one channel per map and create as m,any separate maps as you have channels.

START SMALL
Consider picking a specific scenario or sub -activity of your entire customer experience.

DRAFT THE MAP
Use a large wall or table. Create your first rough draft using post-it notes. When it is complete photograph and share it with as many internal and external stakeholders as possible and ask for their feedback. If insights don't fit on a single map, keep maps simple by creating one map for each persona.

CREATE THE STORY
What are the main elements of the customer experience from a customer perspective? What parts of their experience leave a lasting impression on them either positive or negative.

MAP USER ACTIONS & ACTIVITIES STEP-BY-STEP

271

Experience & Journey Map Process

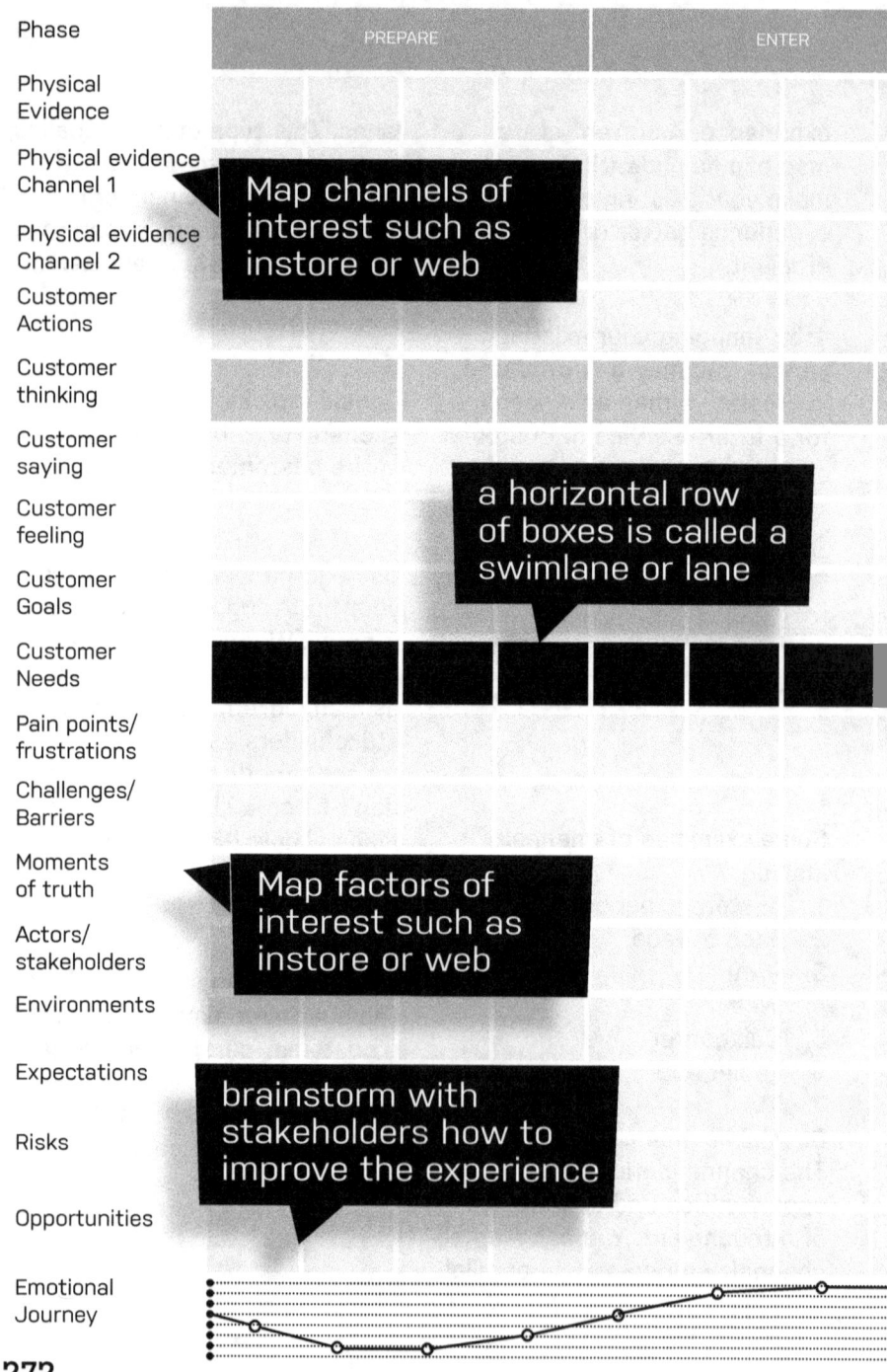

Phase — PREPARE | ENTER

Physical Evidence
Physical evidence Channel 1
Physical evidence Channel 2
Customer Actions
Customer thinking
Customer saying
Customer feeling
Customer Goals
Customer Needs
Pain points/frustrations
Challenges/Barriers
Moments of truth
Actors/stakeholders
Environments
Expectations
Risks
Opportunities
Emotional Journey

- Map channels of interest such as instore or web
- a horizontal row of boxes is called a swimlane or lane
- Map factors of interest such as instore or web
- brainstorm with stakeholders how to improve the experience

PREPARE	ENTER

> understand what your customer is thinking by interviewing them

> understand customer pain points through research

> map positive or negative experience based on your research data for your persona

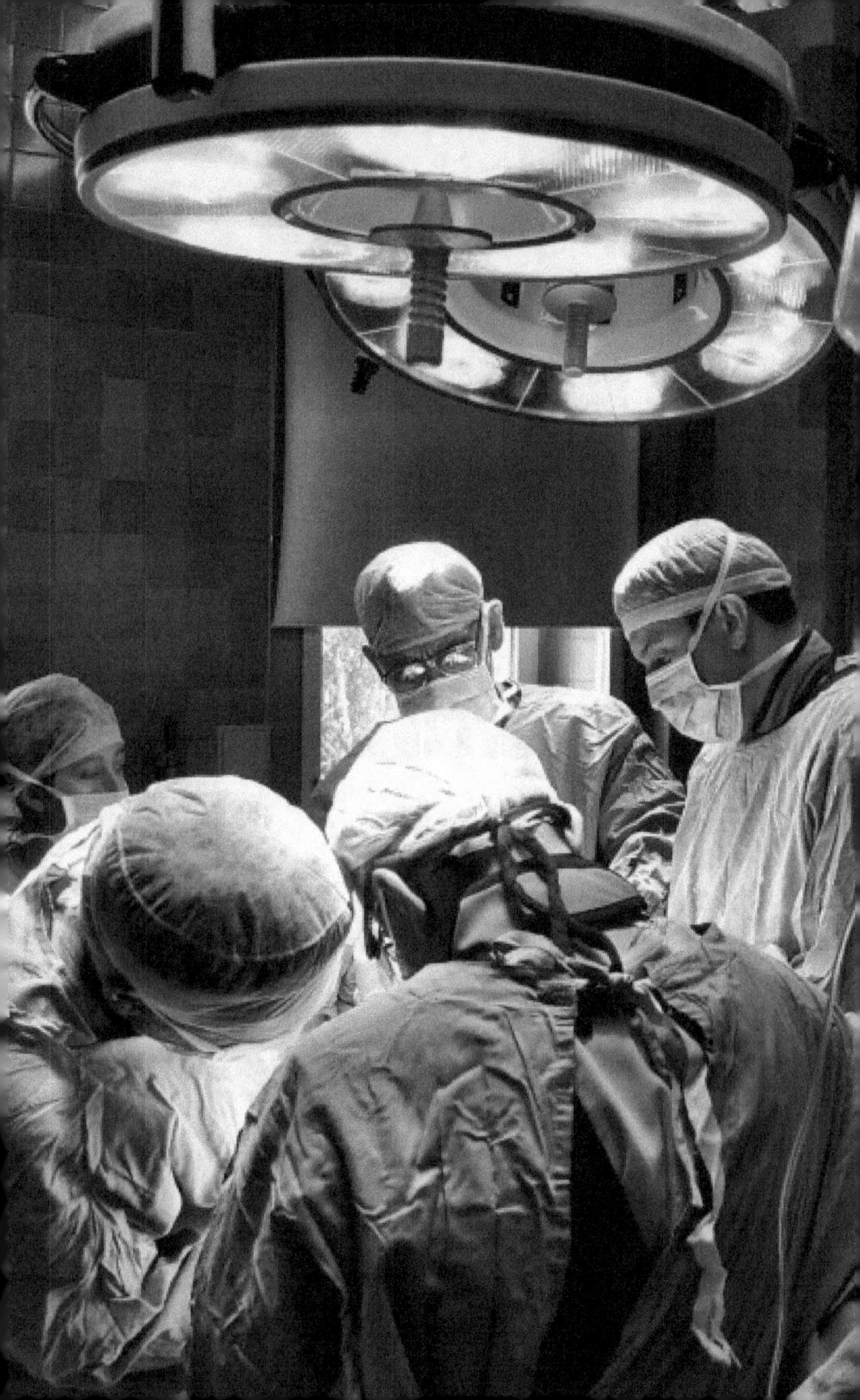

Start at the beginning of the service or experience and list each thing a customer commonly does step by step. Put each sub-activity on a separate post-it note.

For example, if the activity is visiting a coffee shop the activities may include.
1. At work decide to get a coffee on the way home
2. Check the location of coffee shops on the Internet.
3. Select coffee shop
4. Go to car
5. Drive to coffee shop
6. Park
7. Enter coffee shop
8. Stand in line
9. Order
10. Pick up coffee
11. Find table
12. Sit down
13. Drink coffee
14. Read news on tablet
15. Pack up
16. Return to car
17. Drive home
18. Reflect on the experience.

Describe each activity on a separate post-it note and place them in a line on your wall or table. Continue till your team is happy that all important activities have been included.

MAP TIME
How long does each customer activity usually take? Does a stage usually last ten seconds or ten minutes. Place the time taken on a post-it note above each stage of customer activity.

Time to consider:
1. Critical periods service actions, such as response to a proposal.
2. Duration of each service step, such as airline check-in
3. Time between service steps such as walking to a hotel room after check-in.
4. End to end service experience.

BUILD THE MAP
Now you are ready to create the map.

MAP USER ACTION PHASES
Break the list of customer activities into four or six phases of sub-activities. Some examples of phases of activities are:

List the phases of customer actions

PHASES	EVALUATE	ENTER	USE/ENGAGE	EXIT
TOUCH POINTS				
DOING				
THINKING				
FEELING				
PAIN POINTS				
OPPORTUNITIES				

> Review customer activities
> Identify 4 to 6 phases

1. Explore
2. Evaluate
3. Engage
4. Experience

1. Aware
2. Join
3. Use
4. Develop
5. Leave

1. Research
2. Evaluate and compare
3. Commit
4. Use and Monitor
5. Refine and review

MAP THE PHYSICAL EVIDENCE STEP-BY-STEP

Physical evidence is usually the lane shown at the top of a blueprint. Services consist of the interactions with people, the processes, and the physical proof of the experience. Designed objects in the service environment are sometimes referred to as "physical evidence" because they are physical proof of service that has taken place. Physical evidence is the tangible things that help to communicate and perform the service and influence a customer's perception of a service.

Physical evidence is the visible manifestation of service. It conveys to customers whether the service provider cares about their customers and whether they trust their customers. Physical evidence cues are what customers use to evaluate service quality.

Physical evidence can convey intended and unintended messages to customers. Physical evidence is the interface between a service provider and a customer. Key to delivering a successful service is to clearly identify a simple, consistent message, and then manage the evidence to support that message.

" Well-prepared small details represent sincerity in serving guests which reflects the hotel's good service spirit. For example, welcome fruit, an electric kettle and fresh flowers in hotel rooms are service evidence that often evoked delight as they show the hotel's thoughtfulness"

List the stage-by-stage touchpoints for each channel

STAGES	EVALUATE		ENTER	USE/ENGAGE					EXIT	
TOUCH POINTS	Home Interior	Internet Laptop	Car	Car park Coffee shop exterior	Coffee shop interior Menu board	Counter Coffee cup	Coffee shop interior Chair table	Laptop Power socket Internet	Laptop Internet chair table Cup	Cup Trashcan coffee shop Interior	Car Par Car	Car
DOING											
THINKING											
FEELING											
PAIN POINTS											
OPPORTUNITIES											

"For example, a research participant talked about disappointment caused by "fake" hangers in a hotel room's closet. She complained: They're not real hangers, because they're attached to the railing. So
if you want to take out a hanger and then hang it on a chair or hang it on a door, you can't, because there's no hook... That's kind of a fake hanger. It shows that they think I'm going to steal the hangers. So it makes me feel not trusted."
Source: Kathy Pui Ying Lo Loughborough University

Physical evidence includes the service providers building/facilities and staff appearance; and uniforms. Physical evidence should be considered important by the customer and the promise implied by these tangible objects should be delivered. A bank card is an example of physical evidence of a service. It helps a bank differentiate their service from another bank. It separates the service from the seller.

Other examples of physical evidence are
1. The building
2. The interior
3. The car park
4. Internal signage,
5. Packaging.
6. Promotional materials
7. Web pages.
8. Paperwork
9. Brochures.
10. Stationery
11. Billing statement
12. Furnishings.
13. Signage
14. Uniforms and employee dress.
15. Business cards.
16. Mailboxes.

MAP THE PAIN POINTS

A pain point is any part of the customer experience that they find people disturbing, frustrating, urgent or uncomfortable. Many customer needs are for things the end users don't clearly understand or can articulate. A pain point is a problem for you customer and a problem and an opportunity for you. Solving pain points create value for you and your customer. "customer pain" is a synonym for "customer

List the stage-by-stage customer actions

STAGES	EVALUATE	ENTER	USE/ENGAGE				EXIT	
TOUCH POINTS	Home Interior	Car	Car park Coffee shop exterior	Coffee shop interior Menu board	Counter Coffee cup	Coffee shop interior Chair table	Laptop Power socket Internet	Laptop Internet chair table Cup	Cup Trashcan coffee shop Interior	Car Par Car	Car
DOING	Customer At home decides to go out to have a coffee	Drives car to coffee shop	Parks and enters coffee shop	Selects drink and waits in line to order	Pays and picks up coffee	Finds a table and sits down	Drinks coffee and reviews emails on laptop	Writes and sends some emails. Tops up coffee	Finishes coffee and puts cup in trashcan	Returns to car	Drives on to supermarket
THINKING											
FEELING											
PAIN POINTS											
OPPORTUNITIES											

Checks location of coffee shop on internet — Internet Laptop

needs". Customers spend money to combat pain or to pursue pleasure. Examples of service pain points are airport security lines, hospital directions, or the cost of travel. A pain point is the why customers choose you if you offer a solution to their need. If you engage your customers and listen, they'll tell you their pain points

To identify customer 'pain-points':
1. In-depth interviews with customer facing internal employees
2. Requests from your most valuable customers.
3. Customer interviews.
4. Customer focus groups.
5. Review of customer support or warranty claims to identify persistent problems.
6. Review of competitor offerings.
7. You can list the root causes of pain for your customers at each stage.

CUSTOMER OR STAKEHOLDER COMMENTS
List significant or representative comments in a lane. What do customers think?

MAP BRAND IMPACT
List brand impact of touchpoints and customer comments in a lane.

KEY PEOPLE
Identify internal owners of experiences that support customer's needs.

CUSTOMER NEEDS
Do customers have unrecognized needs that could be addressed? What do customers want to accomplish at each stage of interaction?

MAP CONNECTIONS
Use arrows to illustrate the flow of responsibility who is driving the service at any moment and should be initiating service action:

1. Model expectations of "proactive" provider activity.
2. Model the customer responsibility for next steps.
3. Model partner expectations.
4. Define points of handoff between roles, such as from backstage to onstage.

List customer thoughts stage-by-stage

STAGES	EVALUATE		ENTER		USE/ENGAGE					EXIT	
TOUCH POINTS	Home Interior	Internet Laptop	Car	Car park Coffee shop exterior	Coffee shop interior Menu board	Counter Coffee cup	Coffee shop interior Chair table	Laptop Power socket Internet	Laptop Internet chair table Cup	Cup Trashcan coffee shop Interior	Car Par Car	Car
DOING	Customer At home decides to go out to have a coffee	Checks location of coffee shop on internet	Drives car to coffee shop	Parks and enters coffee shop	Selects drink and waits in line to order	Pays and picks up coffee	Finds a table and sits down	Drinks coffee and reviews emails on laptop	Writes and sends some emails. Tops up coffee	Finishes coffee and puts cup in trashcan	Returns to car	Drives on to supermarket
THINKING	Should I call a friend? Will I have a long wait to be served?	Which coffee shop should I go to?	Will be able to park close to the shop?	Will there be a long queue?	Should I have a latte or a drip coffee?	The coffee is more expensive than last time	Is there a seat available at the window?	The coffee is very hot. Is there a plug for my laptop?	Not a plug available. How long will my battery last?	Where is the trashcan?	Will the traffic be heavy?	There was a long queue. I will go to another coffee shop next time.
FEELING												
PAIN POINTS												
OPPORTUNITIES												

MAP MOMENTS OF TRUTH

Map those interactions that have the most impact on the customer. A moment of truth is an interaction between a customer and a service provider that allows the end user to form an impression about the organization. For example waiting in line in a coffee shop. A moment of truth is a point in time when a customer can make a judgment about the value of a service delivery and a business relationship. Identifying moments of truth and improving their outcomes is a focus of service blueprinting.

ROOT CAUSE OF PAIN POINT

Ask why the experience is painful for the customer. If necessary, ask why several times to understand the cause of the pain.

MAP BARRIERS

What are the obstacles to the optimal experience for the customer at each stage of their interaction?

ADD PHOTOS OR PICTURES WHERE POSSIBLE

Maps sometimes have a lane of photographs that show pain points or other aspects of customer activities. Use pictures if they are the best way of communicating something. For example lack of cleanliness on a train platform.

IDENTIFY POINTS OF FAILURE

Where is the experience failing or likely to fail?

OPPORTUNITIES

Brainstorm ways to change to better meet customer needs.
1. Brainstorm ways to change to meet better customer needs.
2. Bullet these ideas in a separate lane stage by stage.
3. What is the ideal customer experience
4. Analyze every touch point
5. Identify physical evidence at each phase - moment of truth
6. Simplify and refine the process

List how the customer is feeling stage-by-stage

STAGES	EVALUATE		ENTER			USE/ENGAGE					EXIT	
TOUCH POINTS	Home interior	Internet Laptop	Car	Car park Coffee shop exterior	Coffee shop interior Menu board	Counter Coffee cup	Coffee shop interior Chair table	Laptop interior Power socket Internet	Laptop Internet chair table Cup	Cup Trashcan coffee shop Interior	Car Par Car	Car
DOING	Customer At home decides to go out to have a coffee	Checks location of coffee shop on Internet	Drives car to coffee shop	Parks and enters coffee shop	Selects drink and waits in line to order	Pays and picks up coffee	Finds a table and sits down	Drinks coffee and reviews emails on laptop	Writes and sends some emails. Tops up coffee	Finishes coffee and puts cup in trashcan	Returns to car	Drives on to supermarket
THINKING	Should I call a friend? Will I have a long wait to be served?	Should I call a friend? Will I have a long wait to be served?	Which coffee shop should I go to?	Which coffee shop should I go to?	Will be able to park close to the coffee shop?	Will be able to park close to the coffee shop?	Will there be a long queue?	Should I have a latte or a drip coffee?	Should I have a latte or a drip coffee?	Is there a seat available at the window?	Is there a plug for my laptop?	Where is the trashcan?
FEELING						Will there be a long queue?	Should I have a latte or a drip coffee?	The coffee is more expensive than last time	The coffee is more expensive than last time	Is there a seat available at the window?	The coffee is very hot. How long will my laptop?	Not a plug available. How long will my battery last?
PAIN POINTS												
OPPORTUNITIES												

7. Remove pain points and surprises.
8. Add touchpoints that are missing
9. Build scenarios.
10. Think about extreme users, new users, average users.

PHOTOGRAPH THE DRAFT
Photograph the whole blueprint and photograph the blueprint in sections with sufficient resolution to enable you to transfer the map into a graphics program such as Adobe Illustrator or InDesign.

CREATE A PRESENTATION COPY
Photograph the whole map and photograph the map in sections with sufficient resolution to enable you to transfer the map into a graphics program such as Adobe Illustrator or InDesign. Templates can be used for future maps.

DISTRIBUTE TO STAKEHOLDERS FOR FEEDBACK
Distribute draft to internal and external stakeholders for feedback. Circulate you map as widely as possible to get feedback from internal departments, executives, external customers and stakeholders.

REFINE THE MAP BASED ON THE FEEDBACK
Does it tell the story of your customer's experience that is complete, from beginning to end? Is it understandable to people outside the team? Are the insights actionable? Does it inspire and support a change in strategy? Does it communicate the necessary information, without further explanation? Simplify the map. Identify gaps and do further research to fill the gaps. Gaps in touchpoints may suggest opportunities to add new touchpoints.

ITERATE
Distribute the refined map to other stakeholders and refine the map again.

BRAINSTORM THE IDEAL EXPERIENCE
Put together what you have learned to generate a better experience for your customers

285

List pain points stage-by-stage

STAGES	EVALUATE		ENTER		USE/ENGAGE						EXIT	
TOUCH POINTS	Home Interior	Internet Laptop	Car	Car park Coffee shop exterior	Coffee shop interior Menu board	Counter Coffee cup	Coffee shop interior Chair table	Laptop Power socket Internet	Laptop Internet chair table Cup	Cup Trashcan coffee shop Interior	Car Park Car	Car
DOING	Customer decides to go out to have a coffee	Checks location of coffee shop on internet	Drives car to coffee shop	Parks and enters coffee shop	Selects drink and waits in line to order	Pays and picks up coffee	Finds a table and sits down	Drinks coffee and reviews emails on laptop	Writes and sends some emails, Tops up coffee	Finishes coffee and puts cup in trashcan	Returns to car	Drives on to supermarket
THINKING		Which coffee shop should I go to?	Will be able to park close to the coffee shop?	Will there be a long queue?	Should I have a latte or a drip coffee?	Is there a seat available at the window?	Is there a plug for my laptop?	Where is the trashcan?	Will the traffic be heavy?			There was a long queue. I will go to another coffee shop next time.
FEELING	Should I call a friend? Will I have a long wait to be served?	Which coffee shop should I go to?	Will be able to park close to the coffee shop?	Will there be a long queue?	Should I have a latte or a drip coffee?	The coffee is more expensive than last time	The coffee is very hot. Is there a plug for my laptop?	Not a plug available. How long will my battery?	Where is the trashcan?	Will the traffic be heavy?	I will go to another coffee shop next time.	
PAIN POINTS	Should I call a friend? Will I have a long wait to be served?	Hard to park at best available coffee shop	No parking place available close to coffee shop	Queue takes 20 minutes	Too many choices on menu	Price has increased	Needs to wait for an available table. Chairs uncomfortable.	Coffee too hot to drink. Coffee shop Music too loud.	No plug available for laptop.	No visible trashcan	Long walk back to car. Traffic heavy	
OPPORTUNITIES												

that you can implement. Develop step-by-step corrective actions for fail points.

RAPID PROTOTYPING

Experience prototyping is the most efficient way to implement an improved service. The goal is to observe customers interacting with the new experience and obtain their feedback about the experience. Use methods such as:
1. Video prototyping,
2. Role playing,
3. Desktop walkthroughs
4. Bodystorming
5. Paper prototyping
6. Empathy tools
7. Wireframing
8. Service staging
9. Wizard of Oz
10. Start with low-fidelity methods and move to higher fidelity prototyping methods as you find clarity with the best design direction.

SERVICE STAGING

Test the refinements in a staged setting. Sets up space that imitates the real environment, but with simple props to represent physical objects. For example cardboard boxes could be used to describe a counter. The design team can work through the experience "on stage" and adapt it based on feedback from customers.

CONDUCT USER STUDIES IN THE TARGET CONTEXT

Test with target users iteratively and refine the service until the pain points have become points of pleasure for customers.
1. Do people understand the service
2. Do people see the value of the service?
3. Do people understand how to use it?
4. Is the experience positive?
5. What ideas do the customers have that could improve the service?

IMPLEMENT THE SERVICE

The end purpose of a blueprint is to take action and improve the journey and drive the ROI to justify the investment.
After the new service design is tested, the design team documents the new experience and creates implementation guidelines to roll out of the new

Brainstorm opportunities to impove the experience

STAGES	EVALUATE		ENTER		USE/ENGAGE						EXIT	
TOUCH POINTS	Home Interior	Internet Laptop	Car	Car park Coffee shop exterior	Coffee shop interior Menu board	Counter Coffee cup	Coffee shop interior Chair table	Laptop Power socket Internet	Laptop chair table Cup	Cup Trashcan coffee shop Interior	Car Par Car	Car
DOING	Customer At home decides to go out to have a coffee	Checks location of coffee shop on Internet	Drives car to coffee shop	Parks and enters coffee shop	Selects drink and waits in line to order	Pays and picks up coffee	Finds a table and sits down	Drinks coffee and reviews emails on laptop	Writes and sends some emails. Tops up coffee	Finishes coffee and puts cup in trashcan	Returns to car	Drives on to supermarket
THINKING	Should I call a friend? Will I have a long wait to be served?	Which coffee shop should I go to?	Will be able to park close to the coffee shop?	Will there be a long queue?	Should I have a latte or a drip coffee?	The coffee is more expensive than last time	Is there a seat available at the window?	Is there a plug for my laptop?	Not a plug available. How long will my battery last?	Where is the trashcan?	Will the traffic be heavy?	There was a long queue. I will go to another coffee shop next time.
FEELING	Should I call a friend? Will I have a long wait to be served?	Should I call a friend? Will I have a long wait to be served?	Will be able to park close to the coffee shop?	Will there be a long queue?	Should I have a latte or a drip coffee?	The coffee is more expensive than last time	Is there a seat available at the window?	The coffee is very hot. Is there a plug for my laptop?	The coffee is very hot. Not a plug available. Where is the trashcan?	Where is the trashcan?	Will the traffic be heavy?	I will go to another coffee shop next time.
PAIN POINTS	Should I call a friend? Will I have a long wait to be served?	Hard to park at best coffee shop	No parking place available close to coffee shop	Queue takes 20 minutes	Too many choices on menu	Price has increased	Needs to wait for an available table. Chairs uncomfortable.	Coffee too hot to drink. Coffee shop cold. Music too load.	No plug available for laptop.	No visible trashcan	Long walk back to car. Traffic heavy.	
OPPORTUNITIES	Improve web site	Differentiate coffee shop from other coffee shops	Make more parking available.	Order coffee Online. Add second cash register.	Reduce number of options	Offer some lower priced menu items	Replace chairs. Open up second room	Adjust coffee temperature. Fix leaky windows.	Add power points	Relocate trash cans. Increase number of trashcans.	Make more parking available.	

Departments of a large organization often send duplicated communications to customers.

Journey maps create alignment to bring all departments together in one seamless mission based on the shared goal of creating the best possible customer experience.

service across the organization. The service blueprint is now a tool to communicate the new design.

1. Use your map for employee training.
2. Map upcoming product launches or your desired future state

MEASURE YOUR PROGRESS TOWARDS YOUR GOALS

Define ways of tracking your progress towards measurable goals. Metrics will help you measure the quality of your customer experience, now and in the future.

1. Net Promoter Score and customer loyalty measures
2. Customer satisfaction measures
3. Quantitative assessments of the customer emotions.
4. Metrics of customer effort
5. The measure of the performance of each touchpoint.
6. New sales.
7. Increased loyalty and retention of customers
8. The increase in revenue per customer.
9. More sales.
10. Reduced costs
11. Better delivery processes.
12. Better quality
13. Increased competitiveness

Phase	PREPARE			ENTER		ACTIVITY						EXIT	REFLECT
Physical Evidence	work building	Internet computer	car	car park	building	chalkboard menu	cash register	coffee machine	table chair	computer	table chair	car park	car
Customer Actions	Decide to have a coffee	Locate coffee shop	Drive to coffee shop	Park	Enter coffee shop	Stand in line	Order	Picks up coffee	Sit down	Drink & Work	Pack up	Finish & return to car	Drive home
Line of Interaction													
Onstage Employee Actions					Greet customer		Take order	Make order	Escort to table		Ask if they need refill	Pick up empty cup	
Line of Visibility													
Backstage Employee Actions							Accounting	Order supplies				Cleans room	
Line of Internal Interaction													
Support Processes													
Opportunities													

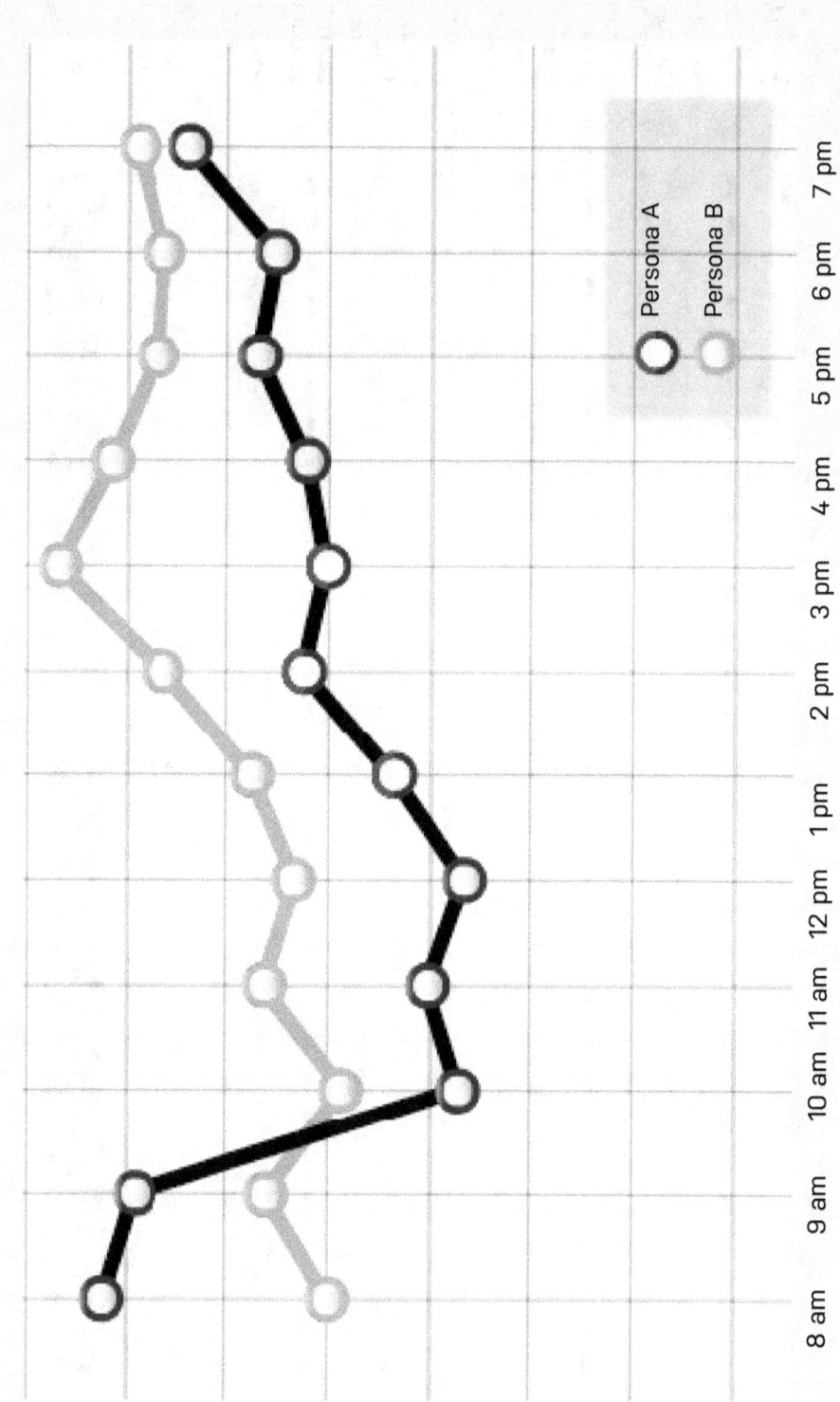

Emotional journey map

WHAT IS IT?
An emotional journey map is a map that visually illustrates people's emotional experience throughout an interaction with an organization or brand.

WHY USE THIS METHOD?
1. It provides a focus for discussion
2. It focuses on what may make your customers unhappy
3. Provides a visually compelling story of customer experience.
4. Customer experience is more than interaction with a product.
5. By understanding the journey that your customers are making, you will be in a position to make informed improvements.

CHALLENGES
1. Customers often do not take the route in an interaction that the designer expects.
2. Failure to manage experiences can lead to lost customers.

HOW TO USE THIS METHOD
1. Define the activity of your map. For example it could be a ride on the underground train.
2. Collect internal insights
3. Research customer perceptions
4. Analyze research
5. Map journey.
6. Across the top of the page do a time line Break the journey into stages using your customer's point of view
7. Capture each persona's unique experience
8. Use a scale from 0 to 10. The higher the number, the better the experience.
9. Plot the emotional journey.
10. Analyze the lease pleasant emotional periods and create ideas for improving the experience during those periods.
11. Create a map for each persona.

RESOURCES
Paper
Pens
Whiteboard
Post-it-notes

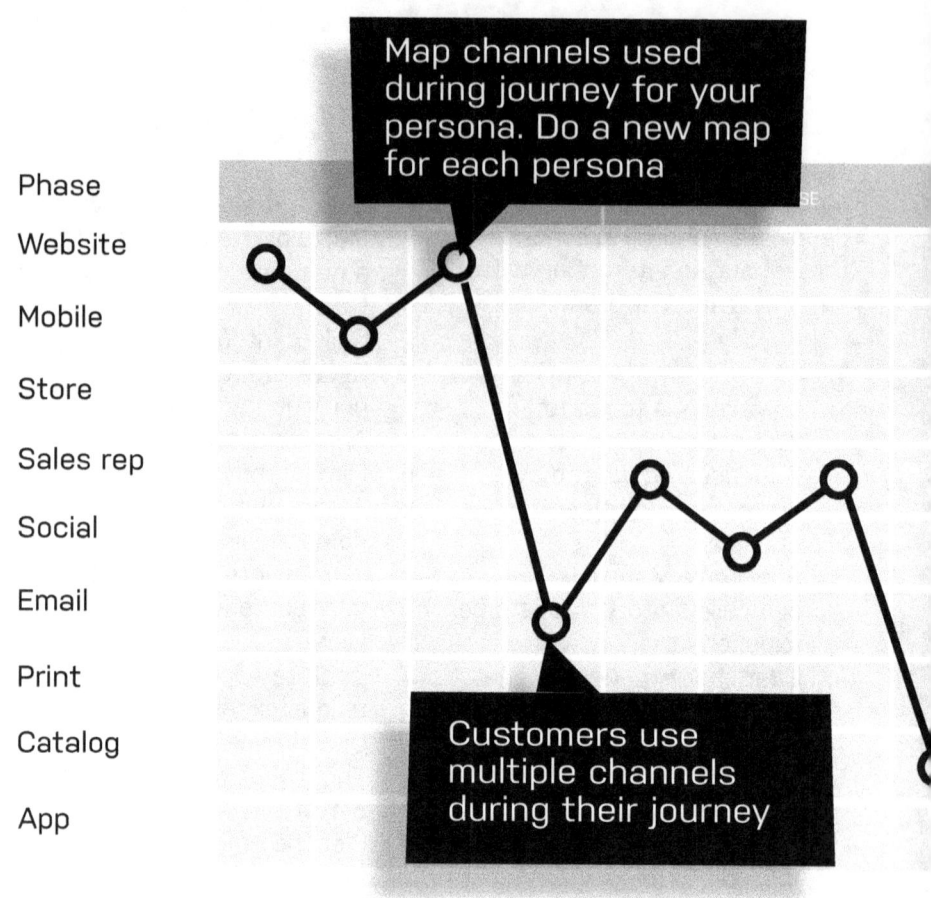

Muli-channel Map

Interactions can cross channels, touchpoints or physical evidence and take place in multiple contexts. More than 50% of companies according to one study have little understanding of the complex nature of their customers typical purchase routes. Customers desire seamless interactions across channels and touchpoints. A multichannel map can help uncover opportunities for your business to improve the customer experience.

Journey phases for the particular persona

USE | POST SALES SUPPORT

Customers may return to the same channel at different times

Experience map example: visit to a coffee shop

STAGES	EVALUATE		ENTER		USE/ENGAGE					EXIT		
TOUCH POINTS	Home Interior	Internet Laptop	Car	Car park Coffee shop exterior	Coffee shop interior Menu board	Counter Coffee cup	Coffee shop interior Chair table	Laptop Power socket Internet	Laptop Internet chair table Cup	Cup Trashcan coffee shop interior	Car Park Car	Car
DOING	Customer at home decides to go out to have a coffee	Checks location of coffee shop on internet	Drives car to coffee shop	Parks and enters coffee shop	Selects drink and waits in line to order	Pays and picks up coffee	Finds a table and sits down	Drinks coffee and works on email on laptop	Writes email and sends some emails. Tops up coffee	Finishes coffee and puts cup in trashcan	Returns to car	Drives car to supermarket
THINKING	Should I call a friend? Will I have a long wait to be served?	Which coffee shop should I go to?	Will be able to park close to the shop?	Will there be a long queue?	Should I have a latte or a drip coffee?		The coffee is more expensive than last time	Is there a seat available at the window?	Not a plug available. How long will my battery last?	Where is the trash can?	Will the traffic be heavy?	There was a long queue. I will go to another coffee shop next time.
FEELING	Should I call a friend? Will I have a long wait to be served?	Which coffee shop should I go to?	Will be able to park close to the coffee shop?	Will there be a long queue?	Should I have a latte or a drip coffee?		The coffee is more expensive than last time	Is there a seat available at the window?	Not a plug available. How long will my battery last?	Where is the trashcan?	Will the traffic be heavy?	I will go to another coffee shop next time.
PAIN POINTS	Should I call a friend? Will there be a long wait to be served?	Hard to park at coffee shop	No parking place available close to coffee shop	Queue takes 20 minutes	Too many choices on menu	Price has increased	Hard to wait for a seat to clear, chairs uncomfortable	Coffee too hot to drink. Coffee shop cold.	No plug available for laptop. Music too loud.	No visible trashcan	Long walk back to car. Traffic heavy.	
OPPORTUNITIES	Improve website	Differentiate coffee shop from other coffee shops	Has more parking available	Order coffee online, add second cash register	Reduce number of options	Offer more loyalty incentives	Replace chairs. Open up second room	Adjust coffee temperature. Fix baby systems.	Add power points	Relocate trashcans. Increase number of trashcans.	Make more parking available	

297

Service Blueprint example: Hotel

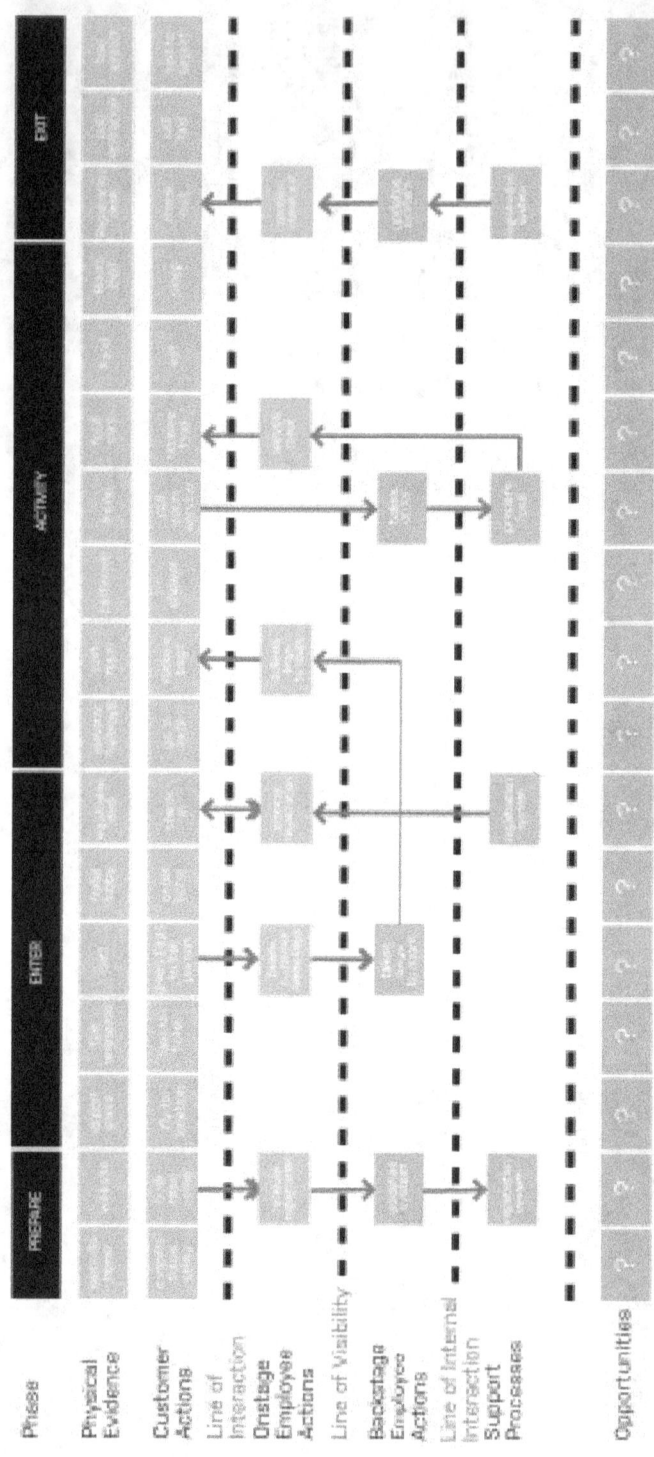

Service Blueprints

A service blueprint is a map showing how a service will be provided, what physical and virtual things that customers will interact with, employee actions, and support systems to deliver the service across channels.

"The idea behind services blueprinting is fairly simple: Companies put themselves in their customers' shoes to find out what's working, what's not, and what needs to be changed."

"It's a very versatile technique that can be used for both innovation and services improvement,"
Mary Jo Bitner

"A service blueprint allows a company to explore all the issues inherent in creating or managing a service."
Lyn Shostack

"The uniqueness of service blueprinting is the unrelenting focus on the customer as the center and foundation of your business."
WP Carey School of Business Arizona State University

Service Blueprints are created by a cross-disciplinary team of internal employees and external stakeholders in an iterative process. A service blueprint is a living document that is refined over time. Blueprints help pinpoint opportunities to improve the efficiency and quality of customer experiences.

Blueprints can also be used to design a new service. A map is produced for each customer segment or persona. Blueprinting has been used by companies across every industry, and it is expected over time that the proven benefits of blueprinting will lead to widespread adoption of the technique.

Services make up 90% of US employment and account for 75% of GDP yet far less attention has been given to design and innovation in services than to manufactured products

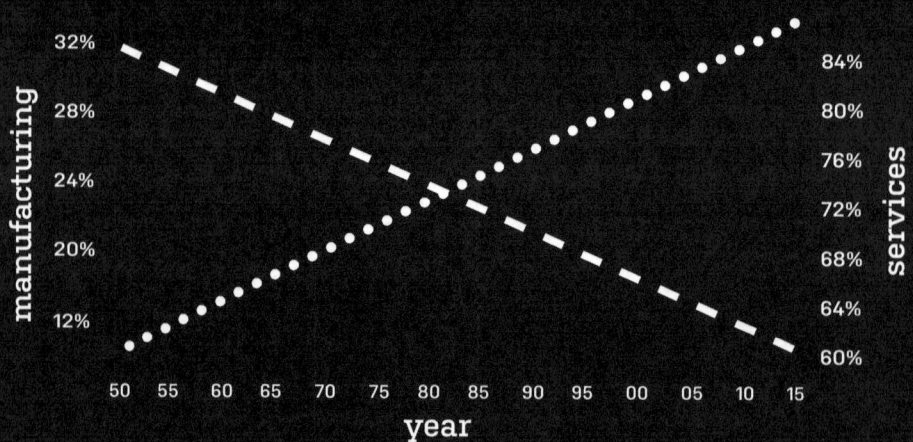

US % total employment manufacturing and services

	PHYSICAL EVIDENCE
	CUSTOMER ACTIONS

Line of interaction

———————————————————————

Frontstage	**FACE TO FACE EMPLOYEE ACTIONS**

Line of visibility

– – – – – – – – – – – – – – – –

Backstage	**EMPLOYEE ACTIONS NOT VISIBLE TO CUSTOMER**

Line of internal interaction

– – – – – – – – – – – – – – – –

SUPPORT PROCESSES

"

67% of on-line shoppers recently made a purchase that involved multiple channels

90% of people move between devices to accomplish a goal

Source: Venturebeat

Why use Service Blueprints?

Service blueprints can be used for the following purposes
1. Understand the structure of a service or experience system.
2. Understand the collective experiences of customer segments
3. To create an improved customer service or experience.
4. Create a more seamless customer experience across business departments, and channels.
5. Design a new service or product customer experience
6. Allocate people and resources efficiently.
7. Develop alignment across departments of an organization.
8. Craft a better customer experience.
9. Expose places where your service or customer experience may fail.
10. Craft a better customer experience
11. Strategic and tactical innovation
12. Building and sharing knowledge
13. Understand competitive positioning
14. Understanding the ideal experience
15. Identify opportunities
16. Empathize with your end users
17. Designing and improving Systems
18. Develop a better product road map
19. Take cost & complexity out of the system
20. Prioritize competing deliverables
21. Plan for hiring
22. Bring different parts of your business together to work to improve the customer experience
23. Identify specific areas of opportunity to drive ideation and innovation
24. Make intangible services tangible
25. Develop customer insights
26. Introduce metrics for what matters most to your customers
27. Align your offerings to brand promise
28. Improve efficiency
29. Imagine future product and service experiences
30. Making better decisions
31. A living document that can evolve with your business

Ginginha Camponesa

How to create a service blueprint

Here is a list of stages that you can complete creating a service blueprint. Consider the blueprint to be a living document that will develop and improve, so it doesn't have to be perfect first time. Concentrate on your customers and their point of view.

CREATE YOUR GOAL STATEMENT

1. What is the problem, unmet needs or opportunities that the blueprint is to realize?
2. A clear map of customer needs should be compatible with your goals and with an outcome that satisfies them.
3. Who are the stakeholders?
4. Where is the service delivered?
5. When is the service delivered?
6. What are the channels?
7. Why is there a need for a new design solution?
8. Are you looking to address issues already identified?
9. Do you want to enhance the customer experience?
10. Do you want to engage your customers more effectively? Do you want to create a more efficient process? Define your goals in a statement and return to that statement as you build your map to ensure that your efforts contribute to reaching the goal.

DEFINE YOUR TARGET AUDIENCE SEGMENT AND THEIR NEEDS

The most successful products and services target precise customer segments. Designs that try to please everyone do not satisfy anyone.

GATHER YOUR EXISTING RESEARCH

Start by auditing internal customer experience data that was gathered. Review existing user data, including call center logs, customer satisfaction surveys, existing personas, mystery shopping data, web analytics and customer satisfaction data. Review the data and determine what new research is necessary to fill in the knowledge gaps. To be useful data should be current. The most significant insights will come directly from engaging

the stakeholders located in their natural context with the service. Engage stakeholders through a variety of possible research techniques in the physical location of the service such as contextual observation and interviews.

Quantitative data is less useful than qualitative research when trying to understand the feelings and emotions of your customers.

Interviews are a common method used to gather data. Ask them to walk you through their experience and talk about their problems, needs desires and feelings at each stage. Start by talking to between five and twenty people as a minimum sample size. Focus your questions on the areas relevant to the lanes of the service blueprint. If you are creating a journey map, ask what are they doing, thinking, and feeling at each stage of the activity. Ask them what touch points they are engaging at each stage. Ask them where they are experiencing problems or frustrations in achieving their goals. Document your interviews or observations by using video or a digital recorder. Quantitative data with a larger sample size is also useful. Create a survey for existing or prospective customers.

To be useful, your service blueprint needs to be based on real and truthful information. Use prototype maps in focus group discussions to validate findings directly with customers..

REVIEW YOUR EXISTING RESEARCH

Review existing research. Identify gaps in data and create a list of recurring customer experience problems.

CREATE A RESEARCH PLAN TO FILL THE GAPS.

1. Create a research plan to fill the gaps.
2. What do you still need to know?
3. What questions do you need to ask?
4. How many people will you involve?
5. What type of people will you

research?
6. What will be the context of the customer?
7. What methods will you use?
8. When will you select and screen the subjects, conduct the research and report on findings?

SYNTHESIZE YOUR RESEARCH

Put each potentially useful piece of information on separate post-it notes. Put the post-it notes on a wall and ask your team to organize the customer's comments into related groups or themes. Which issues are most significant to more customers? Build a hierarchy of problems. Identify themes and patterns from the interviews.
What are your customers' needs and goals at each stage of their activity? What touchpoints are they engaging at each step?

SELECT YOUR TEAM

Care should be taken in selecting your team. As many groups and diverse points of view involved in design delivery and use of the service as possible should be represented.
1. Keep groups to six people or less.
2. If your total group size is larger than twelve people, break the large group into smaller groups of six or fewer people.
3. Have a diverse team with different genders, age, occupations and status represented.
4. Have at least two or three "T" shaped people. "T" shaped people are individuals with two or more areas of expertise such as technology and management or design. This makes the team more flexible and helps group collaboration.
5. Involve external and internal stakeholders such as customers, suppliers, internal business management, engineering, design, and sales.
6. Have customer facing people where possible because they better understand the customer's perspective.

APPOINT YOUR MODERATOR

Create handouts with clear instructions. Provide copies of research summaries. Take

breaks every 90 minutes
Photograph the map as it is being built.

MODERATOR SKILLS

1. Effective Listening Skills
2. Flexibility
3. Customer empathy
4. Sincerely Interested in People
5. Enthusiasm
6. People management skills
7. Able to establishing common direction and buy-in.
8. Understands Group Dynamics
9. Authority
10. Neutral and Objective
11. Patient and Persistent
12. Curious
13. Guide discussion promptly.
14. Able to draw our quieter group members.
15. Able to read between the lines and understand what is not said.
16. Beginner's mind
17. Get Panelists to talk to each other.
18. Get the audience involved early.
19. Able to read body language
20. Able to create an atmosphere where divergent views can be explored
21. Encourage all participants to share their views openly.
22. Keep the conversation focused and relevant
23. Track and record the key themes and ideas expressed by the group.
24. Make sure the best and needed people are in the room.
25. Make sure all roles are clearly defined.
26. State the meeting purpose before or at the start of the meeting
27. Set objectives for the meeting.
28. Define next steps and action items at the conclusion of the meeting.

SELECT AND PREPARE YOUR WORKSPACE

A good space is a large room with plenty of natural light with a large table and sufficient chairs for your team.

Useful materials

1. A large wall
2. Butcher paper
3. Masking tape
4. Mobile whiteboards
5. Dry erase markers
6. Sharpies
7. Adhesive notes in 5 colors
8. Digital camera
9. Tripod

IDENTIFY YOUR TARGET SEGMENT TO MAP
Identifying customer segments.

CREATE PERSONAS
Create your customer personas. Personas are archetypal characters created to represent the different user types that might use a product or service in a similar way. Create 3 to 6 personas to cover all your customers.

IDENTIFY STAKEHOLDERS
A stakeholder is someone who may be in some way influenced by your design. For example in a hospital stakeholders may be patients, relatives of patients, hospital workers, doctors, nurses, health insurance workers. Stakeholders are also people who represent various areas within your organization such as technology, design, business management, sales, customer experience.

HOLD STAKEHOLDER WORKSHOPS
Organize a workshop, and guide internal and external stakeholders through the process of creating the first draft. Go over the user experience and discuss the perspective of customers and diverse interested parties,

SELECT THE SERVICE TO BE BLUEPRINTED
Choose your experience to map. We suggest starting small with part of an experience that is important or problematic. For example rather than mapping an entire customer journey for air travel from New York to London, map a part of it that is important su8ch as selecting the airline and booking online. Explore several challenging sub-journeys before tackling the whole journey.

DECIDE PRESENT OR FUTURE SERVICE TO MAP
It is most usual first to map your existing customer experience. A current state map can help identify ways to make your existing customer experience better or more efficient.

After mapping your current service you may be interested

in creating a map as a concept for a future service or customer experience. You may not have a current service in which case go straight to a map of a future service or experience.

SELECT START AND END POINTS OF THE CUSTOMER EXPERIENCE
Define the scope in terms of time ad customer activities.

SELECT CHANNELS TO MAP
Typical examples of channels include
1. In-store experience
2. Print,
3. Web,
4. Mobile

The channel defines the opportunities and constraints of a touchpoint.

START SMALL
Consider picking a particular scenario or sub-activity of your entire customer experience.

DRAFT THE MAP
Use a large wall or table. Create your first rough draft using post-it notes. Share the first blueprint with as many internal and external stakeholders as possible and ask for their feedback. If insights don't fit on a single map, keep maps simple by creating building one map for each persona.

CREATE THE STORY
What are the main elements of the customer experience from their perspective? What parts of their experience leave a lasting impression on them either positive or negative.

MAP USER ACTIONS & ACTIVITIES STEP-BY-STEP
Start at the beginning of the service or experience and list each thing a customer commonly does step by step. Put each sub-activity on a separate post-it note. For example, if the activity is visiting a coffee shop the activities may include.
1. At work decide to get a coffee on the way home
2. Check the location of coffee shops on the Internet.
3. Select coffee shop
4. Go to car
5. Drive to coffee shop
6. Park

Phase	PREPARE				ENTER		ACTIVITY					EXIT	REFLECT
Physical Evidence	work building	internet computer	car	car park	building	chalkboard menu	cash register	coffee machine	table chair	computer	table chair	car park	car
Customer Actions	Decide to have a coffee	Locate coffee shop	Drive to coffee shop	Park	Enter coffee shop	Stand in line	Order	Wait for coffee	Sit down	Drink & Work	Pack up	Finish & return to car	Drive home
Line of Interaction													
Onstage Employee Actions													
Line of Visibility													
Backstage Employee Actions													
Line of Internal Interaction													
Support Processes													
Opportunities													

customer actions

7. Enter coffee shop
8. Stand in line
9. Order
10. Pick up coffee
11. Find table
12. Sit down
13. Drink coffee
14. Read news on tablet
15. Pack up
16. Return to car
17. Drive home
18. Reflect on the experience.

Describe each activity on a separate post-it note and place them in a line on your wall or table. Continue till your team is happy that all important events are included

MAP TIME

How long does each customer activity usually take? Does a stage usually last ten seconds or ten minutes. Place the time required on a post-it note above each stage of customer activity. Time to consider:
1. Critical periods service actions, such as response to a proposal.
2. Duration of each service steps, such as airline check-in
3. The time between service steps such as walking to a hotel room after check-in.
4. End to end service experience.

BUILD THE BLUEPRINT

Now you are ready to create the map.

MAP USER ACTION PHASES

Break the list of customer activities into four or six phases of sub-activities. Some examples of sets of phases of activities are:

Example One
1. Explore
2. Evaluate
3. Engage
4. Experience

Example two
1. Aware
2. Join
3. Use
4. Develop
5. Leave

Example Three
1. Research
2. Evaluate and compare
3. Commit
4. Use and Monitor
5. Refine and review

Phase

Phase	PREPARE				ENTER		ACTIVITY				EXIT	REFLECT
Physical Evidence	work building	internet computer	car	car park	building	Enter coffee shop		table chair	table computer	table chair	car park	car
Customer Actions	Decide to have a coffee	Locate coffee shop	Drive to coffee shop	Park				Sit down	Drink & Work	Pack up	Finish & return to car	Drive home
Line of Interaction												
Onstage Employee Actions												
Line of Visibility												
Backstage Employee Actions												
Line of Internal Interaction												
Support Processes												
Opportunities												

customer activity phases

320

MAP THE PHYSICAL EVIDENCE STEP-BY-STEP

Physical evidence is usually the lane shown at the top of a blueprint. Services consist of the interactions with people, the processes, and the physical evidence of the experience. Objects in the service environment that customers engage are sometimes referred to as "physical evidence" because they are proof of the service that has taken place. Physical evidence is the tangible things that help to communicate and perform the service and influence a customer's perception of a service.

Physical evidence is the tangible manifestation of service. It conveys to customers whether the service provider cares about their customers and whether they trust their customers. Physical evidence cues are what customers use to evaluate service quality.

Physical evidence can convey intended and unintended messages to customers. Physical evidence is the interface between a service provider and a customer. K

The key to delivering a successful service is to identify clearly a simple, consistent message, and then manage the evidence to support that message.

" well-prepared small details represent sincerity in serving guests which reflect the hotel's good service spirit. For example, welcome fruit, an electric kettle and fresh flowers in hotel rooms are service evidence that often evoked delight as they show the hotel's thoughtfulness."

"For example, a research participant talked about disappointment caused by "fake" hangers in a hotel room's closet. She complained: They're not real hangers, because they're attached to the railing. So
if you want to take out a hanger and then hang it on a chair or hang it on a door, you can't, because there's no hook... That's kind of a fake hanger. It shows that they think I'm going to steal the hangers. So it

Phase	PREPARE			ENTER			ACTIVITY			EXIT	REFLECT
Physical Evidence	work building	internet computer	car	car park	building	chalkboard menu	cash register	coffee machine	table chair	table computer	table chair	car park	car
Customer Actions	Decide to have a coffee	Locate coffee shop	Drive to coffee shop	Park				Wait for coffee	Sit down	Drink & Work	Pack up	Finish & return to car	Drive home
Line of Interaction													
Onstage Employee Actions													
Line of Visibility													
Backstage Employee Actions													
Line of Internal Interaction													
Support Processes													
Opportunities													

physical evidence

makes me feel not trusted."
Source: Kathy Pui Ying Lo Designing Service Evidence for Positive Relational Messages, http://www.ijdesign.org/ojs/index.php/IJDesign/article/viewFile/898/333 (accessed March 23, 2016).

The physical evidence lane on the blueprint appears above the "line of visibility" in a service blueprint. Physical evidence includes the service providers building/facilities and staff appearance; and uniforms. Physical evidence should be considered important by the customer and the promise implied by these tangible objects should be delivered. A bank card is an example of physical evidence of a service. It helps a bank differentiate their service from another bank. It separates the service from the seller.

Other examples of physical evidence are
1. The building
2. The interior
3. The car park
4. Internal signage,
5. Packaging.

6. Promotional materials
7. Web pages.
8. Paperwork (such as invoices, tickets and dispatch notes).
9. Brochures.
10. Stationery
11. Billing statement
12. Furnishings.
13. Signage
14. Uniforms and employee dress.
15. Business cards.
16. Mailboxes.

Blueprint the physical evidence of service. Physical evidence should be refined developed and improved over time. Work cross-functionally.

DRAW THE LINE OF INTERACTION

Separates customer activities from face-to-face onstage and unseen backstage actions.

MAP FRONT STAGE OR ONSTAGE EMPLOYEE ACTIONS

Onstage employee actions are separated from the customer by the line of interaction. Onstage or front stage employee actions are the things that

323

Phase	PREPARE			ENTER			ACTIVITY					EXIT	REFLECT
Physical Evidence	work building	internet computer	car	car park	building	chalkboard menu	cash register	coffee machine	table chair	table chair computer		car park	car
Customer Actions	Decide to have a coffee	Locate coffee shop	Drive to coffee shop	Park	Enter coffee shop	Stand in line	Order	Wait for coffee	Sit down	Drink & Work	Pack up	Finish & return to car	Drive home
Line of Interaction													
Onstage Employee Actions					Greet customer	Take order	Make order				Pick up empty cup		
Line of Visibility													
Backstage Employee Actions													
Line of Internal Interaction													
Support Processes													
Opportunities													

onstage employee actions

line of interaction

your employees do during a face-to-face encounter with the customer. Examples are a waiter in a restaurant taking your order or a hotel front desk employee checking you into a hotel.

DRAW THE LINE OF VISIBILITY
The line of visibility separates actions that are face-to-face from those that are not visible to the end user. Divides actions of onstage employees from backstage actions. Below the line of visibility, actions that involve non-visible interaction with customers such as contact by telephone is described

MAP BACK STAGE OR OFFSTAGE EMPLOYEE ACTIONS
Back stage actions are the activities by your employees to provide the service that the end user doesn't see.

DRAW THE LINE OF INTERNAL INTERACTION
This line separates contact employees activities from noncontact support actions.

SUPPORT PROCESSES
Support functions needed to support the employees. These are internal services, which help the contact employees in delivering the service.
An example is the registration computer system in a hotel.

Support processes are other actions, systems, and resources that the service provider relies upon that must be provided to deliver the service to the customer.

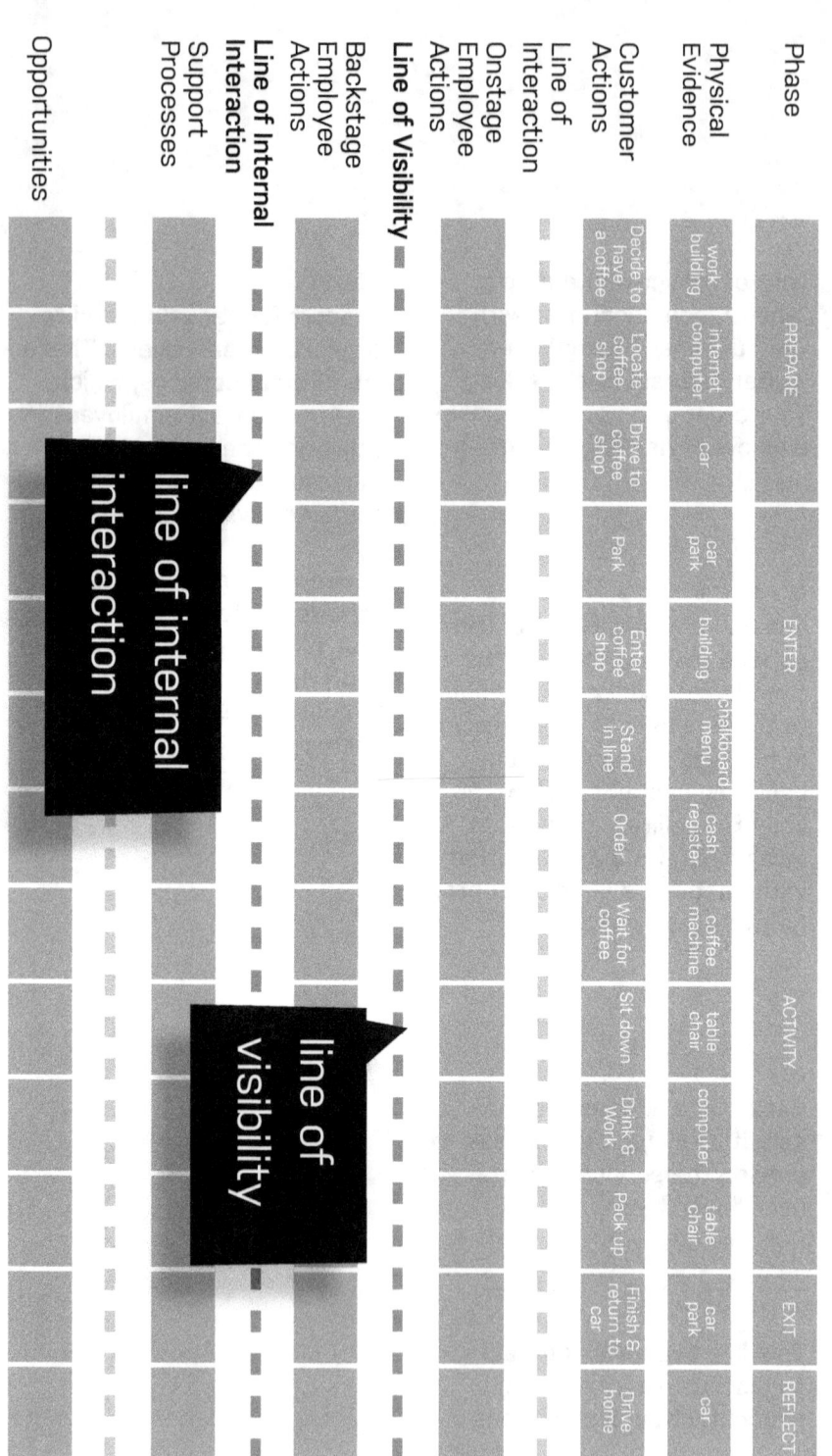

MAP THE PAIN POINTS

A pain pint is any part of the customer experience that they find people disturbing, frustrating, urgent or uncomfortable. Some customer needs are needs which the customers themselves are not aware of and cannot articulate. A pain point is a problem for you customer and a problem and an opportunity for you. Solving pain points create value for you and your customer. "customer pain" is a synonym for "customer needs". Customers spend money to combat pain or to pursue pleasure.

Examples of service pain points are airport security lines, hospital directions, or the cost of travel.

A pain point is the why customers choose you if you offer a solution to their need. If you engage your customers and listen they'll tell you their pain points.

To identify customer 'pain-points':
1. In-depth interviews with customer facing internal employees
2. Requests from your most valuable customers.
3. Customer interviews.
4. Customer focus groups.
5. Analysis of customer calls and warranty claims to identify problems.
6. Review of competitor offerings.

You can list the root causes of pain for your customers at each stage.

CUSTOMER OR STAKEHOLDER COMMENTS

List significant or representative comments in a lane. What do customers think?

MAP BRAND IMPACT

List brand impact of touchpoints and customer comments in a lane.

KEY PEOPLE

Identify internal owners of experiences that support customer's needs.

CUSTOMER NEEDS

Do customers have

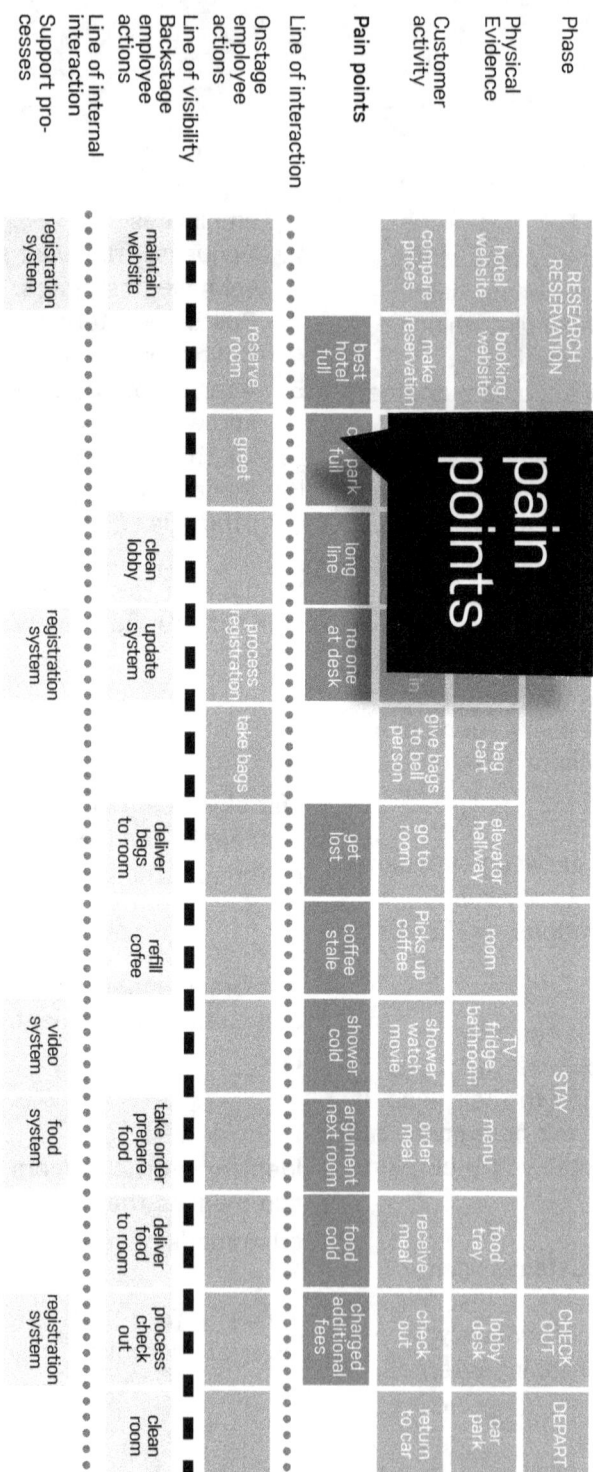

unrecognized needs that could be addressed? What do customers want to accomplish at each stage of interaction?

MAP CONNECTIONS
Use arrows to illustrate the flow of responsibility—who is "driving" the service at any moment and should be initiating service action:

1. Model expectations of "proactive" provider activity.
2. Model the customer responsibility for next steps.
3. Model partner expectations.
4. Define points of handoff between roles, such as from backstage to onstage.

MAP MOMENTS OF TRUTH
Map those interactions that have the most impact on the customer. A moment of truth is a contact or interaction between a customer and a service provider that gives the customer an opportunity to form or change an impression about the organization.

For example waiting in line in a coffee shop. A moment of truth is a point in time when a customer has the opportunity to make a judgment about the value of a service delivery and a business relationship. Identifying moments of truth and improving their outcomes is a focus of service blueprinting.

ROOT CAUSE OF PAIN POINT
Ask why the experience is painful for the customer. If necessary ask why several times to understand the underlying cause of the pain.

MAP BARRIERS
What obstacles are standing in the way of the optimal experience for the customer at each stage of their interaction?

PRIORITIZE TOUCHPOINTS TO IMPROVE OR DEVELOP

ADD PHOTOS OR PICTURES WHERE POSSIBLE
Add photos or pictures where possible
Blueprints sometimes have a lane of photographs that

show pain points of customer activities. Use pictures if they are the best way of communicating something. For example lack of cleanliness on a train platform.
Identify points of failure
Where is the service failing or likely to fail?

IDENTIFY POINTS OF FAILURE
Where is the service failing or likely to fail?

OPPORTUNITIES
Brainstorm ways to change to better meet customer needs.
1. Bullet point these ideas in a separate lane stage by stage.
2. Bullet points these ideas in a separate lane stage by stage.
3. What is the ideal customer experience
4. Analyze every touch point
5. Identify physical evidence at each stage - moment of truth
6. Simplify and refine the process
7. Remove pain points and surprises.
8. Add touchpoints that are missing
9. Build scenarios Think about extreme users, new users, average users.

PHOTOGRAPH THE DRAFT
Photograph the whole blueprint and photograph the blueprint in sections with sufficient resolution to enable you to transfer the map into a graphics program such as Adobe Illustrator or InDesign.

CREATE A PRESENTATION COPY
Transfer the map into a graphics program such as Adobe Illustrator or InDesign.

DISTRIBUTE TO STAKEHOLDERS FOR FEEDBACK
Distribute draft to internal and external stakeholders for feedback. Circulate you map as widely as possible to get feedback from internal departments, executives, external customers, and stakeholders.

REFINE THE MAP BASED ON THE FEEDBACK

Does it tell the story of your customer's experience that is complete, from beginning to end? Is it understandable to people outside the team? Are the insights actionable? Does it inspire and support a change in strategy? Does it communicate the necessary information, without further explanation? Simplify the map. Identify gaps and do further research to fill the gaps. Gaps in touchpoints may suggest opportunities to add new touchpoints.

BRAINSTORM THE IDEAL EXPERIENCE

Put together what you have learned to generate a better experience for your customers that you can implement. Develop step-by-step corrective actions for fail points.

RAPID PROTOTYPING

Experience prototyping is the most efficient way to implement an improved service. The goal is to observe customers interacting with the new experience and obtain their feedback about the experience. Use methods such as:
1. Video prototyping,
2. Role playing,
3. desktop walkthroughs
4. Bodystorming
5. Paper prototyping
6. Empathy tools
7. Wireframing
8. Service staging
9. Wizard of Oz

Start with low fidelity methods and move to higher fidelity prototyping methods as you find clarity with the best design direction.

SERVICE STAGING

Test the service refinements in a staged setting. Sets up a space that imitates the real environment, but with simple props to represent physical objects. For example cardboard boxes could be used to describe a counter. The design team can work through the experience "on stage" and adapt it based on feedback from customers.

CONDUCT USER STUDIES IN THE TARGET CONTEXT

Test with target users iteratively and refine the service until the pain points

have become become points of pleasure for customers.
1. Do people understand the service
2. Do people see the value of the service?
3. Do people understand how to use it?
4. Is the experience positive?
5. What ideas do the customers have that could improve the service?

IMPLEMENT THE EXPERIENCE

The end purpose of a blueprint is to take action and improve the journey and drive the ROI to justify the investment.
After the new service design is tested, the design team documents the new experience and creates implementation guidelines to roll out of the new service across the organization. The service blueprint is now a tool to communicate the new design.
1. Use your map for employee training/
2. Map upcoming product launches or your desired future state

MEASURE YOUR PROGRESS TOWARDS YOUR GOALS

Define ways of tracking your progress towards measurable goals. Metrics will help you measure the quality of your customer experience, now and in the future.
1. Net Promoter Score and customer loyalty measures
2. Customer satisfaction measures
3. Quantitative assessments of the customer emotions.
4. Metrics of customer effort
5. Measure of performance of each touchpoint.
6. New sales.
7. Increased loyalty and retention of customers
8. Increase in revenue per customer.
9. More sales.
10. Reduced costs
11. Better delivery processes.
12. Better quality: i
13. Increased competitiveness

Phase	PREPARE			ENTER		ACTIVITY						EXIT	REFLECT
Physical Evidence	work building	Internet computer	car	car park	building	chalkboard menu	cash register	coffee machine	table chair	computer	table chair	car park	car
Customer Actions	Decide to have a coffee	Locate coffee shop	Drive to coffee shop	Park	Enter coffee shop	Stand in line	Order	Picks up coffee	Sit down	Drink & Work	Pack up	Finish & return to car	Drive home
Line of Interaction													
Onstage Employee Actions					Greet customer		Take order	Make order	Escort to table		Ask if they need refill	Pick up empty cup	
Line of Visibility													
Backstage Employee Actions							Accounting	Order supplies				Cleans room	
Line of Internal Interaction													
Support Processes													
Opportunities													

Connecting the boxes

Single arrow

Arrows show value exchanges through touchpoints

A single arrow shows a single direction value exchange

CUSTOMER EATS MEAL

↑

WAITER BRINGS FOOD TO TABLE

Double arrow

A double arrow indicates that two parties must agree

REGISTRATION EMPLOYEE GIVES CUSTOMER PRICE OF ROOM

↕

CUSTOMER PAYS FOR ROOM

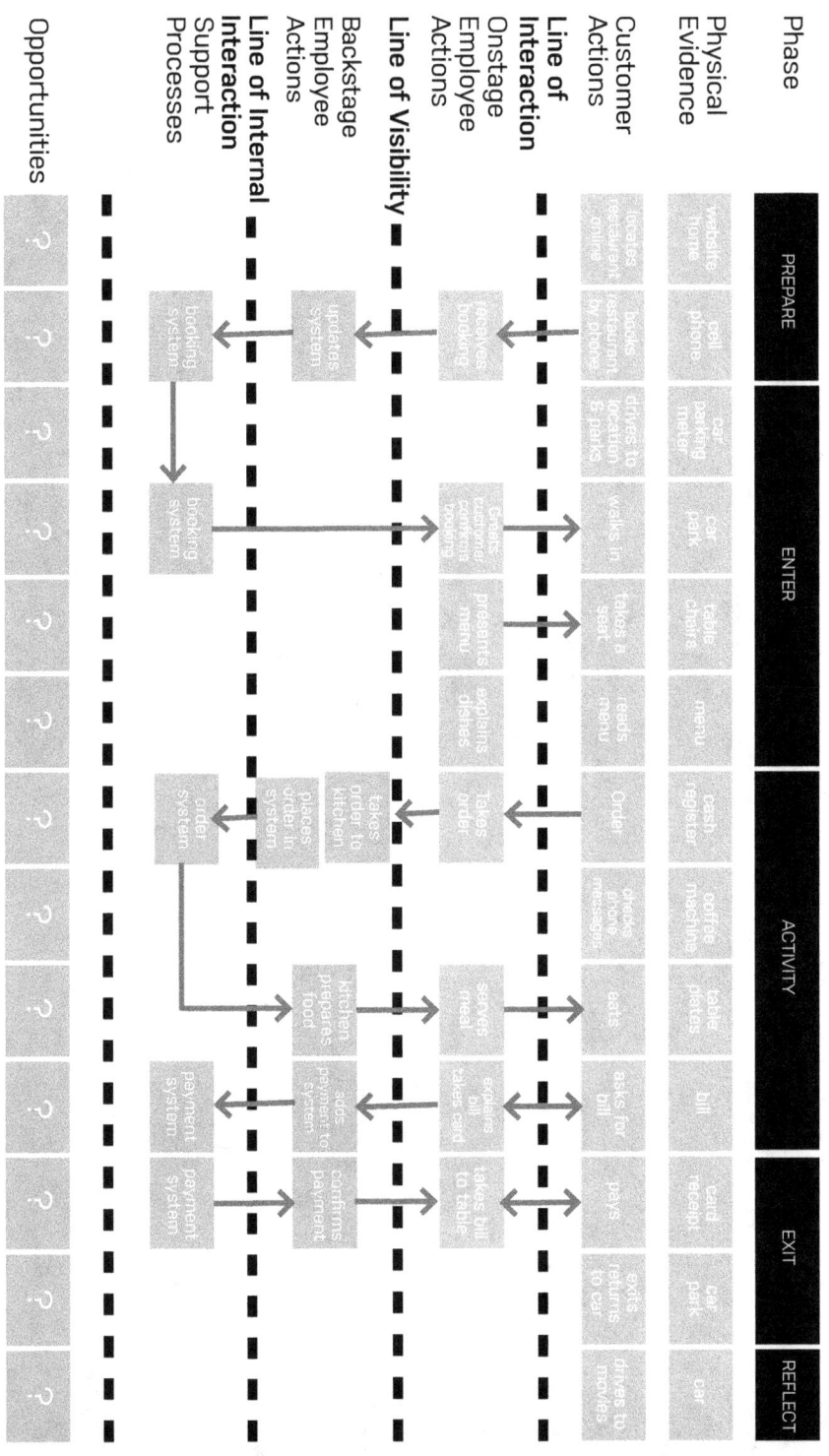

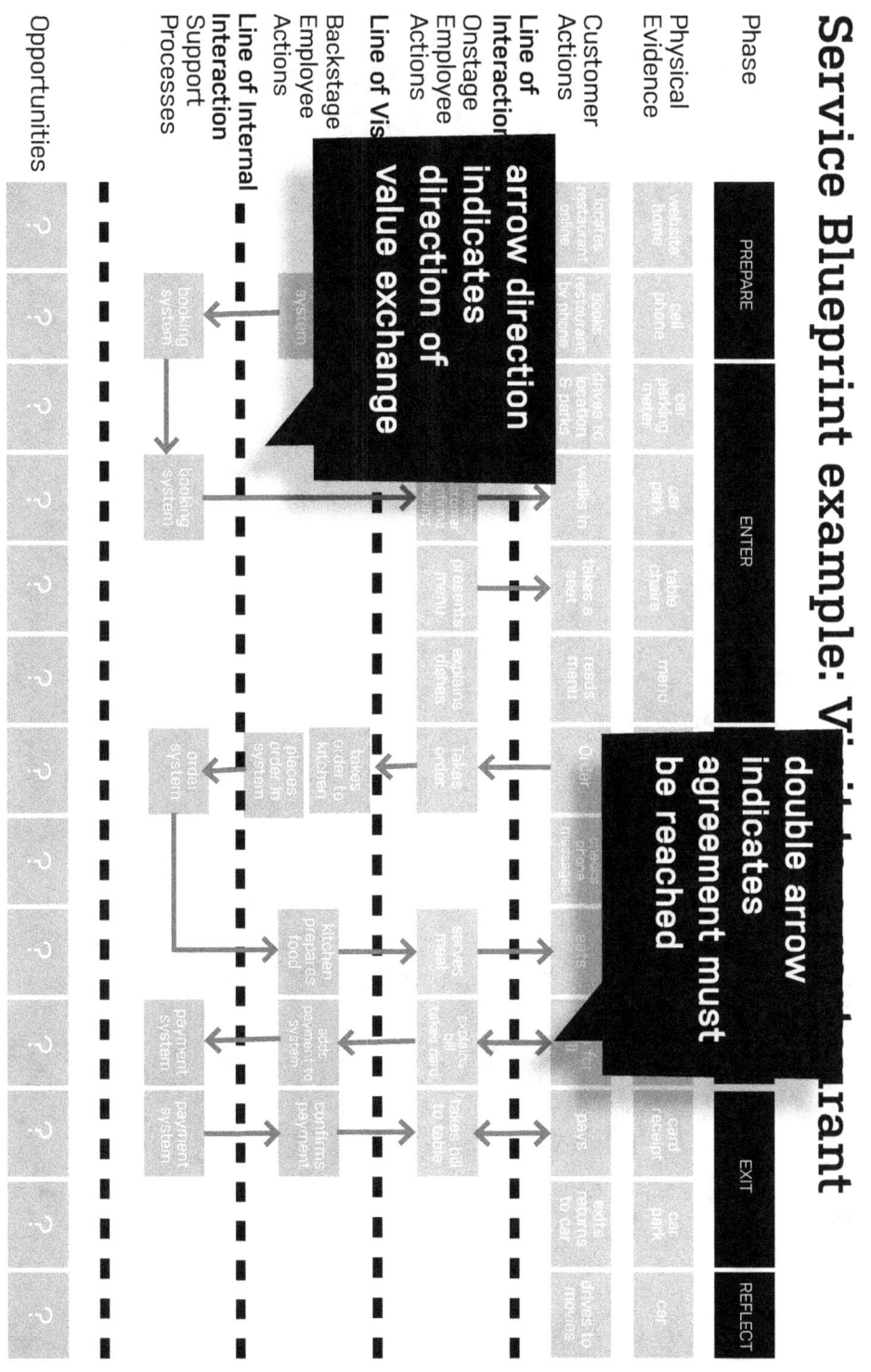

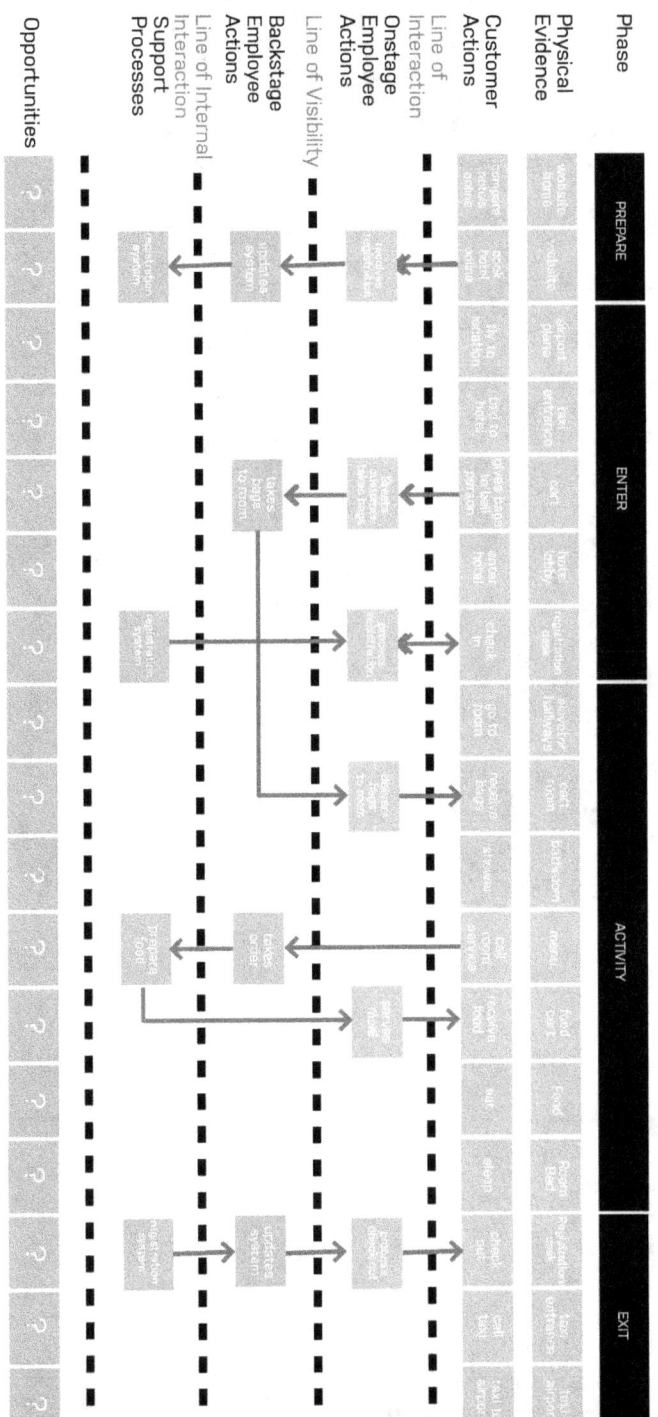

Glossary

A collection of definitions of terms often used with the mapping techniques described in this book

Glossary

ACTOR
A person involved in the creation, delivery, support, or use of a service.

ANALOGOUS SITUATIONS
An analogous situation is a situation from another area or industry that may relate to an area of focus for a design and may suggests ways to improve it.

HEURISTICS
Best practices, principles, or rules of thumb.

ARTEFACTS
Physical service touchpoints. For example the New York Underground map

BACKSTAGE/ BACKOFFICE
Backstage activities are those taken by the service delivering company employees that are not visible to the customer. Backstage actions are actions that impact customers. Backstage actions are separated from onstage service delivery by the line of visibility. Activities above the line of visibility are seen by the client while everything below it is invisible. On an aircraft, the taking of an order for a meal is an onstage or frontstage action, and the preparation of the food is a backstage action if it is not seen by the traveller.

BODYSTORMING
Prototyping method, Service situations are be acted out,for example for example at the hotel reception. The design team cast the roles, practice the situation. often with the input of end users The purpose is to prototype and test interactions to better understand and refine them.

BRAINSTORMING
Brainstorming is a group or individual creativity approach where design solutions are generated by members of the team in a collaborative session.

CHANNEL
A medium for communication or delivery. Most services use more than one channel. For example phone, email, in-store or web site.

CO DESIGN
Process in which the design team directly engages end users to assist in the design to access knowledge that is crucial to develop successful design solutions.

COLLECTIVE INTELLIGENCE
Collective intelligence is shared knowledge that comes from the collaboration of a group of people and is expressed in consensus decision making. Collective intelligence requires openness, sharing ideas, experiences and perspectives.

CONTEXT
Context is external elements that surround and influence design. These items can be physical and non-physical and cultural. The environmental context relates to the time, the day, the location, the type of place and any other physical aspect that could influence your design. The surrounding context influences the success of design.

CROSS-DISCIPLINARY
collaboration
Combines the wisdom and skills of different professional disciplines working in close and flexible collaboration. Each team member requires disciplinary empathy allowing them to work collaboratively with other discipline members. Design teams can include anthropologists, engineers, educators, doctors, lawyers, scientists, etc. in the innovative problem solving process.

CUSTOMER JOURNEY
The customer journey is a graphical representation of how the customer
perceives and experiences the service interface over time It often also shows the phases before and after the interaction with the service. A customer journey map is a tool to explore, visualize, understand and refine an end user experience.

EVIDENCE-BASED DESIGN
Evidence-based design is the approach of basing design decisions on credible research to achieve the best

possible outcomes. Evidence-based design emphasizes the importance of basing decisions on the best possible data for the best possible outcomes. The design is not based just on the designer's opinion.

EXPERIENCE PROTOTYPING

The aim of experience prototyping is to test the feasibility of the design before it is released to the public, It is the most efficient way of ensuring a product or service system will be advantageous from a human and business point of view.

FIVE WHYS

An analysis method used to uncover the root cause of a problem.

Example of the method:
A patient had the wrong leg amputated
1. Why: Patient gave consent for amputation
the night before the proposed surgery to
Registrar (who was not going to undertake
procedure).
2. Why: Amputation site marked with a biro
(wrong leg).
3. Why: Registrar unaware of hospital policy
on amputation sites being marked with a skin
pencil and with bodily part being fully visible
to Doctor.
4. Why: The department had no induction
procedures for new medical staff working in
the department.
5. Why: Because "we've never been asked to".
Root Cause Analysis Tool Kit. NHS

GROUPTHINK

Groupthink is consensus of opinion without critical reasoning or evaluation of consequences or alternatives. Employees may self-censor themselves for fear of upsetting the status quo.

HUMAN-CENTERED

An approach to design that adapts the solution to the end user through understanding the end user. The understanding is developed through engaging the end user and testing a variety of possible solutions through an iterative design process.

ITERATIVE CONSULTATIVE PROCESS
An iterative consultative process is a design process of inviting diverse stakeholders to review a design and give feedback in order to improve the design from their point of view.

ITERATIVE DESIGN PROCESS
Iterative design is the process of prototyping testing and refining a design in a series of repeated steps.

JOURNEY MAP
A visual representation of a particular person or persona's experience with a service. The experience is documented over time and often shows multiple channels.

CONTEXTUAL RESEARCH
Contextual Research is research that takes place in the real-world environment of the service, product or experience.

FRONTSTAGE/ FRONTOFFICE
These are face-to-face between customers and employees. These are separated from the customer by the line of interaction.

ENTRY POINTS
Position of access to a service, where people are able to engage the service as customers, providers, or stakeholders.

EVIDENCE
Service evidences are touch-points that represent parts of a service experience.

EXPERIENCE PROTOTYPING
Service experiences have components that are intangible, and change over time and have multiple touch-points. Services are prototyped different ways then physical products. Experience Prototype is a representation, that is designed to help us understand, explore or communicate what it feels like to engage with a product, space service or system.

EXIT POINTS
Point of disengagement of a service, by stakeholders.

LINE OF VISIBILITY
In a service blueprint this is a line that separates face to face customer employee interactions from customer employee interactions that are remote or not face to face.

MINIMUM VIABLE PRODUCT
A minimum viable product is a simple version of a new product which allows a team to learn the maximum amount about customers with the least effort. The goal of an MVP is to test fundamental business hypotheses as efficiently in the real world as possible.

NEEDS
A necessary function or condition. There are a wide variety of human needs such as food, shelter, security, affection and self fulfillment.

OUTSIDE-IN PERSPECTIVE
This is the perception that people outside of an organization have of the organization and it's products and services such as customers and other stakeholders.

PARTICIPATORY DESIGN
An approach that involves stakeholders such as cleints, end users, community members in the design process to ensure that the designb meets the needs of those it is serving as well as generating buy-in.

PERSONA
A representation of a user segment with shared needs and characteristics. In user-centered design and marketing, personas are archetypal characters that represent different user segments that might use a product or service in a similar way.

PROTOTYPE
A prototype is a model built to test a concept with end users in order to learn from. Prototyping helps understand real, working conditions rather than a theoretical conditions.

ROLEPLAY
Assign roles and act out scenarios with props and end users feedback to refine your

design.

SATISFACTION SYSTEM

The satisfaction system is the system of how the products or services satisfy the customer's needs. It includes the product or service and its related products or service. It involves understanding how related products add value to the main product. Customers are interested in the entire system beyond the individual product.

SCALE

Service design considers micro and macro scales ,detailed interactions, and holistic overviews of an experience.

SCENARIOS

A scenario is a hypothetical narrative illustrating an event or series of events. It is a method of imagining a user experience in the real world.

Use scenarios are a method of prototyping ideas in order to explore and refine them.

Scenarios are short stories about people and activities that describe typical usage and focus on goals, actions and objects.

Scenarios evoke reflection in design and provide a common reference point. Scenarios help express the requirements of the different stakeholders in a format that can be understood by the other stakeholders. They can be written, illustrated, acted or filmed. Scenario generating aims to predict
how people could act in particular situations.

SERVICE DESIGN

Design for experiences that reach people through many different touch-points, and that happen over time.
British Standard for Service Design: BS 7000 -3, BS 7000 -10,BS EN ISO 9000

Service designs can be both tangible and intangible. Service design can
involve artifacts, communication, context and behaviors. It should be consistent, easy to use and have the strategic alliance.
Gillian Hollins, Bill Hollins, Total Design: Managing The Design Process in the Service Sector

SERVICE ECOLOGY
A service ecology is a system of people, objects and the relationships between them that form a service.

System in which the service is integrated: i.e. a holistic visualisation of the service system. All the factors are gathered, analysed and visualised: politics, the economy, employees, law, societal trends, and technological development. The service ecology is thereby rendered, along with its attendant agents, processes, and relations. Mager 2009

Ultimately, sustainable service ecologies depend on a balance where the actors involved exchange value in ways that is mutually beneficial over time.
Live|work 2008

SERVICESCAPE
"the role of physical surroundings in consumption settings" and how physical environments relate to activity. Source: MJ Bitner. There are three kinds of tangible service evidence: people, process, and physical cues.

SERVQUAL
SERVQUAL is a method for measuring service quality. that was created during the 1980's SERVQUAL, quality is defined by the gap between what a customer expects and what the customer perceives. SERVQUAL breaks service quality down to five basic dimensions; reliability, assurance, tangibles, empathy and responsiveness,

SENSUALISATION
Sensualisation is the approach of considering the experience to be the total of the individual experiences of the five senses.

SERVICE
An exchange of value, involving tangible and intangible elements A system of products spaces human interactions and experiences.

SERVICE SYSTEM
The ecology of relationships, interactions, and contexts of a service. channels, resources, and touchpoints, internal and external, that facilitate the

delivering of a service.

STAKEHOLDER
A person, group, or organization directly or indirectly involved or affected by a product, service or experience.

Stakeholders include any individuals who are influence by the design. Specifically, the project team, end users, strategic partners, customers, alliances, vendors and senior management are project stakeholders

Possible stakeholders
1. Employees
2. Shareholders
3. Government
4. Customers
5. Suppliers
6. Prospective employees
7. Local communities
8. Global Community
9. Schools
10. Future generations
11. Ex-employees
12. Creditors
13. Professional associations
14. Competitors
15. Investors
16. Prospective customers
17. Communities

Why involve stakeholders?
1. Stakeholder analysis helps to identify:
2. Stakeholder interests
3. Ways to influence other stakeholders
4. Risks
5. Key people to be informed during the project
6. Negative stakeholders as well as their adverse effects on the project

SWIMLANES
An approach used in service design involving arranging descriptive boxes into rows (the "swim lanes") to provide additional context about how the steps are related. Work flow is represented over time and is usually read from left to right

REFRAMING
Reframe to create different perspectives and new ideas.

How to reframe:
Define the problem that you would like to address.
There is more than one way of looking at a problem. You could also define this problem in another way as."
What if a male or female used it?

351

What if it was used in China or Argentina?
"The underlying reason for the problem is."
"I think that the best solution is."
"You could compare this problem to the problem of."
"Another, different way of thinking about it is"

STAKEHOLDER MAP

A visual representation of the stakeholders in a service and the relationships between them.

SERVICE DESIGN

Service design is a form of conceptual design which involves the activity of planning and organizing people, infrastructure, communication and material components of a service in order to improve its quality and the interaction between service provider and customers.
Service design - Wikipedia, the free encyclopedia, https://en.wikipedia.org/wiki/Service_design (accessed March 20, 2016).

SOCIAL DESIGN

Design done for the social good or top positively impact society.

STRATEGIC DESIGN

Design that focuses on big picture systematic problems in order to increase an organization's future innovative and competitive advantage.

STORYBOARDING

A storyboard is a graphic sequence of illustrations, words or images for the purpose of communicating a user scenario or experience. Storyboarding, was developed at Walt Disney during the early 1930s

TOUCHPOINT
TOUCHPOINTS

A touchpoint is any point of contact between a customer and the provider of a service, product or experience. A touchpoint is where a potential customer or customer comes in contact with your brand before, during and after a transaction.

Identifying your touchpoints is an important step toward creating a journey map or a service blueprint. Each touchpoint is an opportunity to create a better customer experience. A touchpoint can be a physical, virtual or human point of interaction. Chris Risdon from Adaptive Path defines touchpoints in this way. 'A touchpoint is a point of interaction involving a specific human need in a specific time and place.' Laura Patterson of VisionEdge defines a touchpoint as " any customer interaction or encounter that can influence the customer's perception of your product, service, or brand."

Touchpoints classified as three types:
1. Static: such as packaging or an advertisement.
2. Interactive: a website or a kiosk.
3. Human: such as a sales person

Mapping touchpoints is usually started during the process of creating a map by using post-it notes listing touchpoints at each stage of customer activity. A touchpoint inventory is a list of every way a customer can engage your company.

A successful touchpoint strategy should be linked to the organization's goals. Work cross-functionally.
1. Clearly define your organization goals.
2. Define your market audience.
3. Map the Physical Evidence of Service
4. Clarifying the roles played by the each touchpoint.
5. How does each touchpoint contribute to support the value of the brand?
6. Identify Opportunities to improve the effectiveness of each touchpoint.

Make a list of all of those touchpoints that you know exist.
Define the purpose of each touchpoint. Ask you customers which touchpoints work best and poorly from their perspective. Some questions to ask when building your maps:
1. Analyze why each touchpoint exists from a business perspective.
2. Ask which customer need each touchpoint serves.
3. What value is each providing to your audience
4. Who is responsible in your organization for each touchpoint?
5. Can you improve each touchpoint?
6. Are there redundant or

duplicated touch points?
7. How does each touchpoint interact with others?
8. How do touchpoints support your brand promise?

EXAMPLES OF TOUCHPOINTS

1. Advertising
2. Telephone
3. Social media
4. Banners
5. Trade shows
6. Networking
7. Signage
8. Blogs
9. Word of mouth
10. Direct mail
11. Public relations
12. Websites
13. Newsletters
14. Packaging
15. Emails
16. Proposals
17. Employees
18. Products
19. Billboards
20. Business cards
21. Web banners
22. Exhibits
23. Letterheads
24. Customer service rep
25. Brochure
26. Invoice
27. Multi-brand retail
28. Brochure
29. Flier
30. Magazine
31. Annual report
32. Newspaper
33. Catalog
34. Promotions
35. Word of mouth
36. Reviews
37. Employees
38. Space
39. Amenities
40. External Partners
41. Physical devices, buildings, website,
42. Help center
43. Music (in a store)
44. Temperature (in the mall)
45. Smell (popcorn at the movie)

UNMET NEEDS

Six principles that will ensure a design is compatible with user needs:
The design is based upon an explicit understanding of users, tasks and environments.
Users are involved throughout design and development.
The design is driven and refined by user-centered evaluation.
The process is iterative.
The design addresses the whole user experience.
The design team includes

multidisciplinary skills and perspectives.

Some Questions to ask:
Who are the users?
What are the users' tasks and goals?
What are the users' experience levels?
What functions do the users need from the design?
What information will be needed by end-users?,
In what form do they need it?
How do users think the design should work?

USER-CENTERED DESIGN
Design that responds to user needs that is developed through engaging and understanding the point of view of users.

USER PROFILING
Based on research of user groups develop different character profiles to represent your users. These are also called personas.

VALUE EXCHANGE
A service provider makes a promise to the service recipient in exchange for some form of value. The movement of value from the service provider to the recipient is the value exchange.

VANITY METRICS
Data that make you feel good, but is not very useful or actionable such as new users gained per day or number of downloads. Vanity metrics do not reflect the key drivers of a business.

WAYFINDING
Methods for understanding and navigating within an environment. knowing where your desired location is, and knowing how to get there from your present location.

WICKED PROBLEM
A wicked problem is a problem with contradictory, and changing requirements. The term 'wicked' is used, not in the sense of evil but rather its resistance to resolution.

Wicked problems are characterized by:
1. The solution depends on how the problem is framed.
2. Stakeholders have different world views and frames for

understanding the problem.
3. The constraints of the problem and the resources needed to solve it change over time.
4. The problem is never solved definitively.
wicked problem : definition of wicked problem and synonyms http://brevard.ifas.ufl.edu/communities/pdf/SF_Wicked_Issues_Background_Defined_ (accessed March 20, 2016).

WIREFRAME

A website wireframe, is a skeletal framework representing the elements of a website. The wireframe depicts the page layout and shows how the elements work functionally. It focuses on what a web interface does, not
what it looks like. Wireframes can be sketches or computer images.

Index

Index

Symbols

635 83
.X 110, 123, 125, 145, 164, 167, 168, 169, 171

A

Activities 81, 111, 113, 115, 133, 139, 165, 173, 177, 177, 179, 181, 181, 190, 212, 218, 231, 243, 256, 271, 275, 276, 317
Activity 21, 26, 91, 102, 121, 139, 141, 163, 167, 190, 256, 275, 293, 320, 328, 353
Activity 139, 141, 163, 167, 293
Actors 177, 189
Actors 177
Adapt 175
Adhesive notes 267
Affinities 159
Affinity 111, 201
Affinity diagram 111, 201
Age 27
Age 52, 53, 59, 212, 218, 230, 232, 234, 236, 238, 248, 249, 250
Agreement 103, 129, 137, 139, 141, 142, 149, 153, 261, 339
Allport, Gordon 117
Ambiguity 21

Analysis 119, 185
Analytical 19
Analytical thinking 23
Analyze 51
Analyze 22, 71, 73, 83, 83, 87, 87, 110, 113, 115, 119, 137, 155, 161, 163, 164, 165, 167, 168, 169, 170, 173, 174, 174, 177, 177, 256, 293, 353
Appearance 175
Archer, bruce 20
Association 202
At&t 87
Attributes of design thinking 21
Audio 129

B

Back-casting 87
Backcasting 87
Bavelas, Alex 179
  115, 121, 179
Beginner's mind 267
Behave 71, 97, 168
Behavior 110, 139, 149, 163, 164, 165, 167, 168, 169, 170, 171
Behavior 110, 139, 149, 163, 164, 165, 167, 168, 170, 171
Benchmark 27
Bernd rohrbach 83

Blank 117, 205
Block 35, 183, 205
Blueprint 38, 221, 285, 300, 301, 307, 333, 352
Brainstorm 78, 79, 81, 174, 272
Brainstorm 29, 29, 89, 89, 99, 99, 181, 181, 183, 183, 211, 211, 256, 283, 288, 330
Brainstorming 21, 77, 78, 83, 89, 159, 174, 185
Brainstorming 20, 77, 83, 89, 159, 174, 185, 377
Brainstorming: method 635 83
Brainstorming: nhk method 77
Brand 75, 93, 187, 258, 293, 352, 353, 354
Brown, tim 20
Buchanan, richard 20
Building 51, 279, 291, 318, 320, 322, 323, 324, 326, 335, 353
Business 23, 26, 187
Butcher paper 267

C

Camera 23, 35, 71, 78, 79, 97, 111, 113, 115, 117, 121, 129, 139, 141, 142, 143, 145, 147, 149, 151, 153, 157, 161, 163, 171, 179, 181, 185, 189, 190, 269
Camera 95

Cards 105, 111, 183
Car park 279, 323, 328
C-box 89
Challenges 67, 69, 71, 73, 87, 91, 93, 95, 97, 99, 101, 105, 107, 109, 119, 129, 159, 174, 177, 185, 211, 217
Channel 271, 278, 295
Channel 272
Channels 12, 45, 257, 258, 271, 272, 294, 300, 304
Charette 95
Choosing a technique 78
Cluster 183
Clustering 205
Coffee 35, 79, 94, 275, 278, 280, 282, 284, 286, 288, 291, 318, 320, 322, 324, 326, 328, 335, 337, 339
Collaboration 37, 265
Collaboration 26
Collaborative
Collins, allan 159
Color 159, 204, 206
Combine 175
Communications 187
Competitive products 27
Complex 26, 181
Concept 105, 113, 115, 177
Concepts 89, 95, 174, 177
Concepts 23, 89, 123, 177
Conflict 25
Connections 26, 35, 37

Consensus 89
Constraints 27
Constructive 21
Context 15, 15, 21, 21, 21, 23, 23, 26, 26, 27, 27, 69, 71, 73, 91, 95, 97, 101, 109, 110, 110, 115, 115, 115, 119, 121, 121, 121, 121, 129, 133, 133, 133, 133, 133, 135, 135, 135, 137, 137, 142, 142, 142, 145, 145, 147, 147, 147, 151, 151, 155, 155, 161, 161, 163, 163, 163, 164, 164, 165, 165, 167, 167, 168, 168, 169, 169, 170, 170, 171, 171, 175, 177, 179, 179, 179, 189, 256, 265
Context 15, 23, 110, 115, 121, 123, 129, 133, 135, 137, 142, 147, 155, 161, 163, 164, 165, 167, 170, 177, 179, 256, 287, 331
Contextual 91, 129, 133, 135, 142, 143
Contextual inquiry 129, 133
Contextual interviews 129, 133, 143
Contextual laddering 135
Conversation 77, 79, 81, 129, 131, 145, 151, 189, 267
Covert 164
Create a strategy 78

Creative class 20
Creative thinking 23
Creativity 20
Creativity methods 20
Cross, nigel 20
Cultural 26
Culture 27, 123
Curedale, rob 376, 377, 378
Curiosity 21
Customer 7, 12, 13, 19, 21, 31, 33, 38, 39, 45, 51, 73, 75, 85, 121, 125, 135, 221, 225, 229, 231, 239, 243, 251, 256, 257, 258, 259, 261, 262, 263, 267, 269, 271, 273, 275, 276, 279, 280, 281, 282, 283, 284, 289, 290, 291, 293, 294, 301, 315, 317, 318, 320, 324, 327, 330, 333, 335, 337, 339, 352, 353
Customer experience 12, 39, 225, 256, 257, 258, 261, 263, 269, 271, 289, 290, 293, 294, 317, 333, 352
Customers 8, 13, 21, 31, 45, 47, 51, 55, 75, 85, 221, 256, 258, 261, 265, 269, 281, 287, 289, 293, 294, 300, 327, 333, 353

D

Data 47, 51, 67, 69, 71, 73, 110, 111, 113, 115, 117, 121, 135, 137, 145, 155, 161, 163, 164, 165, 167, 168, 169, 170, 173, 187, 199, 200, 202, 204, 225, 256, 263, 273
David kelley 20
Defer judgment 81
Delft 89
Deliverables 27
Democratic 89
Design charette 95
Design methods 20
Design problem 89
Design process 18, 99, 107, 115, 177, 183, 209
Design thinking 19, 26, 27
Design thinking 19, 21, 23, 26, 376, 377
Design thinking process 27
Diagram 183, 201
Dialog. 189
Differentiation 29, 185
Digital camera 23, 117, 121, 181, 190, 269
Director 189
Discussion 83, 177
Disney, walt 181
Divergent 89
Diversity 25, 26, 31

Diversity 25
Document 27, 29, 129
Doing 91, 221, 256
Dot voting 98, 99
Dot voting 209, 211
Draft 269, 271
Dry erase markers 23, 267
Dry-erase markers 77, 87, 95, 159, 177, 185

E

Editing-in-the-camera 189
Einfühlungsvermögen 15
Eisenhower 123
E-mail 137
Emotional 293
Emotional journey map 293
Empathy 15, 21, 113
Empathy 15, 21, 23, 25, 26, 51, 101, 113, 213, 217, 221, 249
Employees 7, 31, 57, 77, 157, 157, 157, 301
Encourage wild ideas 81
Engineering 18, 265
Environmental 26
Environmental 23, 26
Ethnography 51
Evidence 272, 291, 318, 320, 322, 324, 326, 328, 335, 337, 339, 353
Expectations 13

Experience 12, 19, 26, 27, 31, 39, 73, 75, 85, 91, 93, 109, 119, 121, 177, 181, 189, 225, 251, 256, 257, 258, 261, 262, 263, 265, 269, 271, 272, 273, 275, 287, 288, 289, 290, 293, 294, 317, 333, 352, 382
Experience design 20
Experience prototyping 287, 331
Experiences 13, 52, 53, 93, 99, 105, 119, 139, 149, 151, 153, 174, 177, 179, 181, 238, 256, 257, 258, 261, 262, 293, 301

F

Facilitating 79
Failure 22, 258, 283, 330
Faste, Rolf 20
Feasibility 89
Feedback 21, 29, 119, 161, 181, 183, 256, 271, 287
Feel 249, 250
Feeling 256, 272, 284
Findings 69, 265
Flexibility 26, 123
Focus 7, 12, 21, 22, 57, 93, 115, 117, 119, 121, 151, 175, 177, 256, 293, 301
Focus 61, 81, 119, 133, 377

Focus groups 119, 121
Focus groups 377
Frame 23, 89, 95, 123, 129, 177
Framework 87, 177
Fresh eyes 21
Frustrations 55
Functionality 89
Future 18, 21, 38, 87, 177, 191, 258, 261, 271, 290, 333
Future 13, 38, 231, 241, 269, 315
Future scenarios 87

G

Gain 25, 25, 51, 51, 71, 71, 145, 145, 164, 164, 181, 181, 185, 185, 247
Gaver, bill 111
Gender, 27
Goal 87
Goal 143
Goal 12, 221, 233, 262, 307
Goals 31, 43, 45, 51, 55, 69, 87, 91, 97, 133, 168, 168, 169, 169, 175, 177, 191, 212, 218, 261, 290, 333, 353
Goals 43, 51, 133, 177
Goal statement 221, 233, 262, 307
Gray, dave 217

Group 27, 33, 37, 42, 43, 45, 49, 51, 55, 57, 73, 77, 78, 79, 81, 83, 89, 99, 119, 141, 145, 147, 174, 183, 189, 204, 209, 211, 265, 267, 382
Groups 19, 27, 35, 42, 45, 49, 55, 59, 77, 97, 119, 121, 127, 139, 141, 143, 183, 185, 202, 204, 206, 208, 265
Groupthink 99, 211

H

Handouts 267
Hasso Plattner Institute Of Design 81
Headers 204, 206
Hear 15, 15, 26, 101, 245
Hermagoras of Temnos 102, 190
Hierarchy 27, 79, 183, 209
Hierarchy 183
High fidelity prototype 25
History 197
Holistic 21
Holtzblatt 133, 142
Hospital 57, 269
Hotel 275, 277, 279, 328
Human centered design 20
Humphrey, albert 185

I

Idea 17, 21, 25, 29, 79, 81, 83, 89, 99, 105, 159, 211, 300
Ideas 19, 21, 23, 25, 29, 77, 78, 79, 81, 83, 89, 99, 105, 126, 147, 171, 174, 181, 185, 187, 191, 209, 211, 267, 287, 293, 330, 333
Ideation 209, 258, 380
Imitate 175
Implementation 87
Improvement. 261
Information 1, 17, 23, 37, 57, 67, 78, 95, 102, 103, 110, 111, 117, 129, 131, 133, 135, 143, 147, 159, 163, 164, 165, 167, 168, 170, 171, 185, 190, 379, 381
Inhibition 99, 211
Innovate 2, 123
Innovation 31, 81, 89, 123, 125, 127, 382
Innovation 25, 89, 125, 126
Innovation diagnostic 123
Innovative 23, 26, 89, 125, 127, 174
Insight 51, 105
Insights 23, 27, 71, 89, 91, 95, 109, 110, 113, 115, 117, 123, 129, 133, 139, 142, 147, 151, 163, 164, 165, 167, 168, 169, 170, 173, 177,

365

Index

179, 258, 271, 293
In store 271
Instructions 267
Intellectual property 29, 78
Intent 23, 27, 95
Interact 121
Interaction 189
Interactions 12, 37, 105, 177, 189, 212, 218, 258, 261, 294
Interview 27, 117, 129, 131, 133, 135, 137, 139, 141, 142, 143, 145, 147, 149, 151, 153, 155
Interview 27, 117, 129, 133, 135, 137, 139, 141, 142, 143, 147, 149, 153, 155
Interviews 51, 93, 129, 133, 142, 143, 147, 149, 153, 256
Interviews 67, 109, 135, 377, 377
Investment 87, 105, 127, 175, 187
Iteration 29
Iterative 21
Iterative 21

J

Journey 7, 38, 39, 256, 261, 269, 293, 294, 333, 352
Journey map 38, 39, 261, 293, 352
Journey map 272
Judgement 15

K

Kahn, Herman 177
Kimbell, lucy 20
Kipling, rudyard 102

L

Laddering 135
Lane 272, 281, 330
Lanes 261, 271
Lawson, bryan 20
Lego 157
Low fidelity prototyping 105

M

Malinowski, Bronisław 110, 165, 169
Management 126, 157, 265, 267, 269
Manufacture 29
Manzini, Ezio 20
Map 11, 13, 38, 39, 89, 109, 159, 183, 218, 256, 258, 259, 261, 262, 267, 269, 271, 273, 275, 285, 290, 293, 294, 300, 301, 319, 330, 333, 352, 353

Map 89, 159, 183, 256, 293
Mapping 183, 221, 257, 261, 269, 271, 343
Maps 45, 159, 183, 217, 256, 271, 289, 353
Market 127, 187
Martin, roger 20
Masking tape 267
Materials 29, 105, 175
Matthews, scott 217
Mckim, Robert 20
Mead, Margaret 110, 165, 169
Meaning 151, 171, 173

Merton, Robert K. 119

Meta design 20
Method 21, 89, 99, 102, 103, 159, 174, 183
Method 51, 67, 69, 71, 73, 77, 83, 87, 89, 91, 93, 95, 97, 99, 101, 105, 107, 109, 119, 123, 129, 159, 174, 177, 181, 185, 189, 190, 211, 217, 256
Method bank 157
Methods 1, 19, 25, 45, 73, 78, 93, 97, 109, 110, 113, 117, 119, 121, 123, 135, 147, 157, 163, 164, 165, 170, 174, 261, 265, 287, 376
Metrics 290, 333
Mind map 159
Mindset 21

Misuse 177
Misuse scenarios 177
Mitchell 183
Mobile 37, 161, 161, 161, 267, 271, 294
Mobile diary study 161
Moderator 77, 87, 89, 99, 119, 145, 174, 211
Moderator 119, 201, 227, 239, 267, 313
Moderator 201, 227, 237, 267, 311
Moments of truth 258
Monteiro, Robert A. 121, 179

N

Narrator 189
Need 26, 27, 37, 51, 73, 78, 97, 101, 105, 125, 131, 153, 189, 191, 263, 291, 324, 335, 353
Need 26, 27, 51, 87, 105, 153, 191
Needs 12, 13, 21, 25, 26, 57, 73, 85, 91, 109, 113, 115, 121, 126, 173, 179, 209, 212, 218, 258, 283, 300, 330
Needs 117, 191, 249, 250, 272
Nelson, Doreen 173
New products 6
Non judgmental 21

367

Non verbal 15, 161
Norman, don 20
Note 89, 99, 171, 204, 206, 211, 275
Notes 77, 87, 89, 95, 105, 129, 174, 183, 185, 256

O

Objectives 29, 29, 110, 110, 163, 164, 164, 165, 165, 167, 167, 170, 170, 261
Observation 110, 115, 121, 163, 164, 165, 167, 168, 169, 170, 171, 179
Observation 51, 110, 115, 163, 164, 165, 167, 170, 179
Observation: structured 170
Observe 15, 115, 121, 133, 142, 147, 164, 165, 167, 168, 171, 179
Observe 15, 22, 27, 97, 101, 115, 121, 129, 133, 142, 147, 165, 167, 168, 179, 221
Observer 110, 121, 163, 164, 165, 168, 170, 171
Offering 23
One-on-one 129, 133, 135, 142, 147
Open mindset 21
Opportunities 27, 39, 123, 181, 185, 187, 256, 258, 259, 261, 271, 283, 288, 294, 301, 330
Opportunity 22, 258, 352
Organization 87, 123, 127, 159, 185
Organizational 123
Osborn, alex 20
Outcomes 87

P

Pain 246, 276, 278, 279, 280, 282, 284, 286, 288, 327
Pain points 39, 212, 218, 273, 286, 287, 328, 331
Paper 77, 83, 105, 159, 293
Participants 31, 35, 37, 78, 79, 81, 83, 83, 99, 99, 110, 111, 113, 115, 117, 119, 121, 135, 145, 151, 161, 163, 164, 165, 167, 168, 169, 170, 173, 211, 211, 267
Pens 67, 71, 77, 78, 83, 87, 97, 110, 111, 113, 115, 117, 121, 129, 137, 139, 141, 142, 143, 145, 147, 149, 151, 153, 155, 159, 163, 165, 167, 168, 169, 170, 171, 174, 177, 181, 185, 190, 293
People 15, 23, 25, 26, 27, 29, 31, 32, 33, 37, 42, 43, 45, 49, 51, 57, 71, 73, 77, 78, 79, 89, 91, 93, 97, 101,

110, 113, 119, 126, 129,
133, 137, 141, 142, 143,
145, 155, 161, 163, 164,
165, 167, 168, 170, 171,
174, 177, 179, 189, 190,
212, 218, 256, 258, 261,
263, 265, 267, 269, 287,
293, 304, 333
Perceptual map 89, 259
Performance 27
Permission 168, 169
Person 17, 18, 33, 42, 45, 49,
52, 53, 81, 83, 91, 93,
109, 131, 147, 189, 209,
328, 353
Persona 43, 43, 51, 51, 51, 52,
52, 53, 53, 53, 55, 55,
55, 55, 57, 57, 57, 57, 57,
57, 59, 59, 61, 61, 75, 75,
217, 217, 218, 218, 230,
230, 232, 232, 234, 234,
236, 236, 248, 248, 261,
261, 271, 271, 273, 273,
293, 293, 293, 294, 294,
294, 295, 295, 301, 301
Persona 52, 52, 61, 61, 212,
212, 218, 218, 230, 230,
232, 232, 234, 234, 236,
236, 238, 238, 248, 248,
249, 249, 250, 250, 292,
292, 292
Personal inventory 173
Personas 51, 55, 57, 111, 189,
256, 258, 269
Personas 43, 51, 111, 177, 256
Perspective 15, 69, 101, 258,
261, 267, 269, 271, 317,
353
Peter rowe 20
Phase 18, 21, 89, 209
Phases 89
Photograph 77, 267, 285
Photographs 151
Physical evidence 277, 321
Plattner, Hasso 81
Pleasure 287, 333
Point of view 26, 115, 129, 133,
142, 147, 179, 256, 293
Points of failure 283, 330
Points of view 55, 97
Positive 183, 256, 271, 273,
287, 317, 333
Post it notes 35, 77, 183, 205,
271, 353
Post-it-notes 71, 77, 77, 78, 87,
87, 95, 95, 97, 105, 105,
174, 174, 183, 185, 185,
189, 293
Post-it voting 81
Print 159, 271, 294
Problem 18, 21, 21, 21, 21, 21,
21, 22, 23, 23, 25, 25,
27, 27, 31, 69, 77, 77, 77,
77, 78, 79, 85, 89, 89, 91,
102, 102, 103, 107, 174,
174, 174, 177, 177, 191, 261

Problems 17, 18, 19, 21, 22, 73, 105, 139, 181, 191, 225, 256, 263
Process 17, 18, 19, 21, 23, 25, 27, 29, 39, 75, 83, 99, 103, 107, 113, 115, 117, 123, 126, 141, 151, 175, 177, 181, 183, 209, 221, 269, 301, 328, 353, 376
Product 6, 11, 13, 25, 25, 29, 29, 29, 31, 43, 43, 45, 51, 51, 55, 57, 61, 73, 75, 91, 93, 127, 127, 129, 129, 133, 135, 139, 142, 147, 174, 174, 174, 175, 175, 175, 175, 175, 175, 175, 175, 175, 175, 175, 175, 175, 175, 175, 175, 175, 175, 175, 175, 175, 175, 175, 175, 175, 175, 177, 177, 179, 185, 185, 187, 187, 257, 258, 261, 269, 290, 293, 333, 352, 353, 382, 382, 382
Product 25, 29, 43, 51, 129, 133, 135, 139, 142, 147, 174, 175, 177, 179, 185, 187, 293
Props 189, 189, 189
Prototype 25, 29
Prototype 25, 29
Prototype 29
Prototypes 25, 29

Q

Quadrants 89
Qualitative 27, 123
Quantitative 27, 123
Quantitative 73, 309, 333
Questions 15, 69, 73, 78, 101, 102, 105, 117, 119, 127, 131, 137, 141, 143, 147, 149, 151, 153, 155, 164, 171, 174, 175, 185, 187, 190, 191, 263, 353
Questions 129, 137, 139, 141, 142, 143, 145, 147, 149, 151, 153, 190

R

Radcliff-Brown 110, 165, 169
Rause, William 20
Rearrange 99, 211
Refine 29, 177, 181
Refine 29, 91, 99, 139, 181, 211, 277, 319
Refinement 89
Refreshments 79
Relationship 129, 183
Relationships 159, 183
Research 23, 27, 37, 51, 55, 67, 69, 71, 73, 97, 107, 113, 117, 119, 121, 129, 143, 145, 164, 168, 169, 173, 187, 203, 225, 235, 256, 263,

265, 267, 273, 279, 293, 309, 382
Research 32, 33, 63, 67, 69, 73, 93, 119, 131, 225, 277, 293, 319, 377
Research goals 168, 169
Resources 125, 126, 141, 175, 175, 175, 187, 187, 256, 258
Resources 110, 111, 113, 115, 117, 121, 129, 137, 139, 141, 142, 143, 145, 147, 149, 151, 153, 155, 157, 161, 163, 164, 165, 167, 168, 169, 170, 171, 173, 179, 293
Resources 23, 51, 67, 69, 71, 77, 83, 87, 93, 95, 97, 99, 105, 109, 159, 174, 177, 181, 185, 189, 190, 217
Revenue 7, 333
Risks 26, 27, 169
Rittel, Horst 20
Robert Mckim 20
Rohrbach, Bernd 83
Rolf Faste 20
Room 77, 83, 275, 279, 288, 291, 328, 335
Rowe, peter 19
Royal college of art 111

S

Sachichi Toyoda 103

Satisfaction 7, 333
Say and do 245
Scamper 174
Scamper 174
Scenario 177, 271
Scenario 177
Scenarios 27, 87, 175, 177
Schon, Donal 20
Scope 21, 27, 78, 177, 231, 243, 271, 317
Scope 27, 177
Secondary research 27
See 26, 245
Seeing 26
Segment 51
Segment 12, 221, 229, 233, 239, 262, 307, 315
Separate 22, 271, 275, 330
Service 8, 13, 19, 29, 29, 32, 38, 39, 43, 45, 51, 57, 61, 73, 75, 91, 93, 94, 139, 174, 177, 185, 257, 258, 261, 269, 271, 275, 277, 279, 287, 300, 301, 307, 330, 331, 333, 352, 353, 354
Service 20, 32, 32, 33, 33, 43, 45, 51, 94, 139, 174, 177, 185, 299, 299, 301, 305, 337, 339, 353, 353, 377
Service design 20, 377
Services 26, 177, 187
Sharpies 35, 267

Index

Shoshin 79
Simon, Herbet 20
Simple 25
Smart phone 189
Smell 245, 249, 250, 354
Social 52, 53
Space 23, 37, 81, 95, 250
Stage 59, 79, 177, 212, 218, 275, 278, 280, 281, 282, 284, 286, 327, 330, 353
Stakeholder 57, 57, 103, 123, 123, 183, 183, 269, 269, 281, 281, 327, 327
Stakeholder 229, 241, 269, 315
Stakeholder map 103, 183
Stakeholders 27, 27, 27, 29, 29, 51, 57, 102, 102, 107, 123, 123, 177, 183, 183, 183, 183, 183, 183, 183, 183, 183, 183, 190, 256, 261, 265, 269, 271, 272, 301
Stakeholders 27, 29, 95, 183
Stakeholders 229
Step 18, 87, 123, 135, 275, 352
Story 102, 177, 181, 293
Storyboard 115
Storyboards 177, 180, 181
Storytelling 142
Strategic 75
Strategic 123
Strategies 87

Strategy 27, 123
Strengths 184, 187, 197
Strickland, Rachel 173
Structured 170
Structured 83, 129, 133, 142, 147, 149
Subject 97, 113, 131, 137, 143, 151, 153, 155, 173
Subjects 71, 73, 110, 113, 115, 117, 131, 147, 164, 168, 179, 265
Sub-journeys 269
Substitute 25, 175
Success 15, 21, 31, 55, 87, 101, 103, 212, 218, 261
Superheaders 209
Suppliers 265
Swimlane 272
Swot 185, 189
Swot analysis 185, 189
Sympathy 15
Systems 11, 300

T

Table 23, 83, 99, 119, 211, 271, 275, 278, 280, 282, 284, 286, 288, 291, 318, 320, 322, 324, 326, 335, 337, 339
Tablet 61, 271
Tacit knowledge 129, 133, 142, 143

Talk 125, 137, 173, 221
Target audience 221, 233, 262, 307
Task 181
Tasks 105, 129, 133, 137, 139, 141, 142, 143, 145, 147, 149, 151, 153, 177, 190
Tassoul, Marc 89
Taste 245, 249, 250
Team 19, 23, 25, 27, 31, 32, 33, 37, 47, 55, 77, 78, 79, 81, 83, 89, 99, 103, 105, 121, 174, 177, 179, 183, 205, 208, 211, 245, 256, 265, 275, 301, 333, 379
Team 25, 26, 201, 227, 237, 265, 311, 377
Team members 25
Teams 21, 26, 126, 382
Technique 55, 77, 78, 103, 111, 121, 135, 153, 174, 185, 300, 301
Techniques 97, 256, 343
Technologies 123, 187
Technology 18, 23, 26, 161, 265, 269
Telephone 155
Test 18, 25, 29, 110, 164, 165, 167, 170
The environment 81
Themes 168, 169, 209, 267
Think 37, 181, 212, 218, 230, 232, 234, 236, 238, 248, 249, 250
Think and feel 245
Thinking 13, 17, 18, 19, 20, 21, 23, 27, 81, 99, 211, 256, 258, 272, 273
Time 21, 37, 47, 67, 77, 78, 79, 81, 89, 91, 103, 110, 113, 115, 117, 131, 137, 139, 143, 161, 163, 164, 165, 167, 168, 169, 170, 171, 177, 181, 189, 190, 221, 231, 243, 245, 256, 271, 275, 282, 284, 286, 288, 293, 301, 317, 353, 379, 381, 382
Titchener, E.B. 15
Title card 189
Tools 26, 37, 131, 261
Touch 117
Touchpoint 75, 271, 333, 352, 353, 354
Touchpoint 353
Touchpoints 93, 261, 278, 294, 336, 352, 353, 354
Toyota 103
Tripod 269
Trust 95
TV 61, 271, 328

U

Understand 12, 15, 21, 26, 45, 47, 93, 97, 101, 105, 115, 171, 173, 191, 256, 261,

373

267, 273, 287, 333
Understanding 6, 12, 15, 21, 25, 91, 97, 101, 102, 153, 179, 185, 261, 293, 294
Unmet 126
Unstructured 153
User 19, 21, 23, 27, 29, 33, 43, 51, 55, 57, 73, 91, 93, 95, 105, 129, 133, 135, 139, 142, 147, 173, 179, 181, 189, 209, 269
User 123, 129
User centered design 20
User needs 21, 179, 209
Users 19, 23, 37, 43, 51, 55, 57, 73, 105, 107, 113, 129, 133, 139, 163, 177, 179, 189, 261, 287, 331

V

Value 187, 251
Vernile, Lucy 121, 179
Video 35, 110, 129, 133, 143, 147, 157, 163, 164, 165, 167, 170, 177, 185, 189, 328
Video prototype 189
Video prototypes 189
Vision 27, 29, 87, 177, 382
Voice over 189
Vote 79, 83, 99, 211
Voted 209

Voting 98, 99
Voting 209, 211

W

Wall 77, 78, 83, 89, 99, 121, 174, 200, 211, 267, 271, 275
Want 32, 33, 52, 53, 75, 78, 102, 111, 131, 181, 191, 261, 279, 381
Weaknesses 184, 187, 198
Web 61, 69, 271, 279, 323, 354
White board 89, 183, 185
White board 23, 71, 77, 77, 78, 83, 87, 87, 97, 159, 159, 174, 174, 177, 177, 185, 185, 293
Whiteside, Bennet 133, 142
WWWWWH 190

DCC on-line design education

https://dcc-edu.com
info@dcc-edu.com

Start today, DCC expert online programs for designers and managers. More accessible than traditional design education and better value. Classes for different world time zones. Connect to classes anywhere with an internet connection. Study from home or train your whole team in your office. Free textbook with most courses. Check links below for all scheduled dates and local time calculator. Contact us at info@curedale.com for current information.

CREATING EXPERIENCE MAPS, JOURNEY MAPS, AND SERVICE BLUEPRINTS

30 GOOD WAYS TO INNOVATE

DESIGNING WITH COLOR

INTRODUCTION TO DESIGN THINKING

DESIGN THINKING ONLINE PROGRAMS

INTRO TO SERVICE DESIGN

SERVICE DESIGN ONLINE PROGRAMS

INTRODUCTION TO DESIGN RESEARCH

DESIGN RESEARCH ONLINE PROGRAMS

INTRODUCTION TO INDUSTRIAL DESIGN

- INDUSTRIAL DESIGN ONLINE PROGRAMS
- DESIGN RESEARCH: INTERVIEWING & FOCUS GROUPS
- CREATING A SUCCESSFUL DESIGN PORTFOLIO
- PRODUCT DESIGN PROPOSALS
- INTRODUCTION TO HUMAN FACTORS ONLINE
- DESIGN SYNTHESIS
- DESIGN IDEATION METHODS

Do an on-line map class

https://dcc-online.selz.com
info@curedale.com

If you liked this book and want to learn more about experience maps journey maps and service blueprints we offer on-line classes and courses presented by the author. The courses are held at different times of day to suit your schedule and time zone and we can provide a custom class for your whole team.

You can find more information and register at the URL below and order print copies of this book or on Amazon soon.

CREATING EXPERIENCE MAPS, JOURNEY MAPS, AND SERVICE BLUEPRINTS
http://dcc-experiencemaps.eventbrite.com
info@curedale.com

About the author

Rob Curedale was born in Australia and worked as a designer, director and educator in leading design offices in London, Sydney, Switzerland, Portugal, Los Angeles, Silicon Valley, Detroit, and Hong Kong. He designed or managed the design of over 1,000 products as a consultant and in-house design leader for the world's most respected brands. Rob has three decades experience in every aspect of product development and design research, leading design teams to achieve transformational improvements in operating and financial results. Rob's design scan be found in millions of homes and workplaces around the world and have generated billions of dollars in corporate revenues.

Design practice
HP, Philips, GEC, Nokia, Sun, Apple, Canon, Motorola, Nissan, Audi VW, Disney, RTKL, Governments of the UAE, UK, Australia, Steelcase, Hon, Castelli, Hamilton Medical, Zyliss, Belkin, Gensler, Haworth, Honeywell, NEC, Hoover, Packard Bell, Dell, Black & Decker, Coleman and Harmon Kardon. Categories including furniture, healthcare, consumer electronics, sporting, housewares, military, exhibits, and packaging.

Teaching
Rob has taught as a full time professor, adjunct professor and visiting instructor at institutions including the following: Art Center Pasadena, Art Center Europe, Yale School of Architecture, Pepperdine University, Loyola University, Cranbrook Academy of Art, Pratt, Otis, a faculty member at SCA and UTS Sydney, Chair of Product Design and Furniture Design at the College for Creative Studies in Detroit, then the largest product design school in North America, Cal State San Jose, Escola De Artes e Design in Oporto Portugal, Instituto De Artes Visuals, Design e Marketing, Lisbon, Southern Yangtze University, Jiao Tong University in Shanghai and Nanjing Arts Institute in China.

Awards
Products that Rob has managed the design of have been recognized with IDSA IDEA Awards, Good Design Awards UK, Australian Design Awards, and a number of best of show innovation Awards at CES Consumer Electronics Show. His designs are in the Permanent collection of the Powerhouse Design Museum. In 2013 Rob was nominated for the Advanced Australia Award. The Awards celebrate Australians living internationally who exhibit "remarkable talent, exceptional vision, and ambition." In 2015 Rob was selected with a group of leading international industrial designers to provide opening comments for the international congress of societies of industrial design conference ICSID in Korea.

Other titles in the series

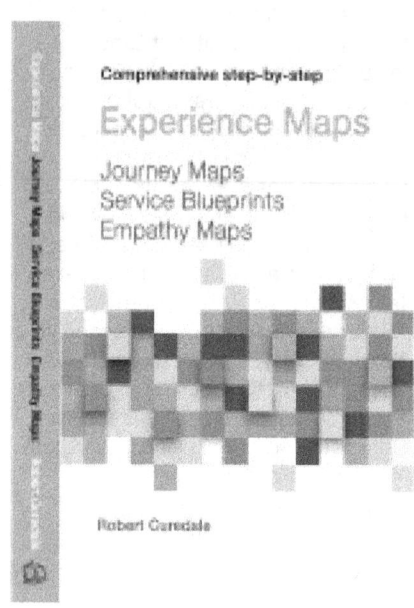 

EXPERIENCE MAPS
JOURNEY MAPS
SERVICE BLUEPRINTS
EMPATHY MAPS
Author: Curedale, Robert A
Published by:
Design Community College, Inc
March 2016

SERVICE BLUEPRINTS
Author: Curedale, Robert A
Published by:
Design Community College, Inc
March 2016
ISBN-10:
ISBN-13:

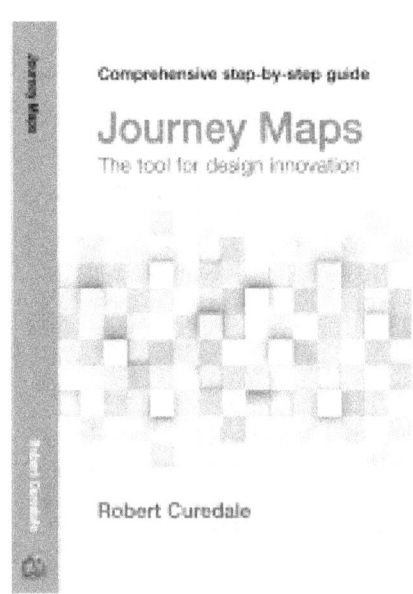 

JOURNEY MAPS
Author: Curedale, Robert A
Published by:
Design Community College, Inc
March 2016

EMPATHY MAPS
Author: Curedale, Robert A
Published by:
Design Community College, Inc
March 2016
ISBN-10:
ISBN-13:

AFFINITY DIAGRAMS
Author: Curedale, Robert A
Published by:
Design Community College, Inc
March 2016
128 pages
ISBN-13 978-1940805269
ISBN-10 1940805269
http://dcc-edu.org/

DESIGN THINKING PROCESS & METHODS GUIDE 2ND EDITION
Author: Curedale, Robert A
Published by:
Design Community College, Inc
January 2016
422 pages
ISBN-10: 1-940805-20-1
ISBN-13: 978-1-940805-20-7
http://dcc-edu.org/

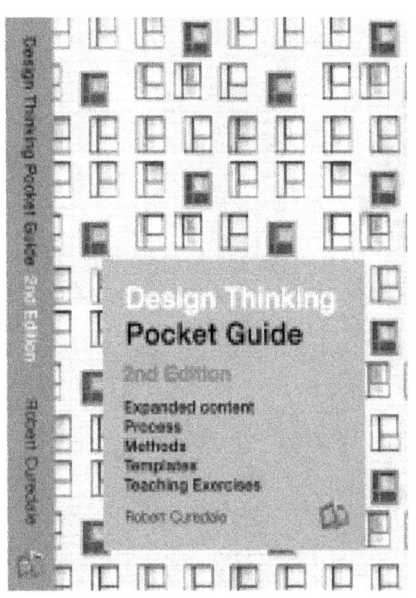 

DESIGN THINKING POCKET GUIDE 2ND EDITION
Author: Curedale, Robert A
Published by:
Design Community College, Inc
Jun 01 2013
ISBN-10: 098924685X
ISBN-13: 9780989246859

30 GOOD WAYS TO INNOVATE
Author: Curedale, Robert A
Published by:
Design Community College, Inc.
Edition 1 November 2015
108 pages
ISBN-10: 1940805139
ISBN-13: 978-1940805139

DESIGN RESEARCH
METHODS
150 WAYS TO INFORM
DESIGN
Author: Curedale, Robert A
Published by:
Design Community College, Inc.
Edition 1 January 2013
290 pages
ISBN-10: 0988236257
ISBN-13: 978-0-988-2362-5-7
http://dcc-edu.org/

50 BRAINSTORMING
METHODS
FOR TEAM AND INDIVIDUAL
IDEATION
Author: Robert A Curedale
Published by:
Design Community College Inc.
Edition 1 January 2013
184 pages
ISBN-10: 0988236230
ISBN-13: 978-0-9882362-3-3
http://dcc-edu.org/

SERVICE DESIGN
250 ESSENTIAL METHODS
Author: Curedale, Robert A
Published by:
Design Community College, Inc.
Edition 1 Aug 01 2013
ISBN-10:0989246868
ISBN-13: 9780989246866

SERVICE DESIGN
POCKET GUIDE
Author: Curedale, Robert A
Published by:
Design Community College, Inc.
Edition 1 Sept 01 2013
ISBN-10:0989246884
ISBN-13: 9780989246880

MAPPING METHODS
Author: Curedale, Robert A
Published by:
Design Community College, Inc.
Edition 1 Apr 01 2013
136 pages
ISBN-10: 0989246825
ISBN-13: 9780989246828
http://dcc-edu.org/

50 SELECTED DESIGN METHODS
Author: Curedale, Robert A
Published by:
Design Community College, Inc.
Edition 1 Jan 17 2013
114 pages
ISBN-10:0988236265
ISBN-13: 9780988236264
http://dcc-edu.org/

DESIGN METHODS 1
200 WAYS TO APPLY
DESIGN THINKING
Author: Robert A Curedale
Published by:
Design Community College Inc.
Edition 1 November 2013
ISBN-10:0988236206
ISBN-13:978-0-9882362-0-2

DESIGN METHODS 2
200 MORE WAYS TO APPLY
DESIGN THINKING
Author: Robert A Curedale
Published by:
Design Community College Inc.
Edition 1 January 2013
ISBN-13: 978-0988236240
ISBN-10: 0988236249

INTERVIEWS OBSERVATION
AND FOCUS GROUPS
Author: Curedale, Robert A
Published by:
Design Community College, Inc.
Edition 1 Apr 01 2013
188 pages
ISBN-10:0989246833
ISBN-13: 9780989246835
http://dcc-edu.org/

DESIGN THINKING
PROCESS AND METHODS
MANUAL FIRST EDITION
Author: Robert A Curedale
Published by:
Design Community College Inc.
Edition 1 January 2013
ISBN-10: 0988236214
ISBN-13: 978-0-9882362-1-9
http://dcc-edu.org/

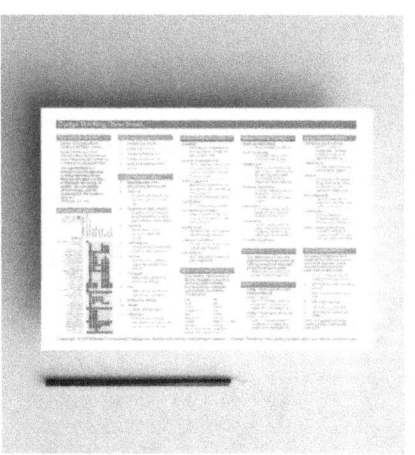

CHINA DESIGN INDEX THE ESSENTIAL DIRECTORY OF CONTACTS FOR DESIGNERS 2014
Author: Curedale, Robert A
Published by:
Design Community College, Inc.
Edition 1 2014
384 pages
ISBN-13: 978-1940805092
ISBN-10 1940805090
http://dcc-edu.org/

DESIGN THINKING QUICK REFERENCE GUIDE
Plastic laminated
Loose leaf one page
Author: Curedale, Robert A
Published by:
Loose Leaf: 1 pages
Publisher: Design Community College Inc.; 1st edition (2015)
Language: English
ISBN-10: 194080518X
ISBN-13: 978-1940805184
http://dcc-edu.org/

DESIGN THINKING TEMPLATES & EXERCISES
Author: Curedale, Robert A
Published by:
Design Community College, Inc
2016

Economic Evolution Model

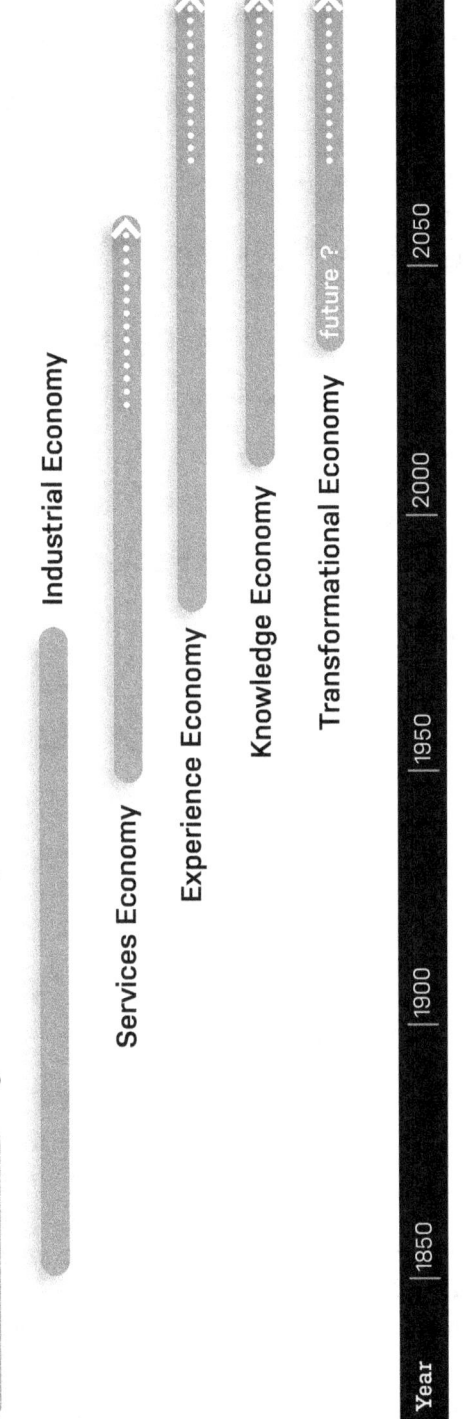

This framework was first proposed by Brand & Rocchi (2011) in a Philips Design document entitled Rethinking Value in a Changing Landscape.

Service Design Tools
Double Diamond Process Model

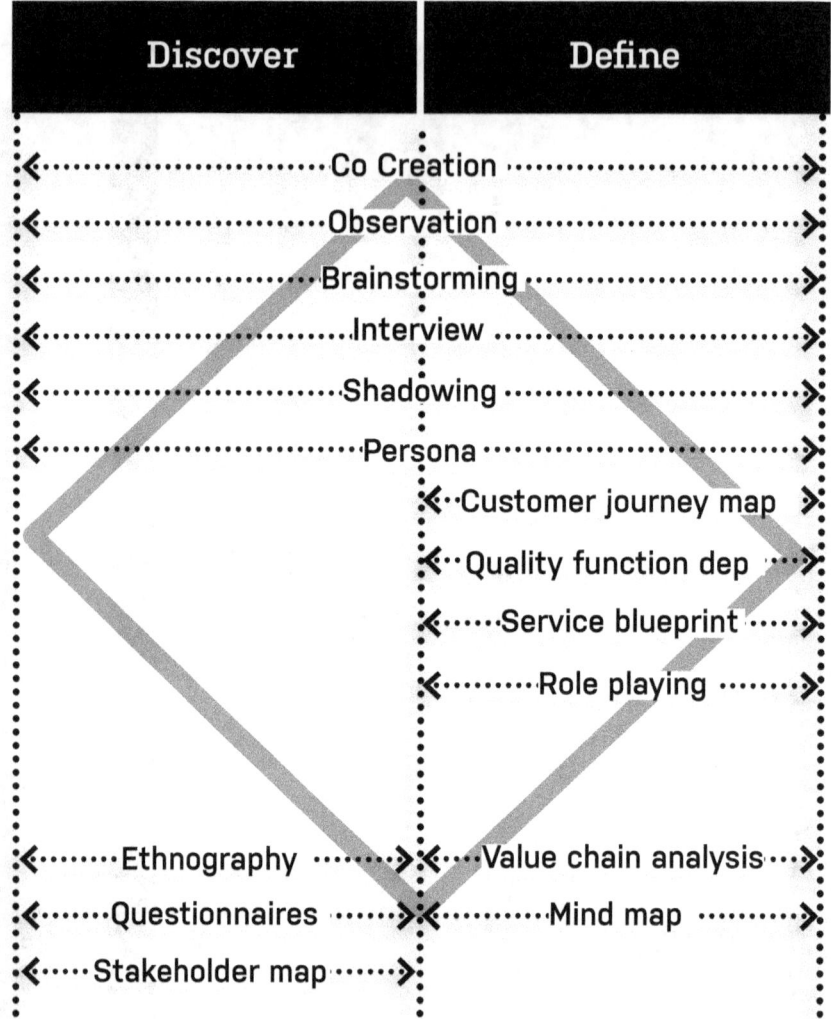

Source: Asia-pacific Journal of Multimedia Services Convergent with Art, Humanities, and Sociology Vol.4, No.2, December (2014), pp. 63-70 Kyung Mi Bae, Kyung Sun Lee, and Youn Sung Kim

Develop	Deliver

⇐·············· Co Creation ··············⇒
⇐·············· Observation ··············⇒
⇐······ Brainstorming ······⇒

⇐·· Customer journey map ·⇒
⇐·· Quality function dep ····⇒
⇐·············· Service blueprint ··············⇒
⇐·············· Role playing ··············⇒
⇐·············· Kano model ··············⇒
⇐·············· Prototyping ··············⇒
⇐·········· Mock-up ··········⇒ ⇐···· Heuristic evaluation ···⇒
⇐········ Usability test ······⇒
⇐········ Task analysis ······⇒

SOCIETY	PRE-INDUSTRIAL	INDUSTRIAL	POST-INDUSTRIAL
Game	Against Nature	Against fabricated nature	Among Persons
Timeline	to 1850	1850 to 1950	from 1950
Pre-dominant Activity	Agriculture, Mining	Goods, Production	Services
Use of Human Labor	Raw Muscle Power	Machine tending	Artistic, Creative, Intellectual
Unit of Social Life	Extended Household	Individual	Community
Standard of Living Measure	Subsistence	Quantity of Goods	Quality of life in terms of health, education, recreation
Structure	Routine, Traditional, Authoritative	Bureaucratic, Hierarchical	Interdependent, Global
Technology	Simple hand tools	Machines	Information
View	Local	Local	Global
Quest	Surviving	Modernizing ones life	
Effect		Productivity & family life	
Skills		Specialization	
Approach		Follow cultural norms	
Focus		Product function	
Qualities		Products	
Value		Commodities	

	SOCIETY	SERVICE	EXPERIENCE	KNOWLEDGE
Game				
Timeline		from 1950	from 1980	from 2010
Pre-dominant Activity		Services	Brand experience	Enabling creativity
Use of Human Labor		Service production and delivery	Raw Muscle Power	Machine tending
Unit of Social Life		Network	Extended Household	Individual
Standard of Living Measure		Service experience	Quality of Experience	Self expression
Structure		Networked	Routine, Traditional, Authoritative	Bureaucratic, Hierarchical
Technology			Simple hand tools	Machines
View		Global	Contextual	Systematic
Quest		Brand Identity	Explore lifestyle identity	Individual empowerment
Effect			Work hard play hard	Develop your potential
Skills			Experimentation	Creativity
Approach			Beak social taboos	Pursue aspirations
Focus		Service experience	Brand experience	enabling creativity
Qualities		Product service mix	Product service mix	Value networks
Value		Sevice experiences	Targeted experiences	Enable self development

This framework was first proposed by Brand & Rocchi (2011) in a Philips Design document entitled Rethinking Value in a Changing Landscape.

The Experience economy

ECONOMY	PRE-INDUSTRIAL	INDUSTRIAL	SERVICE	EXPERIENCE
Function	Extract	Make	Deliver	Stage
Nature	Exchangeable	Tangible	Intangible	Memorable
Attribute	Natural	Standardized	Customized	Personal
Method of Supply	Stored in Bulk	Inventoried	Delivered on demand	Revealed over time
Seller	Trader	Manufacturer	Provider	Stager
Buyer	Market	User	Client	Guest
Factors of Demand	Characteristics	Features	Benefits	Sensations

Source: B. Joseph Pine II/James H. Gilmore "Welcome to the Experience Economy" Harvard Business Review

Notes

Notes